Architecture and Ideology
in Eastern Europe during the Stalin Era

An Aspect of Cold War History

Architecture and Ideology in Eastern Europe during the Stalin Era

An Aspect of Cold War History

ANDERS ÅMAN

THE ARCHITECTURAL HISTORY FOUNDATION, INC., New York, New York
The MIT Press, Cambridge, Massachusetts, and London, England

Originally published as *Arkitektur och ideologi i stalintidens Östeuropa. Ur det kalla krigets historia*

© 1987 Carlsson Bokförlag
© 1992 by the Architectural History Foundation and the
Massachusetts Institute of Technology
Printed and bound in the United States of America.

Library of Congress Cataloging-in-Publication Data

Åman, Anders
        [Arkitektur och ideologi i stalintidens Östeuropa. English]
        Architecture and ideology in Eastern Europe during the Stalin era: an aspect of Cold War history / Anders Åman.
        p. cm.
Translation of: Arkitektur och ideologi i stalintidens Östeuropa. Ur det kalla krigets historia.
Includes bibliographical references and indexes.
ISBN 0-262-01130-1
        1. Architecture—Europe, Eastern. 2. Architecture, Modern—20th century—Europe, Eastern. 3. Socialist realism and architecture—Europe, Eastern. 4. Architecture and state—Europe, Eastern.
5. Europe, Eastern—Politics and government—1945–1989. I. Title.
NA958.A4713 1992
720'.943'09045—dc20   92-8088 CIP

Anders Åman is Professor of the History and Theory of Art at Umeå University, Sweden.

Translated by Roger and Kerstin Tanner
Designed and typeset by Bessas & Ackerman

The translation of this book into English was made possible by a grant from the Swedish Council for Research in the Humanities and Social Sciences.

Contents

Preface

In 1978 I was in Poland, captivated in equal measure by the past and the present in a country where change was already in the air. Yet, when I settled on a topic of study in the history of architecture, it was the most despised of all episodes in Polish architectural history: Socialist Realism, the architecture of the Stalin era. The architectural ideals of Socialist Realism had been defunct for a couple of decades but the same political system was still in power, with background support from the Soviet Union under Leonid Brezhnev. This was long before the fall of the Berlin Wall.

I soon enlarged my plans and decided to write the history of architecture during this period in each of the six countries known in the 1950s as "people's democracies": the DDR (German Democratic Republic, or East Germany), Poland, Czechoslovakia, Hungary, Romania, and Bulgaria. Nowhere in the changeable history of twentieth-century architecture had there been such rapid and drastic twists and turns as here. Three times in little more than ten years, everything had begun all over again: at the end of the war, in 1949, and in 1956. And yet the subject was virtually unexplored. In Eastern Europe, everything relating to the Stalin era was still politically sensitive and Eastern Europeans, when confronted by Socialist Realism, reacted with disgust or embarrassed irony. In the West, the same architecture had been viewed mostly as an anachronism, a deviation from the mainstream of Modernism, barely deserving the name of architecture.

The material to which I addressed myself was not only uninvestigated, it also presented a theoretical problem greatly transcending the history of postwar Eastern Europe: the relationship between architecture and ideology, between the form and the meaning of architecture. How were the two connected? How were they conditioned by each other? These questions are difficult enough when one is dealing simply with the standard select repertoire of architectural history, but in the postwar history of Eastern Europe they are crucial.

By the time this book was published in Swedish, in 1987, much had happened, even though the old rulers of Eastern Europe were still in their positions of power. Now, with the appearance of the American edition, the book deals with a concluded political chapter but a chapter that, for a long time to come, will remain an indispensable background for understanding the countries of Eastern and Central Europe.

During the same 1980s, other architectural historians, from their several vantage points, contributed to the revision of the picture of the twentieth century, with emphasis on the interwar years. We, however, are concerned here with the 1950s and with Socialist Realism—the last and most rabid opponent of Modernism—though not in its relatively familiar, Soviet form. For our purposes, the Soviet Union merely provides a context.

Not many words will be wasted on the difficulties this work entailed. For humanists, the main problems are seldom concerned with theory and method in the narrow sense, but rather with language and style, with empathy versus detachment, with "immediacy" versus perspective, and, not least, with selection and disposition of material. The disposition which I finally opted for has a chronological structure with which studies of various aspects of the subject have been integrated. The theoretical aspects are present throughout the book, but are dealt with mainly in the concluding section.

For inspiration and support I am grateful to many, among them especially Dr. Waldemar Baraniewski, Warsaw; Professor Milka Bliznakov, Virginia Polytechnic Institute and State University; architect Christian Borngräber, Berlin; architect József Fischer, Budapest; Professor Barbara Miller Lane, Bryn Mawr College; Dr. Sergiusz Michalski, Augsburg; and Professor Rudolf Zeitler, Uppsala.

Uppsala and Umeå, January 1992

Two camps are today realizing their contradictory world pictures and ideologies. On the one hand, the camp of democracy, socialism, and peace—with the Soviet Union as its main bastion—and on the other the camp of imperialism, economic crisis, and warmongering. The contest between these ideologies is also being waged in architecture.

From a resolution adopted by the National Congress of Polish Architects, 20–21 June 1949

We are against the Bauhaus. Why? We are against the Bauhaus because Functionalism is the height of imperialist cosmopolitanism, the height of decadence and decay.

Kurt Liebknecht at a cultural conference of the German-Soviet Friendship Union, 2–4 November 1951

Introduction

The period of twentieth-century European history that forms the subject of this book is one and indivisible, but it is difficult to understand unless regarded in three distinct perspectives, against the background of three different kinds of earlier history.

The first perspective is defined geographically. The DDR (East Germany), Poland, Czechoslovakia, Hungary, Romania, and Bulgaria constitute a region, determined by military and political realities, bordering the former Soviet Union in the east and, until recently, bounded on the west by the Iron Curtain. There is no historical precedent for Eastern Europe thus defined, but the course of events stands out nonetheless against the background of the abundant, many-stranded cultural traditions of this particular part of Europe, held together by the boundaries of 1945.

The second perspective is ideological and political: the cultural policy of *actually existent socialism,* or, more briefly, art and communism. Viewed in this perspective, our subject is a continuation of a train of events that began with the October Revolution in 1917 and entered a new phase with the establishment of Socialist Realism in the Soviet Union during the 1930s.

The third perspective is that of architectural history in the more limited sense: the use and survival of traditional architectural vocabulary during the twentieth century. From this point of view our subject is part of the interplay of Modernism and Tradition that is a leitmotif in the history of twentieth-century architecture.

All three perspectives are equally important, but they can hardly be allotted the same amount of space and attention throughout. Accordingly, keeping them alive throughout the story will be a task for the reader as well as the author. All three perspectives are equally important, but as the source material consists primarily of buildings, we have cause to dwell at somewhat greater length on the perspective of architectural history.

There are two rival interpretations of the architectural history of the twentieth century. The first interpretation tells us how Modernism, step by step, vanquished Traditionalism until, at mid-century, it had the stage to itself. This was above all the interpretation of the 1950s and 1960s, launched already in the thirties by Sigfried Giedion and Nikolaus Pevsner and still viable today. Socialist Realism, thus viewed, is a bizarre exception undeserving of close attention—and, indeed, it hardly rates a mention in most surveys of twentieth-century architecture. The second interpretation characterizes the twentieth century as a perpetual trial of strength between Modernism and Tradition, in which there occasionally seemed to be winners and losers, but which, in the eyes of posterity, was really an unending process of interaction. During the 1980s, this view gained support from the return of Tradition to the international debate on architecture. Socialist Realism, thus viewed, can be integrated readily with the course of history, as one of several manifestations of Traditionalism.

Comparing these two interpretations, then, we find that the latter has an important point in its favor. It *tells us more,* it takes in a bigger slice of history, whereas the first interpretation leaves us with significant exceptions and anachronisms. If wealth of content be a quality of historical explanation, the choice is plain enough.

If, however, Socialist Realism is to be thought of as part of the interplay of Modernism and Traditionalism, how does this tally with our knowledge of the political context? We know that Socialist Realism was launched and applied under very definite political conditions, and indeed that without those conditions it would have been unthinkable. Can it, then, at the same time be the product of this interplay or antithesis between two different kinds of architecture?

As we shall see, it is not only possible but necessary to derive Socialist Realism from two independent contexts, one architectural and the other political. So let us now consider how these contexts are related to each other.

Intellectuals during the twentieth century have been faced with two phenomena on which it has been impossible not to take a stand: Socialism in the political arena, and Modernism in the aesthetic arena. For a long time it was commonly supposed that the two were closely interconnected, if not actually interdependent. This was the conviction of many artists and intellectuals, architects not least, who concerned themselves more than others with the relationship between social and aesthetic forms.

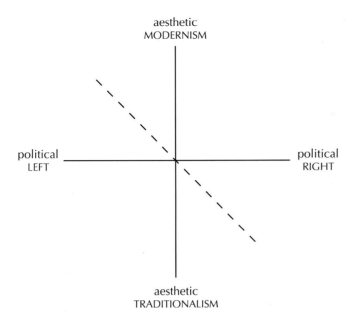

aesthetic
MODERNISM

political
LEFT

political
RIGHT

aesthetic
TRADITIONALISM

Diagram A

This relationship between ideology and aesthetics can be illustrated schematically as in the figure above, with politics varying along the horizontal axis, aesthetics on the vertical (Diagram A). The dashed diagonal line marks the presumed covariation between, on the one hand, Modernism and the left-wing political standpoints and, on the other hand, between Traditionalism and the right-wing political standpoints.

The reader is asked to ponder this little diagram. We will return to it in Chapter Nine, which deals with the architects, but above all it forms the subject of our concluding chapter.

Suffice it to say for the present that the presumed covariation was already contradicted in the 1930s, above all by developments in the Soviet Union, and during the forties and fifties, for example, by the developments in Eastern Europe that form the subject of our story.

Such attention as has been devoted to Socialist Realism previously has been prompted by its implementation in the Soviet Union between the 1930s and the mid-1950s. Its implementation in Eastern Europe between the end of the forties and the mid-fifties has attracted far less interest and has been looked on as a replay of earlier events. What was native to the Soviet Union, however, was extraneous to Eastern Europe, arriving in countries with different traditions, at a different point in time, and at a different stage of historical development.

The Soviet Union is the *precondition* without which Socialist Realism could never have been proclaimed as an architectural ideal in Eastern Europe at the end of the 1940s. But this need not imply—as has often been assumed automatically—that the architecture that was the practical result of Socialist Realism was also imported from the Soviet Union. We shall at all events assume that this was not the case and that differing national traditions were often more influential than the direct influence of the Soviet Union. What was imported was not the actual architecture—other than in exceptional cases—but a constellation of political circumstances that promoted a certain kind of architecture.

The subtitle of this book includes a term that requires comment: *the Cold War*. This, in the West, is the conventional name for an important postwar phase, the duration of which can be variously defined, but the most intensive part of which came between the years 1948–49 and 1955–56.

There are many theories, most of them advanced by American historians, concerning the causes and progress of the Cold War. No such discussion existed until recently in Eastern Europe, but in the West these theories have come to be so numerous that, for the sake of simplicity, their authors have been grouped under various headings, the sequence of which can also serve to indicate a chronology of approaches to the Cold War.

The *Traditionalists* gave their support in all essential respects to the official American policy. The *Realists* employed a more realpolitik-related, less ideological perspective. The *Revisionists* attached great importance to the actions of the USA as viewed in the perspective of the Soviet Union. They adopted an inverted perspective, although hardly any of them were sovietologists. Finally, the *Postrevisionists*, a less united group than the others, have adopted both a skeptical and eclectic approach to earlier research.

For present purposes, we do not have to choose between these different groups of historians, our main concern being not to account for the genesis of the Cold War but to study and interpret its manifestations. But there is another important definition connected with the Cold War.

It takes two sides to make a war, but this is not to say that both are affected by the war in the same way or to the same degree. Even a cold war can be waged far more on one party's territory than on the other's. It can leave profound traces in the history of one side, yet be merely an episode in the history of the other. The Cold War was not symmetrical. On the eastern side it was a total war, affecting every sector of society under a newly established political system. In the West it was more restricted, mobilization was partial. Even in the West, however, architecture was affected, West Berlin being the obvious example.

The term *Socialist Realism*, which we have used several times already, also demands comment. As a term it is both practical and problematic—problematic because, in the West, it is frequently confused with the vaguer term "Social Realism," and because "realism" is a difficult term when applied to architecture. But it is practical because it was used by contemporaries and because it can be employed everywhere in the aesthetic sector.

Christian Borngräber, in his studies of Soviet architecture, has suggested the alternative term *Academic architecture* (roughly corresponding to the term *Beaux-Arts architecture*, as commonly used in the West). This admirably suits the Soviet Union, where academism came to occupy a powerful position, but it can hardly be used in countries here collectively referred to as Eastern Europe. More attractive is the concept of *Socialist Classicism*, launched by Andrei Siniavsky in his book *On Socialist Realism*, published in the West. Although Siniavsky had only literature in mind, it is also an apt description of architecture, and it emphasizes continuity with the past.

But for an account in which the relationship between architectural form and political rhetoric occupies the center of attention, there is really no alternative to the official, contemporary term—*Socialist Realism*.

According to the same official terminology, the antithesis of Socialist Realism is *Constructivism*. For, in the Soviet Union and Eastern Europe during the period we will be studying, this denoted not only the Russian avant-garde of the 1920s but also the whole of modern architecture, even outside the Soviet Union. In this broad sense, however, it is a term that generates confusion. The same is true to some extent of *Functionalism*, a term that again focuses on *one* quality of modern architecture. *Formalism*, frequently used in the Soviet Union, and sometimes in Eastern Europe too, is too negative, too polemical.

There remains *Modernism*. Used as the opposite of Socialist Realism, it is an articulate concept and, like its antithesis, can also be applied to literature, music, and pictorial art.

Very often I have been asked: Why study Socialist Realism? This question has been put to me above all in Eastern Europe, in all of the countries referred to here. Any other interest on the part of a visiting architectural historian from the West would have been more welcome: the architecture of the Prussians, Hapsburgs, or Turks, royal palaces or castles, churches or feudal strongholds—*anything* would have been preferable.

In the countries of actually existent socialism, the attitude toward their own contemporary history was cautious and evasive. This is what made it at all reasonable, and perhaps even necessary, for an outsider to tackle a subject like this.

The Early Postwar Period

From the End of World War II to the Cold War

I

The war ended and, to quote the title of a famous poem by the Hungarian author Gyula Illyés, then came "no man's time." A chapter of history was over, a new chapter was soon to begin. The brief time between the eras forms the subject of Illyés's magnificent poem.

At the Yalta Conference in 1945 the great powers decided that the eastern half of Europe was to be the Soviet sphere of interest, but no one foresaw how *total* that influence was to become. If anything, what was commonly envisaged was the process later known as "Finlandization," that is, there would be far-reaching adjustments to Soviet wishes in matters of foreign and military policy, together with wider economic cooperation.

For a longer or shorter period during the war, this part of Europe had come within the German domain: as occupied territory (Poland, Bohemia-Moravia); as more or less voluntarily allies (Slovakia, Hungary, Romania, Bulgaria); or as part of Germany itself (East Prussia, Silesia, Pomerania, and the region soon to become the Deutsche Demokratische Republic, or East Germany).

As the war continued, ever greater material damage resulted from Anglo-American bombing raids (as in Berlin, Chemnitz/Karl-Marx-Stadt, Dresden, and Magdeburg), from a combination of Russian artillery bombardment and German retreat (as in Danzig/Gdańsk, Breslau/Wrocław, and Budapest), and from systematic obliteration by the Germans (as in the Czech village of Lidice and in Warsaw). But it was the Anglo-American air raids during the last year of the war that caused the most widespread destruction (Fig. 1).

In the wake of the war came an immense movement of population; the evacuation of civilians from the actual fighting zone was

1 One of many shattered German cities in 1945: Chemnitz, later to become Karl-Marx-Stadt in the DDR.

only the beginning. Poles left the region the Soviet Union called West Ukraine, while Germans left what the Poles called "the regained areas" and the old German settlements of Bohemia (Czechoslovakia) and also, before long, the Soviet-occupied zone in Germany. Altogether these movements involved more than 15 million people; according to some estimates, more than 20 million. Earlier European wars had also generated refugee movements, but never on such a scale, and after a time most of the fugitives had returned home, which they were not destined to do this time.

Everywhere in this region, the war had brought terrible destruction, but nowhere more so than in Poland and the future DDR; damage of a more limited nature had been inflicted on the greater part of Czechoslovakia, on Hungary, and on the Balkan countries. In every material sense, the war placed Eastern Europe at a tremendous disadvantage.

Politically, though, the war played into the hands of the regimes soon to be established. A new, previously unknown path to socialism was opened as the Red Army and national Communists combined to achieve "liberation from fascism." Despite the difficulties, the moral, administrative, and economic vacuum left by the Nazis and their allies presented an opportunity for the establishment of new regimes. And these regimes encountered far less resistance than they would have otherwise; to begin with, they could rely on no small measure of goodwill from large sectors of the population.

In the aftermath of the war, left-wing ideology became a dominant force in Europe, and the international prestige of the Soviet Union was greater than at any time before or since. Postwar Eastern Europe, however, was fashioned not on the strength of popular desires but on a basis of military events and agreements between the great powers in Teheran, Yalta, and Potsdam. Any popular legitimacy enjoyed by the regimes thus established was soon lost.

The peoples of Eastern Europe were liberated, but did this also mean that they were free? Opinions differed on this point, and as time went on, more and more people were disposed to answer No.

Political events between the end of the war and the end of the 1940s can be described as follows.

The starting point was "liberation from fascism" by the Red Army (Fig. 2). This is what gave the cachet of legitimacy to the new regimes that began to be built up. The first completely liberated country was Bulgaria (9 September 1944), and the last was Czechoslovakia (9 May 1945). The future DDR remained for the time being, until October 1949, a Soviet zone of occupation.

Restoring order to the ruins and thus making reconstruction possible was the great common task that everybody could agree on (Figs. 3, 4), and by ruins we mean not only shattered buildings but also the wreckage of society.

There was, to begin with, a certain degree of political pluralism, but the different political groupings did not operate on equal terms. It soon became clear that the Communist parties, supported by the occupying power, had a special position and that, within those parties, members who had spent the war years in the Soviet Union had the upper hand over those who had belonged to the resistance in their native country.

Big estates were distributed to small farmers at the same time as the rest of the economy began to be nationalized. Land for building was sequestrated by the state, as were large privately owned buildings.

The Communist parties had been small at the end of the war, but now they grew rapidly and it was not easy to distinguish convinced adherents from those who just wanted to keep in with the new rulers or reluctantly accepted what seemed unavoidable. A

2 "Long live the liberators!" Polish poster, 1946, by Tadeusz Trepkowski. Through the broken bars the flags of the Soviet Union and Poland can be seen against a bright blue sky.

3 Women of Warsaw clearing the ruins of Marszałkowska Street in 1945.

4 Altmarkt in Dresden, 1949, after the ruins had been cleared but before the main work of reconstruction had started.

poem written by Czesław Miłosz in 1946, "A Child of Europe," includes a couple of lines that, ironically alluding to a Biblical text (Matt. 22:21), epitomized the determinist attitude typical of many intellectuals:

> The wielder of power has the logic of history to thank for it.
> Give unto the logic of history that which is its due.

The strength of the Communist parties lay in their determination and discipline, but also in the idealism and commitment of a hard core of veterans and newly recruited young members. Their weakness lay in the gap between reality and political language, between everyday life and rhetoric.

The screening-off of the West soon became noticeable—politically, economically, and culturally. From 1946 onward, *the Iron Curtain* was a term constantly recurring in Western propaganda but seldom mentioned by those who had built it. It was gradually enlarged and reinforced as time went on.

Less talked about was the almost equally hermetic boundary to the east, that is, the western frontier of the Soviet Union, which remained as closely guarded as before, ever since the Revolution, with no opening toward the new sister countries. The latter were also cut off from each other, in striking contrast to conditions during the interwar years.

During 1947, starting in Bulgaria and Romania, the Communist parties achieved complete control of political power everywhere in Eastern Europe, with the exception, for the time being, of Czechoslovakia. The strong agrarian parties of the interwar period had now definitely been pushed aside. A planned economy was introduced along Soviet lines, with two-year plans in Czechoslovakia and Bulgaria, three-year plans in Poland and Hungary. On Moscow's instructions, all the Eastern European countries declined the invitation to take part in the Marshall Plan, America's program for European economic recovery. Cominform, the Communist information bureau located in Belgrade, and from 1948 in Bucharest, was set up as a countermeasure.

The Cold War had been a long time in the making. Its definitive outbreak was signaled by three events in 1948. The Communists' seizure of total power in Czechoslovakia in February 1948 put an end to all thoughts of a popular front in Western Europe as well. By the end of the year there was not a single country in Eastern Europe that still had an independent social democratic party. All of them had been amalgamated with the Communist parties to form united socialist parties. The transition from popular front politics to party dictatorship—"the short march," to quote the title of a book by the Czech historian Karel Kaplan—was complete.

The second event was the breach in June between the Soviet Union and Yugoslavia, between Stalin and "the Fascist Tito clique." The vehemence of the argument, with no invective spared ("hired spies and murderers" was one expression used by the Cominform newspaper), was aimed not only against the Yugoslavs but, to no less an extent, against actual and potential apostates at home, where purges now became the order of the day. Władysław Gomułka, Secretary-General of the Polish party, was deposed in September 1948, charged with "Titoism" and nationalist deviations.

The third event was the Soviet blockade of West Berlin, which began in June of 1948 and only ended in May of the following year, its effectiveness having been countered by the allied airlift.

During 1948 the economies of all six countries were at least 80 percent nationalized, and the politically and economically reformed states were termed "people's democracies." This was a new form of dictatorship of the proletariat, introduced from outside and from the top, instead of from the inside and from below. In his biography of Stalin, written in 1949, Isaac Deutscher referred to a mixture of revolution and conquest. The principles of "socialism in one country" were now also to be applied outside the Soviet Union.

Reconstruction and New Buildings

When building revived, it did so under very different conditions in different countries.

First, the war had affected some countries more than others. The damage in Bulgaria and Romania was on a limited scale. In Hungary, Budapest was badly damaged, and in Czechoslovakia the same was true of the eastern parts of Slovakia. Poland and the future DDR were in a class by themselves. No such widespread destruction had ever been seen before, and reconstruction was bound to take a long time, even though it was pursued with great determination, especially in Poland. All through the 1950s, reconstruction dominated the building agenda. By contrast, it was completed fairly soon in Czechoslovakia and Hungary, and more rapidly still in Romania and Bulgaria, where new buildings became the prime concern after only a year or so.

Second, the suspension of building operations caused by the war lasted for different lengths of time in the six countries. In Slovakia, Hungary, Romania, and Bulgaria—whose regimes had for a long time collaborated with the Germans—building had continued more or less normally until as late as 1943. A decline set in that year, but the period of total stagnation was short, scarcely more than a year. In Poland, by contrast, and in that part of Czechoslovakia formerly constituting the protectorate of Bohemia and Moravia, the intermission had been far longer, equaling almost the full duration of the war. There was also a prolonged hiatus in the future DDR. All building activities not immediately prompted by the war were discontinued in 1942, and reconstruction started more hesitantly here than elsewhere. It did not really get under way until the proclamation of *Das nationale Aufbauprogramm* in 1951.

Third, there were great differences of architectural tradition. In Czechoslovakia, Hungary, and the future DDR, the Modernist tendency was strong and dominant. In Poland it was balanced by a Neo-Classical tendency, while in Romania and Bulgaria the Neo-Classical style predominated. In all six countries, though, both Functionalism and Traditionalism were represented. Both styles were reinstated, but with a different balance of power between them. Traditionalism, in both its Neo-Classical and its national form, had lost authority. In the eyes of many young people it had fallen into disrepute. Modernism, on the other hand, had correspondingly strengthened its position, even in countries like Romania and Bulgaria where it was still fairly weak.

At first sight, the ruined cities of Poland and Germany gave the impression that everything had been destroyed and everything would have to be built all over again. Even in the cities worst affected, however, there were buildings that were undamaged or usable for temporary habitation, if only at basement level. Water and sewerage networks could be put back into operation. Shells and foundations could be reused, and where not even this was possible, there was brick to be salvaged. Everything was reused as far as possible.

The first stage of reconstruction was exclusively a practical problem, a matter of feeding people and giving them roofs over their heads. Very soon, though, decisions were also made concerning the rebuilding of historic monuments: the Zwinger in Dresden and the Łazienki Palace and Stare Miasto (Old Town) in Warsaw. The same went for the ruins of Buda in Budapest.

Reconstruction in Poland came to involve practically the entire nation, because even those who had not actually lost their homes were enlisted for the regularly recurring campaigns mounted above all in support of the reconstruction of Warsaw. Reconstruction was a unifying factor in a country with strong patriotic traditions, a country that had recently been resurrected after its fourth partition but was wracked by fierce internal dissensions. The reconstruction of the old centers of Poznań, Gdańsk, and Wrocław also had another significance: The long historical perspective was a reminder of the ancient sovereignty of the Polish crown over the subsequently German cities that Poland did not recover until 1918 and 1945.

Reconstruction in the future DDR was more hesitant, especially as regards national symbols and in particular where Berlin was concerned. The former royal palace at Lustgarten was sufficiently intact to be used in 1946 for an exhibition (devoted to town planning for Berlin), but it was demolished in 1950. In the DDR, historical associations long remained an argument *against* the reconstruction of historic monuments. In Poland they were an argument *for* such reconstructions. Reconstruction was the riposte to Nazi Germany's bid to deprive Poland of its national identity. And, as in the Soviet Union, there was little scope for the Functionalist aversion to reconstruction that was so influential in West Germany.

Reconstruction of the Nowy Świat in Warsaw was completed in 1949–50. This was the first stage in the rebuilding of the 2-km-long sequence of Nowy Świat–Krakowskie Przedmieście–Stare Miasto–Nowe

5 Warsaw before its reconstruction, looking north from Aleje Jerozolimskie along Nowy Świat and its continuation, Krakowskie Przedmieście. In the distance are Mariensztat and the Old Town.

6 Warsaw, apartment building in Mariensztat. Facade by Zygmunt Stępiński.

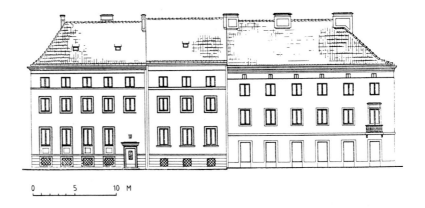

0   5   10 M

7 Warsaw after its reconstruction. The same view as in Figure 5. In left foreground, the International Press and Literature Club, designed, like Mariensztat, by Zygmunt Stępiński.

Miasto, one of the most remarkable historic urban environments in Europe (Figs. 5–8). By the mid-1950s it had been fully reinstated.

The building forming the entrance to Nowy Świat from Aleje Jerozolimskie is inscribed in capital letters: CAŁY NARÓD BUDUJE SWOJĄ STOLICĘ, that is, "the entire nation builds its capital city," a motto that occurred frequently in postwar Poland (see Figs. 7, 72). The building, designed by Zygmunt Stępiński, is not a reconstruction but a new edifice alluding to the historical context. So too is the same architect's Mariensztat housing development, constructed in 1947–49 on the east side of Krakowskie Przedmieście (see Fig. 6). This was part of the big Trasa W-Z project, the east-west throughway tunneled underneath Krakowskie Przedmieście (*Architektura*, 1949:11–12).

Wartime destruction and reconstruction stimulated the erection of new buildings in traditional styles, but only on a limited scale. The

8 Warsaw, Mariensztat, photographed in 1980.

crucial factor was the return of Modernism. Before any new buildings had been completed, Modernism was being promoted by the journals, by *Tér és forma* in Hungary, *Architektura ČSR* in Czechoslovakia, and *Architektura* in Poland. In the absence of finished buildings, they published projects, competition entries not least. And these were strikingly numerous.

One new building that attracted a good deal of attention at the planning stage during the early postwar years in Czechoslovakia was the collective housing block in Litvínov, an industrial town to the northwest of Prague (Fig. 9). There were far-reaching plans here for the production of synthetic petroleum, and a great deal of housing was needed. The demand was to be met partly by means of collective housing blocks, and a prototype of such a block intended for eight hundred residents and designed by Václav Hilský and Evžen Linhart (*Architektura ČSR*, 1946:7) was the winning entry in a competition held in 1946. The collective housing idea, probably derived from the Soviet Union, had already existed in Czechoslovakia during the thirties.

Strict functional differentiation was applied to the layout, with communal facilities in a low-rise central body, and with single rooms and two- and three-room apartments in thirteen-story high-rise wings. The vocabulary and the program ("new ways of living") as well as the layout were rooted in the radicalism of the interwar years, which probably explains why the scheme took so long to realize. The bulk of the complex was only completed in 1952, and the west wing

9 Litvínov, Czechoslovakia, collective housing by Václav Hilský and Evžen Linhart. Model, 1946.

10 Budapest, MÉMOSZ, house of the builders' unions, designed 1946. Architects: Lajos Gádoros, Imre Perényi, Gábor Preisich, and György Szrogh.

not until 1957. This big collective block did not fit in at all well with the Czech fifties.

Another strikingly modern building was the headquarters of the builders' unions in Budapest, frequently known by the acronym MÉMOSZ (Fig. 10). After a competition in 1946 it was built, between 1947 and 1950, on the broad Dózsa György út, Budapest's demonstration square, complete with a tribune for the party leaders and, before long, a statue of Stalin. This building is a six-story office block,

11, 12 Two Polish department stores designed in the postwar era: (above) by Marek Leykam in Poznań, and (right) by Ihnatowicz and Romański in Warsaw.

with a large congress hall, seating 1,250, adjoined to it at the rear. The main facade is a demonstration of modern construction technology: the wall is a thin screen, separated from the slender concrete pillars composing the main structure. This structural relationship provides the motif of the facade. Before long, in the language of Socialist Realism, that kind of thing was to be castigated as "technology fetishism." MÉMOSZ was also to be singled out for special reference in 1951 when the Minister of Culture, Révai, denounced Hungarian Modernism.

Examples of the return of Polish Modernism included two department stores, in Warsaw and Poznań, both designed and started immediately after the war but not completed until the 1950s. Marek Leykam's department store in the center of Poznań is a nine-story cylinder in which the stairwell forms a central core and the tone of the facades is set by the closely spaced verticals of the prefabricated concrete elements (Fig. 11). The Central Department Store (CDT) in Aleje Jerozolimskie, only two blocks away from Stępiński's reading room at Nowy Świat, was designed by Zbigniew Ihnatowicz and Jerzy Romański, who won the brief in a competition in 1948 (*Architektura* 1948:5; Fig. 12). Its sweeping horizontals echo the department stores of Erich Mendelsohn, for example, the Kaufhaus Petersdorff (1927) in Breslau/Wrocław.

Before long, buildings like these were to be fiercely criticized and condemned out of hand as Formalistic. Like MÉMOSZ in

13 Interior of the Băneasa airport building in Bucharest. Architects: Mircea and Cleopatra Alifanti, Nicolae Bădescu, and Ascanio Damian; completed 1948. Beneath the center of the dome, the somewhat later sculpture *Lenin and Stalin in Smolny,* by Constantin Baraschi.

Budapest and the collective housing unit in Litvínov, they were too provocative and far too closely in touch with architectural developments in Western Europe.

This was not the case with the first postwar buildings in Romania and Bulgaria. The airport building at Băneasa in Bucharest, designed in 1946, follows the tradition inherited from Auguste Perret: simplification of form and modern concrete structure, but no demonstrative break with tradition (Fig. 13). After the proclamation of Socialist Realism, the domed concourse of the arrivals hall could be presented in the guise of new Romanian architecture. And from the Town Hall in Burgas on the Black Sea, built in 1946 but designed before the war (Fig. 14), it was but a short step to Dimitrov's mausoleum in Sofia three years later, both buildings in fact being the work of the same architect, Georgi Ovcharov (see Figs. 151, 152).

Elsewhere, it was, above all, the projects that displayed the strength and breadth of Modernism, and especially the attraction it held for architects. Those projects also showed how the 1950s could have developed—for better or worse—given different conditions from those that were soon to divert the course of development.

From 1946 we have a scheme for the renewal of the Erzsébetváros district in Budapest, worked out while reconstruction was still in progress, by the architects of the city building office—József Fischer, Pál Granasztói, and Jenő Kismarty-Lechner (Fig. 15). This inner city area had a dense concentration of old three- and four-story buildings, covering nearly 60 percent of the land area. The scheme now was to replace them with sixteen slab blocks of nine and

14 Burgas, Bulgaria, Town Hall by Georgi Ovcharov, 1946.

15 Budapest, redevelopment scheme for the Erzsébetváros district. Perspective, 1946.

16 Czech project for the United Nations headquarters in New York, design by Josef Havlíček, 1947.

thirteen stories, which would provide 40 percent more dwelling space while occupying only 22 percent of the land area. This scheme demonstrated the alliance of Modernism with Rationalism and progress. The prospective drawings were reminiscent of Gropius, Hilberseimer, and Mies van der Rohe.

From 1947 we have the Czech architect Josef Havlíček's design for the United Nations headquarters in New York, which although not intended for his own country still conveys something of the situation there (Fig. 16). Havlíček had been a big name since the 1930s and was now one of ten architects from all over the world invited to submit designs for the UN building. Czechoslovakia still ranked as a bastion of modern architecture, and the UN was to be *modern*, in every way something different from the League of Nations in Geneva. Havlíček's design is dominated by a forty-story tower block with converging walls: a steep pyramid consisting of three volumes grouped round a single elevator well. It was modern enough, but it was not accepted. One year later the odds are that the Czech Socialist government would not have allowed this submission.

From 1948 we have a scheme for offices and housing in Warsaw, designed by the abovementioned architects Ihnatowicz and Romański for the site that, later on, came to be occupied by the Palace of Culture (Fig. 17). This too features high slab blocks, and once again several precincts have been amalgamated and treated as a single unit, emulating Rockefeller Center in New York City. The design was judged one of the two best entries in a competition for this district, which had been completely destroyed during the war. The other entry (Bogusławski and Łowínski) was based on the same principle, but its high-rise buildings took the form of tall cylinders.

From 1949, finally, we have a design by Hans Scharoun and his associates for Nachbarschaft Friedrichshain in East Berlin (Fig. 18). During the Weimar Republic, Scharoun had made a name for himself with his expressive, Modernist housing. After the war he was in charge of reconstruction in Berlin while it still had a single administration. After the administration split up, he remained very prominent in West Berlin but worked as well for a while on the eastern

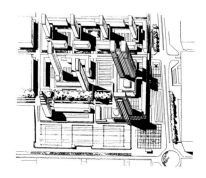

17 Warsaw, prize-winning project by Ihnatowicz and Romański for an office and housing development, 1948.

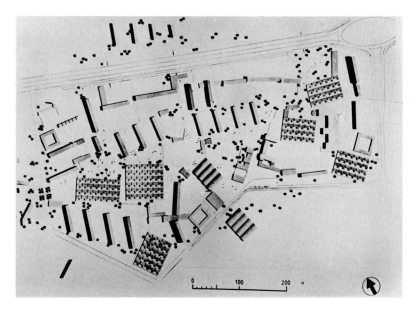

18 East Berlin, plan by Hans Scharoun and his collective, 1949, for a housing development south of Frankfurter Allee, renamed Stalinallee later that year. The area was a Nachbarschaft, or neighborhood unit.

side. His idea for the future of the city was not reconstruction in the true sense but a city of a new kind, an open city or *Stadtlandschaft*. His plan for Friedrichshain was a concretization of that idea, and it shows dwelling units of various kinds grouped freely in a park. Before long, however, Scharoun was to relinquish his post in East Berlin. A couple of years later Hochhaus Weberwiese and Stalinallee were built and laid out in the position intended for Nachbarschaft Friedrichshain.

The radical Modernism of these four projects never really came to fruition, but it played an important part as a target for the new cultural policy already in the making in 1949. Architecture of this kind was condemned as "cosmopolitan," the cat's paw of an imperialism bent on subversion by every possible means, even in countries that had already gone over to "the camp of peace and socialism."

The allusion of these projects to the interwar period and to Western European traditions was contradicted, in both form and content, by the first monumental project to be realized in postwar Eastern Europe: the Soviet victory monument in Berlin-Treptow, *Sowjetisches Ehrenmal* (Figs. 19, 20). There are many such monuments in Eastern Europe, but Treptow is the most overwhelming of them, being not just a single monument but a whole ensemble of park and monuments.

Following a competition under Soviet auspices in 1946, with a number of Germans among the forty-five participants, the brief was awarded to the sculptor Evgenii Vuchetich and the architect Jakov Belopolskii. In Berlin, where reconstruction had not yet got seriously

19, 20 East Berlin, Soviet victory monument at Treptow, constructed 1947–48. General plan and photograph from about 1970: (1) entrance gates, (2) The Mother Country, (3) flags, (4) the marble tombs, (5) mass graves, (6) The Liberator.

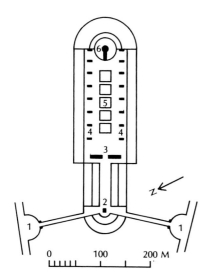

under way, the work was done between 1947 and 1949 by German labor under Soviet direction, partly using materials from Hitler's Chancellery.

At the beginning of the 400-meter central axis there stands the marble statue of a sorrowing Mother Country; 150 meters in front of her, two immense, stylized flags of red granite (bearing the hammer and sickle) are lowered in tribute to the memory of the fallen. Two soldiers kneel beneath the flags. At the end point of the central axis is a burial mound (*kurgan* in Russian) with a mausoleum surmounted by a 12-meter-high bronze soldier, "The Liberator." With the sword in his right hand he has shattered the swastika, which lies in fragments at his feet. On his left arm he lifts up a child, in the protective manner of a victor.

Five mass graves and sixteen relief-carved marble tombs (one for each of the Soviet republics) form the last resting places of 6,800 Soviet soldiers. A special grave contains four "heroes of the Soviet Union": a general, an officer, an NCO, and a private. The mosaic vault of the mausoleum is set with a five-pointed crystal star emblazoned with the words USSR and VICTORY (the Victory Order founded in 1945).

The monument at Treptow honors the fallen, but only those who fell on the winning side. It is a victory monument in the land of the vanquished—or, in the words of the victor, "in the land of the liberated."

A few years earlier, as they advanced through Belorussia and the Ukraine, the Germans had had the same idea: monuments to their own troops in a foreign land. This is an ancient tradition among liberators with historic missions, aspirants to world domination, and imperialists.

This chapter began by emphasizing the differences between the six countries as regards the conditions applying to building. But it ends with a significant similarity among them: the organization, in 1948–49, of state planning bureaus. This was a decisive change, both professionally for the architects and for subsequent architectural developments. Once building activity had been subsumed by the five-year plans and had come to be dominated entirely by big state-sponsored commissions, there was no longer any room for private architectural practices.

The state planning bureaus were large workplaces, often with a couple of hundred employees and consultants of all kinds gathered under one roof. Most of them operated at the regional level, but some of them specialized in hospitals, factories, or military buildings. The organizational pattern came from the Soviet Union. The new scheme of things was introduced quickly, starting with Bulgaria early in 1948. Czechoslovakia and Hungary followed suit that year, next came Poland, at the end of the year, and finally, at the beginning of 1949, Romania and the DDR. A completely new organization was in place in all six countries within the space of a year—with serious practical and ideological consequences. The state planning bureaus were a precondition without which the sequel would hardly have been possible.

The Cold War

II

From 1949 to the Mid-1950s

During 1949, increasing demands were made for the welding together of Eastern Europe into a homogeneous ideological bloc. Purges within the ranks gathered intensity. Even in the uppermost echelon there were "traitors," "Titoists," and "American agents." Lázló Rajk in Hungary and Traicho Kostov in Bulgaria were sentenced to death and executed—unjustly, as it was later to prove.

The theoretical basis of the purges was Stalin's thesis of the intensified class struggle: The greater the success of one's own cause, the more dangerous the opponent becomes, the greater is the vigilance required in tracking him down, even where he is least expected, and the more ruthlessly he has to be fought.

The same orthodoxy as in the Soviet Union was now insisted on not only in political and economic affairs but also in science and art. There was bourgeois, reactionary science and there was proletarian, progressive science. Biology and genetics provided the stock example of this. "Mendelists and Morganists" were contrasted with the doctrine of Michurin and Lysenko, which, being firmly rooted in dialectical materialism, was an example to other sciences.

The same antithesis prevailed in art: on the one hand, Cosmopolitanism, and on the other, Socialist Realism. In the Cominform newspaper *For a Lasting Peace, for a People's Democracy* (1949:16), Jerzy Albrecht, one of the leaders of the Polish party wrote as follows.

> The sharpening struggle between the forces of progress, peace, and socialism, led by the Soviet Union, and the imperialist camp has faced us with the urgent task of fighting cosmopolitanism in culture, for it is with the help of this weapon

that American imperialism hopes to weaken the peoples ideo-logically.

The cosmopolitan, accordingly, was dangerous. It came close to trea-son. And "cosmopolitan" was a dangerous word bordering on other dangerous words: Trotskyist, Titoist, Zionist. Thus it was no trivial matter that Modernism in arts of all kind was now classed as Cosmopolitan.

This was an extension to the people's democracies of Andrei Zhdanov's campaign against Western cultural influences. The new signals were proclaimed at national, sectorially organized confer-ences. Albrecht's article referred to three such conferences in Poland during June 1949, dealing in turn with the theater, pictorial art, and architecture.

In the three Cominform resolutions adopted in November 1949 at a meeting in Hungary, the three archadversaries were said to be Anglo-American warmongers, right-wing socialists in Western Europe, and the Yugoslav renegades (*For a Lasting Peace,* 1949:28). The common denominator here was the threat of an imminent war against the Soviet Union and its allies, with reference among other things to the signing, in April of that year, of the North Atlantic Treaty. The result was still greater vigilance against the West, in all fields.

The world picture disseminated through political speeches, newspapers, and periodicals was founded on antitheses. Light was contrasted with darkness, peace with war, success with defeat, the future with the past, the victors of history with its losers. The chess game of world history was already over. That, at least, was the description conveyed by a political cartoon occupying a full page of the German-language Romanian newspaper *Neuer Weg* in August 1949 (Fig. 21). White moves Labor and Peace (king and queen) to the center of the board. They are supported by Science and Art and also by Agriculture. Behind them they have the invincible collective, made up of all classes and peoples—of workers, peasants, and intel-lectuals, of whites, blacks, and Chinese. In the distant background is the heavy support of industrial expansion and agricultural mecha-nization under the five-year plan (rooks).

On the black side, by contrast, all is confusion. The USA and the Vatican—capitalism and the Church (king and queen)—are about to slither off the board. The shot-up tank and the wrecked warship (rooks) have already done so, and the rats are literally leaving the sinking ship. Remaining on the board is a motley array of effete politicians and military leaders: Winston Churchill and the "right-

21 The contest between East and West as a game of chess. East (white) is about to win. West, in the foreground, is on the point of utter collapse. Political cartoon from the Romanian newspaper *Neuer Weg*, 1949.

wing socialist" Bevin, Chiang Kai-shek, and Field Marshal Montgomery, each riding backward on a donkey. Generals Franco and de Gaulle have already been knocked over. De Gasperi, the Italian premier, is portrayed as a monkey and the Benelux countries as Siamese triplets. Dollars and munitions of war instead of peaceful implements. Contemptible, ridiculous figureheads instead of the collective of workers and peasants.

During the years that followed, this world picture was reiterated in many different ways. The antithesis between the political systems permeated everything, or rather, it *ought* to have. Wherever it was not sufficiently in evidence—in architecture, for example—something was wrong.

A tremendous manifestation of the ideological front and of support for the Soviet Union occurred with the celebration of Stalin's seventieth birthday in December 1949, an event that merits a study in its own right, to at least the same degree as other ceremonial climaxes of history, national jubilees, coronations, and royal funerals.

The celebrations were almost as important a concern in the people's democracies as in the Soviet Union. Varna, the second largest city of Bulgaria, was renamed Stalin. East Berlin announced the building of its Stalinallee. Budapest and Bucharest resolved to erect statues of Stalin, and the same happened in Prague, where the monument thus planned was to dominate the urban scene for a few short years. Congratulatory addresses from Bulgaria, the Cominform weekly reported, had been signed personally by more than one out of every two Bulgarians, at mass meetings organized all over the country (*For a Lasting Peace*, 1949: 28).

On the stage of the Bolshoi Theater in Moscow, Stalin's portrait was surrounded by the flags of the Soviet republics (Fig. 22). In front of this display, Stalin himself stood joining in the applause, together with the other Soviet leaders, Mao Zedong, the leaders of Eastern Europe, and representatives of the French, Spanish, and Italian Communist parties. Above the stage the audience could read: LONG LIVE THE GREAT LEADER AND TEACHER OF THE COMMUNIST PARTY AND THE SOVIET PEOPLES, COMRADE J. V. STALIN. For months after, *Pravda* went on reproducing congratulatory addresses. And for years, museum galleries were cleared for exhibitions of the birthday presents.

During the early postwar years, the standard of living in Eastern Europe had risen quickly and conspicuously. In the early 1950s it improved less rapidly, if at all. Industrial investment and armaments preempted a large share of the gross national product, relatively speaking a bigger share than in the West. Private consumption was stinted. Apart from basic essentials, there was little for people to buy. There was a world of difference between the gray scarcity of everyday life and the propaganda image of the economic situation.

The official view of economic conditions was formulated *ex cathedra* in Stalin's *The Economic Problems of Socialism in the USSR*, his last publication, which appeared in 1952. In it we read that no capi-

Пролетарии всех стран, соединяйтесь!

Всесоюзная Коммунистическая Партия (больш.).

ПРАВДА

Орган Центрального Комитета и МК ВКП(б).

№ 356 (11463) | Четверг, 22 декабря 1949 г. | ЦЕНА 20 КОП.

Имя Сталина—самое дорогое для наше народа, для простых людей во всем мире. Им Сталина—это символ грядущей победы ко мунизма. Сердца советских людей и миллион тружеников земного шара преисполнены горяче любовью к тебе—Великий Сталин!

ДА ЗДРАВСТВУЕТ ВЕЛИКИЙ ВОЖДЬ И УЧИТЕЛЬ КОММУНИСТИЧЕСКОЙ ПАРТИИ И СОВЕТСКОГО НАРОДА ТОВАРИЩ И. В. СТАЛИН !

Торжественное заседание в Большом театре, посвященное семидесятилетию со дня рождения Иосифа Виссарионовича Сталина. В президиуме (слева направо) товарищи: Пальмиро Тольятти, А. Н. Косыгин, Л. М. Каганович, Мао Цзе-дун, Н. А. Булганин, И. В. Сталин, В. Ульбрихт, Ю. Цеденбал, Н. С. Хрущев, И. Коплениг, Долорес Ибаррури, Г. Георгиу-Деж, М. А. Суслов, Н. М. Шверник, В. Червенков, Г. М. Маленков, В. Широкий, Л. П. Берия, К. Е. Ворошилов, В. М. Молотов, А. И. Микоян, Матиас Ракоши. *Фото Ф. Кислова.*

talist country could have given the people's democracies such competent, advantageous assistance as the Soviet Union, that the people's democracies will soon be able to manage without imports, while Western Europe, as a result of the Marshall Plan, is becoming embroiled in "the general crisis of the world's capitalist system."

This could also be put across pictorially. A drawing in *Pravda*, also distributed in the people's democracies and reproduced here from *Neuer Weg*, shows the trial of strength between the economic systems, measured in terms of the growth of industrial output between 1937 and 1952 (Fig. 23). It is of no consequence for our purposes that the comparison, because it says nothing about absolute figures, is of limited statistical worth. The picture conveyed is what counts.

22 Moscow, officials gathered on the stage of the Bolshoi Theater on Stalin's seventieth birthday, 21 December 1949, as pictured the following day on the front page of *Pravda*. Stalin, the only participant in uniform, can be seen in front of the portrait, to the left.

Zwei Wirtschaftsentwicklungen

23 Two graph lines of economic development. One for the East, is nearly vertical, while that for the West is a heavy chain. Political cartoon in *Neuer Weg,* January 1953, after *Pravda.*

In front of the heroic worker of the people's democracies, with his five-year plan in hand, the development graph climbs, arrow-like, steeply upward. In the background we see tremendous chimneys, and in the foreground tractors working in fields. The graph line for the Western European countries, by contrast, rises but slowly and takes the form of a heavy chain, which of course is the chain referred to in the Communist Manifesto, the chain that the proletariat will cast off in the coming revolution. The old capitalist is making off with the profits in the Marshall Plan's dollar bag. The so-called help is just a new form of exploitation. In the background can be seen an obsolete factory, tanks, and artillery.

The austerity of the early 1950s was accompanied by a massive propaganda of success, founded—as was soon to become apparent—on a programmatic overestimate of the economic potential of the system and on a no less programmatic underrating of the world at large. This was a misjudgment based not so much on observations of reality as on theoretical deliberations.

Since the Soviet Union was the leading force of world progress and had attained a higher level of historical development, then the Soviet Union, and in its wake the people's democracies too, must automatically be the leader in all fields of social life, from economics to science, art, and architecture. A Russo-nationalistic caricature of this thesis could also be applied to history. All the big inventions had been devised by Russians, indeed, all that was great was of Russian origin. "Russia is the native country of the elephants," as we read in the composer Shostakovich's memoirs—a desperate, irreverent joke on the part of Soviet intellectuals during the Stalin era. And the response was no greater in the people's democracies, entirely foreign as they were to the traditions of Russian absolutism.

The new order was victorious. Its opponents were beaten but still they approached from all quarters, all the time, and in every context. Surveillance and suspicion followed in the wake of the ideological mobilization, accompanied in due course by reprisals, dismissals, and arrests. Failures were blamed on bourgeois elements, reactionaries, class enemies, infiltrators, and saboteurs. The culmination came with the Slanský trial in Czechoslovakia in 1951–52, named for the Secretary-General of the Czech Communist Party, Rudolf Slanský, who, together with ten other accused persons, was sentenced to death and executed for antistate activities. The public confessions of the accused, culminating in improbable self-denunciations, were reminiscent of the Moscow trials of 1936–38.

Karel Kaplan, the Czech historian, maintains that the Slanský trial and its ramifications—affecting all levels of political life—were

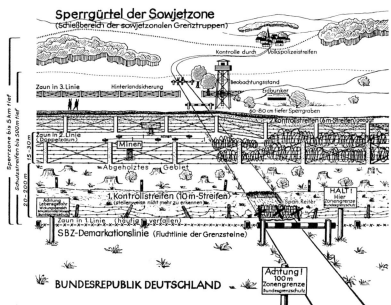

only one side of what he terms the "militarization" of society. At a secret conference in the Kremlin in January 1951, Stalin and Molotov had declared to the leaders of the people's democracies that, for the next three or four years, politics would have to be entirely subordinated to one objective: the military occupation of the rest of Europe. The right opportunity had come. The Americans were tied up in Korea.

Kaplan's story was made possible by temporary relaxations, during the Prague Spring of 1968, of the secrecy surrounding official records, and much remains to be confirmed. Even so, his militarization concept makes a good summary of known facts concerning conditions in the people's democracies during Stalin's last years: further escalation of the targets for an economy already under heavy strain, additional favors for heavy industry, the acceleration of armaments, curbs on private consumption, stronger positions for the military in every connection, a further rise in the ideological temperature, rigid censorship, purges, a cult of the leader.

The system was superior, but at the same time it had to be protected and screened off from the rest of the world. The Iron Curtain was enlarged and reinforced (Figs. 24, 25). The stretch of it through Germany was the most closely guarded of all. A resolution in 1952 by the DDR Council of Ministers made a 5-km belt inside the frontier (the line of demarcation) a restricted zone to which only the holders

24, 25 Left: Map showing the course of the Iron Curtain, from the Baltic to the Caucasus. Right: Schematic drawing of the rigorously guarded border, looking from West Germany toward the DDR, here referred to as SBZ, meaning the "Soviet-occupied zone."

of a special permit could be admitted. The closer one came to the frontier, the denser the surveillance and the exclusion devices became.

It is no exaggeration to say that the Iron Curtain, throughout its massive extent from the Baltic to the Black Sea, was one of the great construction projects of postwar Europe. But it was very different from such historical precursors as the Great Wall of China or Hadrian's Wall in Britain. Then again, it had a completely different task—not just keeping intruders out, but keeping its own population in. And it was quite devoid of the impressive, deterrent exterior of a fortress. It was much more similar to the barriers surrounding a maximum-security camp, with barbed wire supported by concrete posts, forest cut down for a better view and a clearer field of fire, mines, *chevaux-de-frise,* lookout towers, and armed guards with dogs. The rigidly guarded frontier was both an instrument and a symbol of the screening-off of Eastern Europe from the West and, accordingly, of the division of Europe.

Only the sectorial boundary through divided Berlin was open and unguarded, and it would remain so until August 1961. Between the formation of the DDR in September 1949 and the end of 1953, more than a million fugitives entered West Berlin and the Federal Republic from the East. Another 700,000 arrived between 1954 and 1956, and so it went until 1961, a copious flood of more than 200,000 refugees a year, on average more than six hundred a day. In the West they were welcome, both for ideological reasons and because there was a shortage of labor for the expanding industry of the West German miracle. In the East, if they were caught, they were severely punished for "deserting the republic."

Describing this dramatic phase of events in just a few words is difficult for many reasons, not least because those actively involved often had little scope for maneuver and their motives were of a complexity to which it is hard to do justice. But to supplement the account already given, here are some reflections by two Eastern European writers on this critical period in the history of their countries. First, Adam Zagajewski, the Polish poet and novelist, born in Lwów in 1945:

> Beginning all over again, refashioning society, creating a new
> human being, building up a culture for the masses—can
> there be a more inspiring task anywhere in the world? And
> yet the group of enthusiasts was not all that large, and
> indeed it was hard to tell the difference between enthusiasm

and fear. One sentiment merged with the other, like the colors of the rainbow.

(*Polen. Staat im Schatten der Sowjetunion*, 1981)

Second, the Czech author Milan Kundera, born in Brno in 1929, and himself once numbered among the enthusiasts:

> . . . old wrongs were righted, new wrongs perpetrated, factories were nationalized, thousands of people went to jail, medical care became free of charge, small shopkeepers lost their shops, aged workers took their first vacations ever in confiscated country houses, and we smiled the smile of happiness.

(*The Book of Laughter and Forgetting*, 1978)

Iconography, Rhetoric, and the Cult of Stalin

The new society was accompanied by new symbols: the *red flag,* symbol of the power of the working class; the *hammer and sickle* or other symbols of the unity of workers and peasants, the *five-pointed star,* symbol of communism, the morning star. Together these three symbols made up a fourth, the *flag of the Soviet Union.* The red flag, showing hammer and sickle and the five-pointed star, symbolized the leading role of the Soviet Union.

The new symbols also included the stylized group portrait of *Marx-Engels-Lenin-Stalin,* all depicted in profile and symbolizing the ideology of Marxism-Leninism. Then there was the Soviet soldier, symbolizing liberation from fascism. Furthermore there was the *white dove,* although peace could be just as frequently symbolized by the very word *peace,* often presented in several languages and in capital letters: PEACE! MIR! PAIX! Or in the languages of the six people's democracies: FRIEDEN! POKÓJ! MÍR! BÉKE! PACE! MIR!

All seven of these symbols, however, could be replaced by just one: *Stalin* (Figs. 26, 27). Stalin was everything. According to a frequently employed turn of phrase, he was "the immortal genius of the working class"; as "the greatest strategist of all nations and all ages" he had led the liberation from fascism. He was "the Lenin of our time" and "the life-giving force of socialism." He was "the coryphaeus of science" and "the children's friend." In all pictures referring to the revolutionary year of 1917, he was portrayed at Lenin's side, as the man who was destined right from the beginning to take over. His name symbolized peace. He was synonymous with

26 Stalin portrayed as the children's friend, met with flowers, a dove of peace, and embraces. *Stalin with the Pioneers,* by the Bulgarian sculptor Ivan Funev and his collective. Plaster sculpture, intended to be cast in bronze. Exhibited in Sofia, 1952.

27 Stalin as generalissimo and great master builder, next to a model building in a room at the Kremlin. Visible through the open window is the tower block at Kotelnicheskaia Naberezhnaia. From model to finished building, from plan to victory. Oil painting by the Romanian artist Ştefan Szönyi, exhibited in Bucharest in 1952.

peace. It could be invoked on *all* occasions. There was "Stalin's concern for mankind" and there was "Stalin's plan for the transformation of nature."

But launching new symbols was not enough. They also had to be integrated with everyday life and tradition, and since most of the old traditions were bound with the Church and the old political order of things, new traditions had to be created or, as the British historian Eric Hobsbawm puts it, one had to *invent traditions.* The religious festivals were degraded. May Day and the anniversary of the October Revolution (7 November) became great national festivals, representing respectively the traditional festival of the labor movement and the day on which history definitely took a new turn.

To these festivals were added the new "national days." The old ones had recalled national rebirth in 1918 (Poland, Czechoslovakia), liberation from the Turks (Romania, Bulgaria), or the death date of St. Stephen in 1038 (Hungary). The new ones recalled instead liberation from fascism by the glorious Soviet Army, the formation of the so-called Lublin government (Poland), or the proclamation of the new republic (DDR). The anniversaries of these and other important political events were celebrated as jubilees: the second anniversary, the third anniversary, the fourth anniversary, and so on.

Then there were international events of various kinds, including the grandly orchestrated World Youth Festivals. Prague in 1947 was followed by Budapest in 1949, East Berlin in 1951, Bucharest in 1953, and Warsaw in 1955. These festivals were a grand venture by the country arranging them. New stadium facilities, sports centers, theaters, and cinemas were completed in time for the official opening. The signature tune of the festivals was "the hymn of democratic world youth."

One annual event was the International Race for Peace, a bicycle touring event through the DDR, Poland, and Czechoslovakia ("Internationale Radfernfahrt für den Frieden," "Międzynarodowy kolarski wyścig pokoju," "Mezinárodní cyklistický závod míru"), first held in 1948 and arranged by the party newspaper in each country.

With the exception of Czechoslovakia and Poland—whose white eagle, however, had lost its crown—new national coats of arms were introduced on Soviet lines (Fig. 28). All of them included wreathed ears of wheat together with stripes showing the national colors and various symbols of technology and industrialization: hammer, compasses, oil derrick, and gear wheel. The Romanian coat of arms included a rising sun, those of Hungary and Bulgaria featured the five-pointed star. The DDR emblem alone lacks a symbol of this kind for the bright future ahead, but then it was only finalized in 1955. After Stalin's death—and in the case of the DDR, after the rebellious events of 17 June 1953—the future was no longer what it had been. It was treated with more circumspection.

In reality, the new national coats of arms were also a weapon of the parties. In the newly formed people's democracies, it was only a short step from state to party.

The new political order was also proclaimed in coins, bank notes, and postage stamps (Fig. 29). In addition to national coats of arms and the other new symbols, these also featured a complete new iconography. The obverse of the Polish National Bank's new 100-zloty note in 1948 featured—instead of the kings, presidents, and national heroes usually displayed on bank notes—the portrait of a miner. The reverse showed a landscape, a close-packed industrial scene with a forest of smoking chimneys, factory buildings, cooling towers, and railway lines (Fig. 30). Perhaps this picture represented an existing landscape, but above all it was a picture of industrial society, of the spirit of progress and industry in the new, socialist Poland. In 1948 the smoke coming from the factory chimneys was still the smoke of industriousness and progress. And in Western Europe, too, the time was still far ahead when smoke would instead begin to mean pollution.

Monuments to the Soviet Army were erected before any other permanent symbols of the new political order existed. Most of them were put up by the army itself, with the assistance of Soviet artists and architects. These monuments proliferated, being erected in military cemeteries and battlefields, in parks and in downtown open

28 Four new national coats of arms, from top: DDR (1955), Hungary (1949), Romania (1948), and Bulgaria (1946). Bulgaria was liberated on 9 September 1944.

29 Sixteen Polish stamps, issued 1948–55.

a *Marx-Engels-Lenin-Stalin. "Congress for the unity of the working class, referring to the amalgamation of the Communist and Social Democratic parties, 1948.* **b** *Three bricklayers. "The rebuilding of Warsaw" (compulsory surcharge, as in several of the following cases), 1950.* **c** *Miner and farm worker. "Forward into battle for the 6-year plan," 1950.* **d** *Felix Dzerzhinsky, Bolshevik of Polish origin, founder of the Cheka. Marking the quarter-centenary of his death, 1951.* **e** *President Bierut. "Town"(left), "Country" (right),"7 years of the people's Poland," 22 July 1951.* **f** *Housing construction. "The 6-year plan means 223,000 new homes," 1951.* **g** *Rural electrification. "The 6-year plan means 2.3 times more electrical energy," 1951.* **h** *The Lenin Steelworks (Nowa Huta). "We are building Nowa Huta," 1952.* **i** *Women on a demonstration march, placards with the word "peace" in various languages. "International Women's Day" (8 March), 1952.* **j** *May Day demonstration, 1952.* **k** *Stalin. "Month for the deepening of Polish-Soviet friendship" (November), 1952.* **l** *President Bierut surrounded by little girls in a field of flowers. "International Children's Day" (1 June), 1952.* **m** *Miner. "Miners' Day" (4 December), 1953.* **n** *Warsaw, MDM, Plac Konstytucji (Constitution Square), 1953.* **o** *Monument to Polish-Soviet comrades in arms, in the Praga district of Warsaw, 1955.* **p** *Dove with olive branch and the Palace of Culture in Warsaw. "Vth World Youth Festival, Warsaw, August 1955."*

STO ZŁOTYCH

100 100 100 100

BILETY NARODOWEGO BANKU
POLSKIEGO SĄ PRAWNYM ŚROD-
-KIEM PŁATNICZYM W POLSCE.

30 Reverse of 100-zloty note issued by the Polish National Bank in 1948. Drawn by Wacław Borowski and printed in Czechoslovakia.

spaces. The Treptow monument in East Berlin, mentioned above, was in a class of its own (see Figs. 19, 20), but a guidebook from the DDR mentions another two hundred monuments, and a similar guide from Poland lists more than three hundred.

The monuments were of three main types: the Soviet soldier, in bronze or stone; the pillar or obelisk; and, taken from the battlefield, the Soviet tank or gun put up on a stone base. Here are some examples, all of them from the DDR.

In Seelow, near Frankfurt an der Oder, the victorious Soviet soldier stands on a high plinth of rough-hewn ashlar (Fig. 31). At his feet is the shattered turret of a German tank. The monument is named officially *Denkstätte der Befreiung,* but it really takes the form of a victory monument, rather than a memorial to liberation or to the fallen. One of the last great battles of the war, claiming an estimated thirty thousand Soviet lives, took place here between 16 and 18 April 1945. The monument, designed by the Soviet sculptor Lev Kerbel, was erected in 1946–47.

In Torgau, Saxony, on the banks of the Elbe, there stands a monumental memorial stone, erected in 1946 (Fig. 32). It is surmounted by bronze flags and rifles, resembling a trophy display. The sides of it display the hammer and sickle, and on the front and back it is emblazoned with the five-pointed star. The front is inscribed, in Russian: LONG LIVE THE VICTORIOUS RED ARMY AND THE HEROIC TROOPS OF OUR ALLIES, VICTORS OF A FASCIST GERMANY. Advance parties of the American and Soviet forces met here on 25 April 1945, a "historic moment," hence the unusual mention of the Red Army's allies in the struggle against Nazi Germany. It is a mar-

31, 32, 33 Three monuments to the Soviet Army, all in the DDR. From left: Seelow, Torgau, and Klein-Machnow.

tial monument in the Russian tradition, of the kind associated with the victory over Napoleon in 1812 and revived in 1945. The plinth is signed: ERECTED BY ARMY FIELD POST 42603, 1946.

In Klein-Machnow, near Potsdam, a Soviet T 34 tank, No. 157, stands on a stone base inscribed, in German and Russian: HONOR TO THE SOVIET ARMY (Fig. 33). This tank took part in the final battle for Berlin, which began on 25 April 1945. The stone base is a modern version of the plinth of Falconet's famous equestrian statue of Peter the Great erected in St. Petersburg in 1782, thus intimating, to the initiated beholder (until the tank was removed in the summer of 1990), a parallel between Peter the Great's advance to the Gulf of Finland and the Soviet Army's march on Berlin.

The new monuments did more than commemorate historic events. Every year they provided the venue for celebrating, with military honors and the deposition of wreaths, both the anniversary of "liberation from fascism" and that of "the great October Revolution." And so they did until 1989.

The monuments had a message over and above that conveyed by their inscriptions: Soviet influence was to endure. A victorious army does not erect stone and bronze monuments to itself in places where it proposes to relinquish control. For the artists, these monuments conveyed a special message. *Realism* and *tradition* were two of the fundamental principles of Socialist Realism, and the Soviet victory monuments were the first implementation of this doctrine in the future people's democracies.

An important part of the political message was concerned with *the plan*—the five-year plan or, in Poland, the six-year plan. The focus

34, 35 Two Polish posters from 1949. Left: "Forward into battle for the 6-year plan!" by Włodzimierz Zakrzewski." Right: "We are forging the foundations of socialism: the 6-year plan," by Jerzy Srokowski.

of attention here was on the industrial worker and heavy industry. But the message was also conveyed in figures: 5 and 6 took on a symbolic pregnancy. They were depicted monumentally in political posters, they were incorporated in the decor of monumental tenement buildings, and they even penetrated private life. In Poland, Christmas tree decorations were sold in the form of a 6—a step toward the secularization of Christmas and one way for Party stalwarts to display their fidelity.

Banners and posters proclaimed the new political objectives, constantly reminding people of what had been achieved already: liquidation of the old political system, abolition of the private ownership of the means of production, establishment of the people's democracy, friendship with the Soviet Union—eternal friendship with the Soviet Union (Figs. 34, 35).

The daily papers, of course, did the same. The powerful Party newspapers—*Neues Deutschland* (New Germany), *Trybuna Ludu* (People's Tribune), *Rudé Právo* (Red Justice), *Szabad Nép* (Free People), *Scînteia* (The Spark), and *Rabotnichesko Delo* (The Workers' Cause)—emulated *Pravda* in both content and outward design. All of them were the organs of central Party committees with mastheads reading: "Proletarians in all countries, unite!" They even had the same style of writing—ponderous, overexplicit, self-congratulatory. One journal common to all six countries and also intended for the Western Communist parties, was the Cominform weekly. The English edition

36 Warsaw, 22 July 1949, Poland's new national day. The marchers carried portraits of Stalin, Bolesław Bierut, Engels, Mao Zedong, and others, as well as a banner reading PEOPLE'S POLAND 5 YEARS.

was named "For a Lasting Peace, for a People's Democracy!"

Everywhere there were portraits of the leaders—in school class-rooms, in factories, on demonstration marches (Figs. 36–38). Often they were matched so as to illustrate the alliance with the Soviet Union: Pieck and Stalin in the DDR, Bierut and Stalin in Poland, Gottwald and Stalin in Czechoslovakia, Rákosi and Stalin in Hungary, Gheorghiu-Dej and Stalin in Romania, Dimitrov (later Chervenkov) and Stalin in Bulgaria—just as the national flag was

almost invariably shown together with the flag of the Soviet Union.

The same sentiments could be expressed as slogans, by chanting crowds. In Bulgaria: *LE*-NIN, *STA*-LIN, DI-MI-*TROV*! Or in Poland, on its national day in 1950, after the DDR had confirmed the Oder–Neisse frontier: *STA*-LIN, *BIE*-RUT, *WIL*-HELM *PIECK*, or also in Poland: *LE*-NIN, *STA*-LIN, RO-KOS-*SOV*-SKY! Rokossovsky was the Soviet marshal of Polish origin who, between 1949 and 1956, was Poland's Minister of Defense and Supreme Commander and also for a time second in command of the government.

Important factories and public buildings were surmounted with red stars, often with built-in lighting, so that after dark they would be visible everywhere in the city. Loudspeakers in many public places helped to disseminate the political message. Practically all buildings had fixtures for flags and bunting to be displayed on national festivals. Along the main streets used for parades and demonstration marches, it was the expected thing for every household to put out a red flag. Anyone failing to do so risked incurring unwelcome attention—like the greengrocer, in a philosophical text by Václav Havel, who omits to show a slogan in his shop window (*Tidskriften Östeuropa*, 1981:1).

Many factories and other big workplaces had what was called a "red corner," a bust of Lenin, Stalin, or Dimitrov against a background of red cloth and with a political motto—about exceeding the planning targets, for example. Ideological altars of this kind could also be seen in the homes of keen Party members. But a red corner could also be a special room containing books and magazines for the workers' ideological instruction.

It has often been observed that, in the Soviet Union, these red corners—like the portraits of the leaders carried on demonstration marches—can be viewed as a continuation of an old, Orthodox icon tradition. For our purposes, it is more important to note that only a minority of the populations of the people's democracies had such a background.

Streets, squares, and parks were renamed. Hindenburg, Piłsudski, Masaryk, and Andrássy were dropped, together with the kings of Romania and the tsars of Bulgaria. They were superseded by Marx and Engels, Lenin and Stalin, Pushkin and Gorky, the Paris Commune and the October Revolution. Or else by names from a country's own radical and revolutionary tradition: Liebknecht, Marchlewski, Fučík, Petőfi, Bălcescu, Blagoev. Or names of the Soviet generals and marshals who had led the Red Army at the liberation. New official names, but by no means always accepted by the population.

Following a pattern already established in the Soviet Union during the 1920s, there were also instances of places being named after a country's own leaders while they were still alive. In 1948, the Czech industrial city of Zlín was renamed Gottwaldov. Gheorghiu-Dej and Dimitrov also bestowed their names on cities. And it was common practice for large industrial concerns to be called after eminent Party officials.

The leader and the mass were the poles of political life and this polarity was most clearly apparent on the big festivals such as May Day and the national day (see Figs. 36–38). Both the following descriptions come from Romania in 1950 and are taken from official accounts in the journal *La Roumanie Nouvelle* (nos. 43 and 51), which was intended for a Western European readership.

In the May Day parade in Bucharest that year, hundreds of thousands of marching workers chanted their absolute determination to fight to the last ounce of their strength "for peace, for socialism, for life." That parade lasted for five hours. There were veterans of the resistance to fascism and young pioneers with red scarves rhythmically shouting "*STA*-LIN, *PA*-CE-A! *STA*-LIN, *PA*-CE-A!" (Stalin, peace!). There were factory workers with red flags and big painted charts illustrating the ample accomplishment of the planning targets. There were construction workers from the Danube–Black Sea Canal and others from the recently started polygraphic combine Casa Scînteii. They carried an enormous painting showing what the building would look like when finished. There were people from collective farms, craftsmen, students, sportsmen, artists, and composers. There were representatives of the national minorities—Germans and Hungarians from Transylvania, wearing their picturesque folk costumes. There were portraits of Gheorghiu-Dej and Ana Pauker, of Marx and Engels, of Lenin, Stalin, and Mao Zedong. Spectators applauded and gave loud voice to their solidarity with the Greek delegation "in its struggle against Anglo-American imperialism, abetted by the traitor Tito." Before the parade, everybody had affirmed a letter to Stalin in which the workers of Romania expressed their devotion and their trust in "our people's best friend, the ingenious leader of all the world's workers." Afterward, we read, Bucharest resounded with singing and dancing far into the night.

And so to the Romanian national day that year, on 23 August ("the anniversary of our people's liberation by the glorious Soviet Army"). That day was celebrated in all the towns and villages of Romania, but particularly this year in Braşov, Transylvania. From the thirteenth century until 1867 the city had been called Kronstadt. For about fifty years after that it bore the Hungarian name of Brassó. When, as a result of the Treaty of Versailles, it was ceded (with the rest of Transylvania) to Romania, its name was altered to Braşov. But now it was to change names again. The day before the national day, the leaders of state had agreed to a request from the workers of Braşov for their city to be called after Stalin, "the great genius of laboring humanity."

The demonstration marchers carried signs displaying the new name of Oraşul Stalin (Stalin City), as well as red flags and portraits of Stalin (see Fig. 37). Biggest of all was a head and shoulders portrait of Stalin, 4 meters high, moving on wheels. Young Pioneers released white doves and everyone chanted the name of Stalin.

After a mass meeting in the big medieval square, the local political leader declared, in the name of the workers: "I assure the Central Committee that, through new successes in the struggle for peace and socialism, we will make ourselves worthy of the new name." By way of conclusion, the participants spread out through the city, taking down all old signs showing the name of Braşov and replacing them with new ones reading ORAŞUL STALIN.

The author of the account summarized here explains that the enthusiasm shown by the workers of Oraşul Stalin is typical of the entire Romanian people and that it will lead to new victories—at work, in the study of Stalin's teachings, and in the acquisition of experience from the Soviet Union. The article ends with a sentence in bold print: **"The name of Stalin is dear to our people, for it is a synonym of peace."**

In the capital city, the "Permanent J. V. Stalin Exhibition" had been opened the day before. This was an exhibition of photographs, paintings, sculptures, books, and documents, all dealing with Stalin, "the glorious leader of the Soviet peoples, the ingenious educator of all the world's workers, leader of the world front for peace, democracy, and socialism." The exhibition was arranged by the Historical Institute of the Central Committee of the Romanian Workers' Party.

But political rhetoric was also a feature of everyday life. In a photograph taken during the 1950s in Dimitrovgrad, the first socialist city in Bulgaria, we see the entrance to the Stalin Chemicals Combine and, in the foreground, a group of women workers (Fig. 39). The picture, of course, is carefully worked out and composed, but its elements were to be found in many places. Similar photographs could be taken at any number of factory gates.

The Bulgarian text on the architrave of the triumphal arch-like entrance translates: "The Stalin Chemicals Combine is a Child of Bulgarian-Soviet Friendship." In the original language the words are easy to remember because "child" and "friendship" rhyme (*rozhba-druzhba*). The central arch is hung with the hammer and sickle, but the emblem is partly concealed by the white dove of peace. On the left pillar is a placard showing Lenin in speaker's pose, with the date 1917 in the background in big (red) figures, while on the right pillar we see "Dimitrov" and the date 1944—the founders and foundation years of the socialist state in the Soviet Union and Bulgaria, respectively. In the planted circle in front of the entrance, we have a full-length statue of Stalin. This is the commonest representation: Stalin as military commander, wearing a long greatcoat and with his right hand imperiously stuffed inside the front of it, as befits the leader of "liberation from fascism." But here, in front of the big chemicals combine named after him, he is also the Stalin whose name, in the unceasing flood of political rhetoric, was associated with "the great plan for the transformation of nature."

Visible in the background are parts of the factory complex, one of the "great projects of the five-year plan." Through the left-hand arch we glimpse a tower surmounted by a red star. Beneath the star we can also make out the word *mir*, which is both Russian and Bulgarian for "peace." The women leaving the factory after their day's work are young, cheerful, and strikingly well-dressed. It is *young persons* who sustain the new state. Dimitrovgrad is *The City of Youth*, and Dimitrovgrad belongs to *the future*. Moreover, Dimitrovgrad epitomizes Bulgaria and the entire socialist camp.

39 Outside the gates of the J. V. Stalin Chemicals Combine in Dimitrovgrad, 1950s.

Finally, the ideological content of this picture also includes the architecture—the entrance to the Stalin Chemicals Combine, conceived of as an architectural composition. With its arches and keystones, its pilasters and profiles, it conforms to a long tradition of city gates and triumphal arches, deliberately rejecting "Formalism" and "Cosmopolitanism" as practiced in the countries of capitalism and imperialism.

Already in the 1920s, the Soviet Union had been portrayed as a strong young worker and the capitalist world as a worn-out old man. In the age of the Cold War, this iconography took on a new relevance, and we have already encountered it in "the game of chess" and in the chart comparing the economies of Eastern and Western Europe. We also find it in a drawing from the political weekly *Novoe Vremia* (The New Age), published in Moscow and with parallel editions in most European languages (Fig. 40). The economic success of the Soviet Union—and of the people's democracies with it—is illustrated here by a runner coming up to the finishing line in splendid trim. Displayed on his breast are the hammer and sickle. "Hopelessly outdistanced," in the background, sweating and staggering, is a bespectacled man with a dollar sign on his chest. He is the loser, the USA, floundering under the burden of a gun barrel. This is a renewal of the iconography associated with the sporting successes that, especially from the 1952 Helsinki Olympics and onward, were an impor-

40 "Hopelessly outdistanced." Drawing by I. Semionov in the Soviet weekly *Novoe Vremia*, 1954.

tant part of the image of the Soviet Union and the other socialist countries.

Thus the contest between the two systems was depicted as a forgone conclusion, and one could put together a whole world of pictures and a whole corpus of literature under the two headings *them and us* and *then and now*. The first of these was quite unambiguous, while the second was more complicated, for—as we shall see in Chapter Six, on national form—the past was both positive and negative.

The most important messages were stated in positive terms: *for* peace, *for* the working class, *for* socialism, *for* the Soviet Union, and so on. But large groups of the population, growing in numbers as the volume of the political loudspeaker was turned up, put a negative interpretation on those same messages: *against* national independence, *against* every hint of organization not under Party control, *against* the individual right of free expression and free movement.

For the political message was not only interpreted literally and in terms of its symbols but also in accordance with what happened in the surrounding community, in the name of the slogans and symbols. Propaganda was tinged by the course of events and the course of events in turn by propaganda. Impact and repercussion. All was interconnected in a way that is possible only in a society where the political power claims to represent *all* the interests of the people.

One description of these political conditions towers above all the others. It is not one of the main books about totalitarianism and its essence, but a poem by the Hungarian Gyula Illyés, "On Tyranny" (*Egy mondat a zsarnokságról*). It was written as early as 1951, but it did not become public until 2 November 1956, two days before the

Hungarian uprising was put down. It is a long poem, forty-five verses, but its message can be stated briefly and simply. Where tyranny prevails, Illyés writes, it is present in everything—*as if a gas pipe were leaking somewhere in the house*. The important point here is not Illyés's polemic against Stalinism, not the dangerous and malodorous character of the gas, but its ability *to penetrate everything*.

There were differences among the six countries, for example, as regards their tributes to Stalin. The Poles, in this respect, were restrained, especially when compared with the Romanians and Bulgarians. Essentially, though, the iconography and the rhetoric were the same in all countries, and the similarities—as in so many other fields of social life—were so great that both contemporaries and posterity implied a common aegis—in other words, "an order from Moscow," since nearly all the similarities could be traced back to common Soviet prototypes.

Perhaps such an order existed, but in the political situation prevailing in the people's democracies from 1949 onward, it was not really needed. The example of the Soviet Union was followed in any case. There was little scope for independent action and the unspoken demands were as powerful as the spoken ones.

The Example of the Soviet Union: Socialist Realism

III

The compulsion to adapt themselves to "the example of the Soviet Union" did not come to the architects as an order. It came upon them as a heavy pressure that was just as hard to resist as its consequences were hard to accept.

Many of those who were young in the 1920s had taken a very sympathetic view of the Soviet Union, but not even those who had gone the whole hog and become Communists had been able to acquiesce when, from 1932 onward, modern architecture was thrust aside in favor of the new Traditionalism, dubbed *Socialist Realism*.

Within the intellectual left outside the Soviet Union, there were many who tried to understand or excuse both the brutal collectivization of agriculture and the astounding Moscow trials. But hardly any architect—with the exception of those who were living inside the Soviet Union as exiles or as foreign specialists—had endorsed Socialist Realism, neither in the 1930s nor during the early postwar years. The aesthetically unpleasing was less easy to accept than the politically repugnant. Architecture was *visible* and could not be argued out of sight. Acceptance became even harder at the end of the 1940s, when Socialist Realism was elevated to an ideal, to the sole tolerated ideal.

What, then, was the meaning of this Soviet ideal, expressed in architectural terms? How and why had it been established? What had happened since the breakthrough years of the 1930s?

Basic Architectural Concepts

Function and *form* were the basic concepts of Modernist architecture. It was the business of the architect to analyze function and, on the basis of that analysis, to give the building its form: *form follows function*.

The corresponding concepts in Socialist Realism were *socialist content* and *national form.* A building—like a novel or a symphony—had to be "socialist in content and national in form." But these two concepts, which we shall be studying more closely in the following sections, did not, any more than did their Modernist counterparts, convey any concrete idea of what architecture ought to look like. On the other hand, palpable indications were obtainable merely by leafing through a Soviet architectural journal. Here the concepts of Classical architecture and Classical town planning still held sway, from *the ornament, the architectural detail,* and *the facade* via *the street, the square,* and *the block,* to *the city as an artistic entity.* To this must be added a couple of more recent concepts, albeit of ancient descent: *the ensemble* and *the silhouette.* Or, summing up: *monumentality* was an important concept here, and tribute was still paid to *architecture as art.*

All these concepts had been rejected by the Functionalists. Ornament and architectural detail were superfluities, unconnected with function. The facade, interpreted as the artistically designed display side of the building, was a false appearance commanding far too high a price: the indifferent quality behind the scenes. By dint of similar arguments, the street in its spatial sense had been discarded in favor of the untrammelled communication route on the one hand and, on the other, the free grouping of buildings. And because the Functionalists thought of the whole as the sum of its parts, they also rejected the square in the Classical sense, the ensemble and the city as an artistic entity.

To the historians and the traditionally schooled architects, on the other hand, these concepts had a positive substance, which had been true at least from the Renaissance. To them the difficulty lay not in the concept as such but in the new ideological context.

How are we to explain this controversial return of tradition? Why had architecture in the Soviet Union developed in this way?

The Breakthrough of Socialist Realism in the Soviet Union

The crucial impediment to an understanding of Socialist Realism has nothing to do with the political background. Instead, the crucial impediment is the widespread overestimation, above all in the West, of the status of Modernism in Russian architecture from 1917 to the beginning of the 1930s. And that overestimation in turn is connected with the idea that a new society meant a new art and a new architecture and that the political left and aesthetic Modernism both pointed in the same direction.

In 1919–20 Vladimir Tatlin produced his famous design for a

Monument to the IIIrd International, a spiral tower that, in its final state, would have been 100 meters higher than the Eiffel Tower (Fig. 41). It soon became known also in the West as the supreme manifestation of the encounter between art and revolution. "Die Kunst ist tot. Es lebe die neue Maschinenkunst Tatlins," we read on a placard held up by George Grosz and John Heartfield in a famous photograph from the Dada Exhibition in Berlin in 1920. Several attempts have been made to find Tatlin's precedents—from the Tower of Babel to the Eiffel Tower—but it was the negation of tradition that gave the tower its impact. In the words of Mayakovsky, it was "the first monument without a beard."

Far less known and seldom reproduced is another attempt at giving artistic expression to the new society: Ivan Fomin's design for a Workers' Palace in Petrograd, a competition entry in 1919, intended for the workers of the immense Putilov Works, later renamed the Kirov Works (Figs. 42, 43). This is a monumental structure in strict, solemn Doric style, rooted in Russian and French Neo-Classicism. Above the main entrance is a charioteer with six horses, a parallel to the layout of the building, in which the dome in the background dominates six projecting temple porticos.

This is a gigantic "house of the people," more monumental than many royal palaces in the history of architecture. And this, according to Fomin and his successors at the Petrograd Academy of Art, is in no way contradictory. Their heroic architecture—"the red Doric style"—matches the spirit of the state in which the proletariat have assumed power. This was a "left-wing Classicism."

Contrary to what many people in the West still seem to imagine, the Revolution of 1917 did not end the age of traditional architecture. From 1917 and all through the 1920s, Classicism was an alternative to Modernism. Coexisting with El Lissitzky, Konstantin

41 Photograph taken in 1920 of the completed model for Tatlin's Monument to the IIIrd International, with Tatlin himself standing next to the monument. Banner in foreground reads, "Long live the IIIrd International."

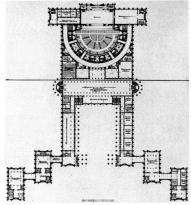

42, 43 Ivan Fomin's design for the Workers' Palace in Petrograd, 1919. Perspective of the central section and ground plan.

44, 45 Two designs for a building to house the Arcos foreign trade organization in Moscow, 1924: (left) by Fomin, and (right) by the Vesnin brothers.

Melnikov, Ivan Leonidov, Moisei Ginzburg, Ilya Golossov, and the Vesnin brothers, there were the Academicians: Ivan Zholtovskii, Alexei Shchusev, Alexander Tamanian, Vladimir Shchuko, Evgenii Levinson, Lev Rudnev, and Ivan Fomin. Among them, Zholtovskii was the leader in Moscow, Fomin in Petrograd/Leningrad.

The extremes of Soviet architecture in the 1920s were miles apart, as witness two entries in the 1924 competition for offices in Moscow for Arcos Ltd., the Soviet foreign trade organization (Figs. 44, 45). On the one hand, we have a project by Fomin and on the other a frequently depicted project by the Vesnin brothers: Russian Classicism versus Constructivism. But not necessarily the new versus the old, because Fomin too was looked on as new and aesthetically radical. The old, rejected by Modernists and Academicians alike, was nineteenth-century eclecticism and the Art Nouveau style.

For a long time the ideological climate seemed to be favoring the Modernists, especially in the closing years of the 1920s, when many of the Classicists too were swept along. The first five-year plan brought a revolution in cultural life. It was now, for example, that the famous workers' clubs were designed by Melnikov and Golossov, and it was this architecture of the cultural revolution that was presented in El Lissitzky's *Russland: Die Rekonstruktion der Arkitektur in der Sowjetunion*, published in Vienna in 1930 and more influential than any other publication in shaping the image of Soviet architecture.

Beginning in 1932, however, the situation gradually changed, against the Modernists and in favor of the Academicians. An important stage in this process was the competition for the Palace of the Soviets in 1932, in which both foreign and native Modernists were thrust aside (Fig. 46). Another was the formation that year of a single organization of architects to replace the rival organizations, representing different schools, that had existed until now. This was the same kind of cultural one-party system as was introduced at the same time for literature, pictorial art, and music.

It soon became clear that, within the new organization of architects, the Academicians—represented by Fomin's Classicism and Zholtovskii's Renaissance—stood for the official and only acceptable line. The concept of Socialist Realism was launched at the great authors' congress in Moscow in 1934, and before long, in all fields of art, architecture included, it came to denote the line supported by both the Party and the professional establishment.

The initial stage of the Moscow underground rail system, the first big example of the new socialist monumentality, was opened officially in 1935 (Figs. 47, 48). Formal confirmation came with the first congress of the Federation of Soviet Architects in Moscow in 1937. Widespread international attention was aroused by the Soviet pavilions at the Paris and New York expositions, in 1937 and 1939 respectively. More important to the native public was the great agricultural exposition in Moscow, opened in 1939 and discussed in Chapter Six (see Fig. 49, see also Figs. 80–82).

Causes and Implications

The conventional explanation for the genesis of Socialist Realism says that the revolutionary enthusiasm of the 1920s, with its

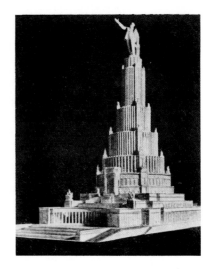

46 Boris Iofan's winning entry in the competition for the Palace of the Soviets in Moscow, modified in collaboration with Vladimir Gelfreich and Vladimir Shchuko. Model, 1934.

47, 48 The Moscow underground rail system, opened in 1935, was a breakthrough for the new monumental architecture, but the Modernist idiom lived on, for example, in Sokolniki Station (left), designed by the architects Nadezhda Bykova and I. Taranov. Contrast this with the new style (right): Komsomolskaia Station by Dimitrii Chechulin. In the Modernist setting, a woman with a tennis racket; in the magnificent Socialist Realist station (right), a becapped worker.

amenability to new forms, was followed by the totalitarian ossification of the 1930s and a reversion to tradition.

This, however, is an oversimplification. As we have already seen, the twenties in the Soviet Union accommodated both Classicists and Modernists, though by the end of the decade the Modernists appeared to have seized the initiative. It looked as if they had won the day, but their position was tenuous for many reasons. Their projects incorporated not only a new, revolutionary vocabulary but also a new, revolutionary technology. This technology did not exist, however, at all events not in the everyday life of the Soviet Union. The country was short of glass, steel, and concrete, and there was also a shortage of skilled workers. Not so for the Classicists. Their projects might look exclusive, but they were more closely adapted to the realities of existing technology, materials, and skills. The necessary resources were less available to the Modernists than they were to the Classicists.

The same was true of the Modernists' relations with clients and users. Experimental modern architecture was poorly rooted both among the people and among the political leaders. It derived its main support from the radical intelligentsia, in Russia and elsewhere. But that kind of support quickly declined during the 1930s.

What is more, Modernism had a more difficult task to face in the Soviet Union than in Germany, Czechoslovakia, the Netherlands, or Scandinavia. Most building assignments there were of a practical, everyday nature: housing, offices, factories. Architects in the Soviet Union, moreover, had to represent and make plain a new social system whose objective was to "build socialism." Building was a picture of politics. Political language made demands on architecture, demands that, in the eyes of many people, Modernism was not strong enough to meet.

The defeat of Modernism in the competition for the Palace of the Soviets did not come as a bolt from the blue. A large sector of the architectural profession appears to have been prepared for and in agreement with it. But this does not explain the depth of the defeat or the conclusiveness of the Traditionalist victory. That kind of explanation has to be looked for in the political situation.

In his biography of Stalin, Isaac Deutscher refers to the late 1920s and the early 1930s as "the great change." This was a second revolution, just over ten years after the first. It was led by Stalin and it had much more far-reaching effects on people's lives than the first.

It resulted in Russia's rapid industrialization; it compelled more than 100 million peasants to abandon their small, primitive holdings and to set up collective farms; it ruthlessly tore the primeval wooden plow from the hands of the muzhik and forced him to grasp the wheel of a modern tractor; it drove tens of millions of illiterate people to school and made them learn to read and write; and spiritually it detached European Russia from Europe and brought Asiatic Russia nearer to Europe. The rewards of that revolution were astounding; but so was its cost: the complete loss, by a whole generation, of spiritual and political freedom.

The State turned against its own people, in the name of historical necessity, and in the name of the People millions of people lost their lives.

When this revolution began, cultural radicalism was at its apogee. By the end of the revolution it was a thing of the past. The political power had revoked the vague, noncommittal contract with cultural radicalism in all of its manifestations. It was looked on as a spent force, just like its representatives insofar as they were not prepared to change. Instead, the power in the land—Stalin and his administration—entered into a new, more binding contract with Traditionalism, not only with those who had launched a "left-wing Classicism" or a "red Doric style" but with the old cultural establishment in its entirety. This was part of the stabilization of the political system. Everything positive was associated with this new Traditionalism. Everything negative—from Trotsky to Wall Street—was lumped together with vanquished Modernism.

This did not mean that architecture was entirely subordinated to tradition. Still less that it was to look old-fashioned. The architecture of Socialist Realism would certainly not be called modern, but it would be *new*. New, but based on tradition and allied with "socialist content," a content inserted in the form. It was a contradictory content with powerful elements of personal cult, terror, and the propaganda of success. And it was content, much more than form, that was to be the problem of the new Soviet architecture.

Victory Architecture of the 1940s

Primarily, it was not the Soviet ideals of the 1930s with which the people's democracies were confronted, it was the postwar elaboration of Socialist Realism, more completely formulated in terms of both vocabulary and ideological arguments.

To a certain extent, Soviet Classicism of the 1930s stayed in touch with Modernism, often in such a way that the motifs were tra-

49 Typical of the postwar era was the main pavilion opened in 1954 at the great agricultural exposition in Moscow. Architects: Yuri Shchuko et al.

ditional but the composition was modern, just as in many parts of Europe during the interwar years. But Academism was in the offing, and Shchusev's building for the Marx-Engels-Lenin Institute in Tbilisi (1938) was an important example.

Then, after the war, the new architecture advanced on a wide front. It was an ostentatious, eclectic architecture, an *architecture of victory*. It was now that the basic architectural concepts we have already referred to—from architectural detail to the city as an artistic entity—acquired their full substance. Their implementation was demonstrated by reconstruction in Leningrad, Kiev, Minsk, Stalingrad, and other cities destroyed during the war, as well as by tremendous new buildings in Moscow (Fig. 49). The results were summarized in special yearbooks and the most deserving architects were rewarded with the Stalin Prize.

Leningrad Classicism, one of the original points of departure of Socialist Realism, still mattered, but no less important now was the Moscow or Kremlin tradition. The seven high-rise buildings in Moscow are the supreme example. Originally eight of them were planned, one for each century, and their foundations were laid to mark the eighth centenary of Moscow in 1947. In practice they were both successors of and substitutes for the great Palace of the Soviets, the paramount monumental project of the 1930s, on which work had come to a standstill at the outbreak of war.

The ideological messages that Soviet architecture had to convey had been superimposed on one another over the decades. There was from the beginning "the great October Revolution." To this was added in the 1930s the myth of Stalin and his superior leadership, and in 1945 the victorious conclusion of "the Great Patriotic War." Lastly came the role of the Soviet Union in the Cold War, as the leader of the "camp of peace and socialism" in the struggle against reaction and imperialism. A more strident tone was introduced in 1948, signaled by an article in *Pravda* on 25 September: "Front against the pernicious influence of Western architecture!" This was the same campaign—associated with the name of Andrei Zhdanov—that had already been started in literature, music, and pictorial art. Zhdanov had recently died, but the campaign rolled on. Before long it would reach the people's democracies.

Both the architectural and the ideological content of postwar Soviet architecture are summarized in a drawing showing the silhouettes of the old and new Moscow (Fig. 50). The message is unmistakable: *The present rests on the foundation of tradition. The present surpasses tradition. The example of the Soviet Union is outstanding.*

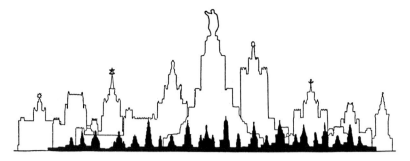

50 Silhouettes of the old and the new Moscow, in a drawing published frequently during the 1950s. It shows both the Palace of the Soviets (center) and the tower blocks that emerged in the 1940s as the new Moscow skyline.

51, 52 The government building in Baku, Azerbaijan, 1952: main facade and statue of Lenin atop the tribune.

This could be realized in many different ways, as for example in the government building of the Soviet republic of Azerbaijan in Baku (1952), designed by Rudnev, Munts, and Tkachenko (Figs. 51, 52). It combines Russian Academism, arches and other details of the local Islamic tradition, and, beneath Lenin's feet, a tribune for the political leaders.

Realization of the Example in the People's Democracies

A meeting of Party-affiliated Polish architects took place in Warsaw on 20 and 21 June 1949, ending with a resolution, part of which read as follows:

> Two camps are today realizing their contradictory world pictures and ideologies. On the one hand, the camp of democracy, socialism, and peace—with the Soviet Union as its main bastion—and on the other the camp of imperialism, economic crisis, and warmongering. The contest between these ideologies is also being waged in architecture.

The conclusion was obvious: In architecture as well, one must rally around the Soviet Union. And like everything else in the people's democracies at this time, it had to be done quickly, with a revolutionary urgency. The greater the importance, the greater the urgency. In some cases we can see how architectural drawings were altered right up to the last minute.

One such case is the office block at Ulica Krucza in Warsaw, built for "the Central Administration for the Electrical Engineering Industry and Resenoid Industries" (Fig. 53). Anyone can see that the three big windows on the first floor are a last-minute addition, a central emphasis in order at least to hint at a facade in the traditional sense in the middle of the Modernist grid. The architects received praise for their "break with Constructivism" from scrutinizing colleagues. A similar instance was the Central Committee building at Aleje Jerozolimskie in Warsaw, the modern character of which was softened by means of sculptural decoration and a crowning upper story.

But things of this kind were merely retouching, necessary expedients in a transitional period. In the somewhat more long-term perspective, an entire profession had to be retrained. But this too had to

IV

53 Ulica Krucza, Warsaw, as rebuilt in the 1950s. Left foreground, "Central Administration for the Electrical Engineering and Resinoid Industries," early 1950s. Architects: Jerzy Kowarski and Mieczysław Piprek.

be done quickly. Knowledge of "the example from the Soviet Union" had to be disseminated quickly and put into practice.

The result was a highly unusual campaign in the history of architecture. No country had ever changed direction so quickly, still less six countries at once. In the history of the people's democracies, however, this was one of many simultaneous campaigns. Events in architecture were paralleled by events in art and music, biology, the study of history, and so on.

How the Example Was Transmitted

The change was made easier by the new social order. Nearly all building land was publicly owned and the same public sector was in reality the one and only developer, just as it was the one and only publisher of books and periodicals. All architects were employed in state planning offices.

All organs and channels could be enlisted, from ministries to schools of architecture. The architects' organizations held congresses, adopted resolutions, and put on exhibitions. The periodicals acquired new content, even going so far as to mark their divorce from the West and from Modernism in their typography and layout. There were only a few episodes, highlighted as cautionary, instructive examples—Teige, Major, Henselmann—to suggest that the consensus was not complete.

A small but important group consisted of architects who had spent the war years in the Soviet Union and were already schooled in the theory and practice of Socialist Realism. Kurt Liebknecht in the DDR, Edmund Goldzamt in Poland, and Imre Perényi in Hungary all served, in their various countries, as the ideological leaders of the architects. Their experience, knowledge of languages, and personal contacts gave them an authority that brooked no contradiction. Others who had been decisively influenced in the Soviet Union and passed on their experience to others were Tibor Weiner and Petur Tashev, the architects respectively of Sztálinváros and Dimitrovgrad.

There was more direct transmission of experience through the "Soviet advisers" who fleetingly appeared in magazines and other publications. They included Alexander Vlasov and Sergei Chernyshev, who scrutinized the plans for Stalinallee in East Berlin and criticized them for steering too close to Soviet precursors (*Neues Deutschland,* 23/12 1951). They pointed to Schinkel as a point of departure for Socialist Realism on German soil. Similar advisory visits were paid by Georgii Orlov to Budapest and Alexei Galaktionov to Prague (*Magyar Építőművészet,* 1952:2; *Architektura ČSR,* 1954:6). The new detailed development plan for Sofia was submitted to a whole group of leading Soviet architects, among them Karo Alabian, Arkadii Mordvinov, and Alexei Shchusev. The same Mordvinov, together with Grigorii Simonov, was commissioned to examine the project for Casa Scînteii in Bucharest and provided the crucial impulses for its ultimate design.

Still more important, however, was the widespread publicity given to Soviet architecture, above all through periodical publications. Articles on the Soviet Union were a regular feature in the architectural journals of the six countries. Often they were translations of articles from *Arkhitektura SSSR, Arkhitektura i stroitelstvo,* and other Soviet periodicals, articles, for example by Zholtovskii or Tsapenko. The latter ranked as the theoretician of Socialist Realism, and he was also the author of a history of Bulgarian architecture.

Czechoslovakia actually had a special journal on this subject: *Sovětská architektura.* Published in Prague between 1951 and 1955, its contents included not only translations but also native ideological articles and surveys of architectural developments in the other people's democracies. It was published by the Czech-Soviet Institute in Prague. In 1953 the Polish-Soviet Institute in Warsaw issued Edmund Goldzamt's booklet on Soviet high-rise buildings, *Wieżowce radzieckie.* Haus der Kultur der Sowjetunion in East Berlin published, in 1951, proceedings from a conference on Socialist Realism, at which Kurt Liebknecht spoke about architecture under the title "Das grosse Vorbild" (The great model).

The most sumptuous publication was the *Dreissig Jahre sowjetische Architektur in der RSFSR,* an impressive photographic survey published by the Academy of Architecture (Bauakademie) in the DDR in 1951, one year after it appeared in the Soviet Union. Like the original, this was a folio volume weighing more than 4 kilos, and as a book production too it exemplified Socialist Realism. On the bookshelf it more than held its own against the classic folios of architecture. Two years later there came a Czech version, *Vývoj sovětské architektury.*

The Polish anthology *Architektura radziecka 1946–1947,* published in 1951, contained not only articles on Soviet architecture but also Andrei Zhdanov's assault on the authors Anna Akhmatova and Michail Zoshchenko in 1946 and the notorious Party resolution on Vano Muradeli's opera *Deep Friendship* from 1948. The impact of these writings greatly transcended that of Akhmatova's poetry, Zoshchenko's satires, and Muradeli's music. They heralded the postwar crackdown on Soviet culture, the same crackdown that, after some delay, had now also come to the people's democracies.

Knowledge of "the example of the Soviet Union" was promoted in every way. At the same time, links with the Western countries were severed. Architectural journals from Britain, France, or Scandinavia became virtually unobtainable. And the journals of the six countries themselves withdrew nearly all coverage of "the non-Socialist foreign world," except when condemning Le Corbusier on ideological grounds or presenting horrific portraits of the big cities of the USA, "the cities of the yellow devil," in the words of Maxim Gorky.

Realization, Country by Country

Publicity and propaganda, however, do not automatically engender a new architecture, not even under the heavy pressure that now prevailed. Although the basic political conditions were the same in all six countries, events took different courses. And for all the urgency, not everything happened at once. First there was the rejection of Cosmopolitanism and Western influence. Next came the construction of Socialist Realism on a national basis. As time went on the screw was given a new turn.

An attempt will now be made to characterize the course of events in each individual country. The countries themselves are taken in geographical order, here as in other parts of the book, moving from north to south.

The DDR. It was fairly obvious that the realization of Socialist Realism would take time in the DDR. It was not until October 1949 that the Soviet zone of occupation became an independent state, and architecture was not the first item on the agenda. Once broached, however, it was prosecuted with great vigor, partly by Walter Ulbricht in person. More than any other politician in the people's democracies, he seems to have taken an interest in architecture, and in several of his speeches he held forth at length on its ideological content.

The first step, however, was a sixteen-point enactment, adopted by the government in July 1950: *Grundsätze des Städtebaues,* "principles of urbanism." Those principles rejected the ideas of Functionalism in urban development as realized, for example, in Scharoun's Stadtlandschaft or his neighborhood unit for the Friedrichshain district of Berlin. Socialist Realism was not mentioned by name, but the fourteenth point required architecture to be based on "the experience of the people, embodied by progressive tradition." The delegation drafting these maxims had made a study of urban-development questions in the Soviet Union in April and May of the same year. On 6 September the maxims were incorporated in a special *Aufbaugesetz.*

The criticism leveled the following year against Hermann Henselmann and the new housing development in Stalinstadt demonstrated the determination of the authorities in their campaign against Formalism and led to an immediate rectification. In November 1951, speaking at the conference organized by the German-Soviet Friendship Association, Kurt Liebknecht declared:

> We are against the Bauhaus. Why? We are against the Bauhaus because Functionalism is the height of imperialist Cosmopolitanism, the height of decadence and decay.

At the end of the year Ulbricht made a long ideological speech at the official opening of the Deutsche Bauakademie, which was established on Soviet lines. By Western standards it was not only an academy but also a governmental authority, exerting a strong influ-

54 The Big Five among DDR architects: (from left) Edmund Collein, Kurt Liebknecht, Hermann Henselmann, Richard Paulick, and Kurt W. Leucht. Photograph from the press conference on *Das nationale Aufbauprogramm,* March 1952. In the background, a plan of Stalinallee.

ence on the entire building sector. From 1952 onward the Academy published the journal *Deutsche Architektur,* the first volumes of which expounded Socialist Realism more vigorously and consistently than any other journal in the people's democracies.

Events in the DDR culminated with *Das nationale Aufbauprogramm* (Fig. 54), inaugurated in February 1952 with the construction of Stalinallee in East Berlin and continuing with Lange Strasse in Rostock, Altmarkt in Dresden, Rossplatz in Leipzig, and Zentraler Platz in Magdeburg. In these monumental projects the new DDR architecture moved quite close to the academic ideals of the Soviet Union—closer, in fact, than in any other people's democracy except Bulgaria.

Poland. Events in Poland took a different course. Socialist Realism was established sooner and manifested in somewhat different forms than in the DDR. The turning point was a meeting of the Party-affiliated architects on 20 and 21 June 1949, ending with the resolution we have already quoted. That resolution called for an "unmasking of the influence of the imperialist camp on architecture," in other words, resistance to Modernism. But it also appealed to national sentiment in postwar Poland: "Polish architecture must be revived, as great, social art." SARP, the Polish Association of Architects, made the resolution its own. A select group of architects spearheaded reconstruction (Fig. 55).

In February 1950 a coordinating committee was set up for the planning offices in Warsaw, and in May of that year it organized an

55 Studying the model of the MDM housing development and Plac Konstytucji in the center of Warsaw are the authors of the project: (from left) Zygmunt Stępiński, Józef Sigalin, Stanisław Jankowski, and Jan Knothe. This group, with Sigalin and Jankowski as organizers and Knothe and Stępiński as designers, spearheaded Poland's reconstruction.

exhibition at Politechnika Warszawska (the Warsaw Institute of Technology). The exhibition featured 156 new projects, and a jury of twenty eminent architects was appointed, above all in order to address two problems. To what extent did the projects meet the requirements of Socialist Realism? And how did they fit in with the architectural environment of Warsaw? Five hundred architects attended a three-day seminar at which the jury's verdict was presented and followed by a discussion. There was no criticism of the principles of Socialist Realism. Its *implementation,* on the other hand, could be criticized, and here there was a certain amount of scope for intraprofessional criticism, as long as it did not come into conflict with the overriding objective. The architects were given the task of scrutinizing and correcting themselves.

A new exhibition was held in 1951, with much the same adjudication procedure, but this time with projects from all over the country. Two more exhibitions, covering different parts of the country, were held the following year.

These public scrutinies were summed up in a large album, *Architektura polska 1950–1951,* published in 1953 by Bohdan Garliński. It contains abstracts and commentaries, but above all a detailed account of thirty-two different projects that display a rapid move toward richness of form and monumentality, with only a few attempts to achieve a completely new architecture. A modernist Classicism has been adjusted to the basic concepts of Socialist Realism. Polish architecture is heading in the right direction, but it is still excessively Formalistic (often pointed out in the commentaries). The architects must *deepen* their understanding of the principles of Socialist Realism. And as long as those principles remain in force, that demand will be constantly reiterated, both in Poland and in the other countries: deepening, deepening, deepening. And that was also the tune of things in other problem fields of social life, such as the economy.

Czechoslovakia. Three somewhat contradictory factors left their mark on the course of events in Czechoslovakia: first, the comparatively negligible destruction wrought by the war—Czechoslovakia did not have the same practical needs as the DDR and Poland for a new representational architecture; second, the strict canons of ideological orthodoxy in the people's democracy where the contrast between the old and new systems was most blatant; third, the strong position that Modernism had held among architects ever since the 1920s. Their practical capacity for complying with the principles of Socialist Realism was even less than in other countries.

After February 1948 the ideological temperature of *Architektura ČSR* rose remarkably. Jiří Kroha became national artist and the advocate of a new relationship between architecture and politics. Functionalism was declared "cosmopolitan and hostile to the people." All information about Western European architecture was cut off. In the first issue of the journal for 1950, Socialist Realism was proclaimed as the one and only ideal. Oldřich Starý, like Kroha a former Modernist, addressed the ideological subject of "What architecture can learn from J. V. Stalin's article Marxism and Linguistics." With the publication of the 1950 volume, even typography and layout ceased to be modern. To readers of *Architektura ČSR* it now seemed that there was nothing left of Czech Modernism but the names of some of its architects. Behind the facade, though, resistance lived on and, even at a national conference of architects in July 1953, the recalcitrants among the avant-garde were still being called upon to mend their ways.

New housing took on a *national* form which in practice meant a national decor. More far-reaching implementation of Socialist Realism was demonstrated in the plans for the expansion of Ostrava—Nová Ostrava. The orthodox projects were many in number, but only one monumental edifice in the grand Soviet style actually materialized—the Hotel International in Prague (see Fig. 75).

Hungary. Of all the six people's democracies, the case of Hungary is the most complicated.

In November 1949 the organization of Party-affiliated architects adopted a resolution to campaign *against* the cosmopolitan influence of the West and *for* Socialist Realism (*Építés-Építészet*, 1949:5). In

Rákosi's Hungary, a resolution of this kind should have been law, but it was not, at all events not in practical building. The contest that took place over the next two years centered around words and periodicals, not buildings. *Tér és forma* (Space and form), which had existed since the 1920s, closed down in 1948, and so too in the following year did *Új építészet* (New architecture), which had been founded in 1946. *Építés-Építészet* (Building-architecture) completed just three years of publication (1949–51) before being closed down and superseded by *Magyar Építőművészet* (Hungarian architecture), which first appeared in 1952. Behind every closure and every start-up there was an ideological conflict, and the very names of the journals hinted at the movement away from Modernism and toward Socialist Realism.

The crucial campaign opened in the spring of 1951, culminating with a grand ideological speech by the Minister of Culture, József Révai, addressed to the architects of Hungary (*Építés-Építészet*, 1951:9-10). In the background was Imre Perényi, now returned from the Soviet Union. The direct target of his and Révai's criticism was the architect Máté Major and, indirectly, the whole architectural profession.

Socialist Realism, however, was short-lived here, more so than in other countries, because Hungary was the first to deescalate and abolish it. The first step in this direction was taken in the spring of 1954, when architects were criticized for overzealously misinterpreting the directives from 1951.

Romania. Here we can distinguish two phases in the introduction of Socialist Realism.

At the center of the first phase was the project for the immense polygraphic combine Casa Scînteii in Bucharest (see Figs. 106, 108, 109, 139–150). Several schemes were rejected in 1949 as unduly Constructivist, hollow, cold, and brutal. The architects went to Moscow, where they consulted two members of the Academy—Simonov and Mordvinov. Returning home, they brought with them the striking composition of the Casa Scînteii and a recommendation to study their own national tradition. Eventually Casa Scînteii met the requirements of Socialist Realism, but the project dragged on and was not finished in time to exert a truly seminal influence.

The second phase concerned the building sector as a whole. In November 1952 the Central Committee and the Council of Ministers announced three important resolutions. The first of these concerned urban development and the work of architects (see below, article from *Neuer Weg*, 8/11 1952), the second a new plan for Bucharest, and the third an underground railway for the same city (*Neuer Weg*, 15/11 1952). The first of these resolutions resulted in a new organization and strict insistence on conformity to the principles of Socialist Realism: "Our architects must allow themselves to be guided by the teaching of Stalin on culture which is socialist in content but national in form."

Perhaps the background was the exhibition of Romanian architecture put on in June that year in Moscow, and subsequently in Leningrad and Kiev as well (*Neuer Weg*, 25/6 1952). Many of the buildings on display had been designed during the early postwar years or even earlier than 1944. In their Classical Traditionalism they had long escaped being branded as Formalist, but when confronted by the academic architecture of the Soviet Union, they were found to be vague and inadequate. This, at all events, is what *might* have happened.

Bulgaria. Soviet architects were engaged as advisers long before Socialist Realism was even being talked about. They were first called in as early as 1945 to assess the urban plan for Sofia. When construction of Dimitrovgrad was begun in 1947, the very idea was Soviet Russian: a newly laid-out industrial city, launched as its country's "first socialist city." But the urban plan and the buildings complied with the discreet Classicism of the interwar years. Here, as in Romania, tradition seemed good enough at first, but in Bulgaria the crackdown came sooner.

In December 1948 the Party Congress called for a campaign against capitalist ideology in the fields of science, culture, and art, architecture included (*Arkhitekturata v Bălgarija*). The plans for Dimitrovgrad were thoroughly revised, as far as possible, and from 1950 onward development was a true application of Socialist Realism. This, moreover, was not confined to Dimitrovgrad and the new center of Sofia. The new ideals were more widely implemented in Bulgaria than in the other people's democracies.

Although most of the architects had been trained in Central Europe and in France—architecture studies at home had got going only during the last years of the monarchy—Bulgaria became something of a "model satellite" in architecture as in other things. ("Model satellite" was a term readily used by political observers from the West.) The common allegation that the architecture of the Stalin era in Eastern Europe looks as if it had been imported directly from the Soviet Union is nearly always wrong. Only in Bulgaria does it, occasionally, come close to the truth.

The demands confronting the architects were the same in all six countries, but the results differed (Figs. 56, 57). Most compliant were

56, 57 Two contrasting examples of the practice of Socialist Realism, in Hungary and Bulgaria respectively, both dating from 1953. Left: Vocational school for miners in Várpalota by Gyula Rimanóczy. Right: South front of the Party building in Sofia, by Petur Zlatev and his collective. The difference here is more than one of function. There is also a difference in conformity to "the example of the Soviet Union": in the first instance, a free, asymmetrical Classicism that may recall the Scandinavian twenties; in the second instance, a ponderous, richly decorated architecture closely related to both Soviet and Classical precursors.

the Bulgarians, followed by the Germans in the DDR, the Romanians, and the Poles in that order. The Czechs and Hungarians were more recalcitrant. The Hungarians in particular seemed to have made a big distinction between practice and ideology. Why? If the answer is a reference to the powerful Modernist tradition, then this in turn raises a new question: Why was there no such resistance in the DDR? There as well the Modernists were in the majority among the leading architects. The answer must be that the Cold War antithesis between East and West Germany put added pressure on the architects of the DDR, making it more important there than elsewhere for ideology to be *outwardly visible.*

The DDR was a special case. In the other five countries the results can be related to the architects' differing capacities for meeting the demands of Socialist Realism. It was easiest for the Bulgarians and Romanians to do so and perfectly possible for the Poles. But it was a good deal more difficult for Czechs and Hungarians.

But there is another aspect to the degree of compliance. As new states, with new boundaries, the DDR and Poland had to build up their national institutions from scratch and they needed a monumental architecture. So too did Romania and Bulgaria, being relatively underdeveloped architecturally by Central European standards.

Hungary and Czechoslovakia had richer architectural traditions. In Budapest and Prague especially, there was a wealth of public buildings from the past hundred years, undamaged by the war. Those two cities had no new assignments requiring a new monumental architecture—at all events, nothing like as many as in East Berlin, Warsaw, Bucharest, and Sofia.

The Ideological Context—a Newspaper Article from 1952

In all six people's democracies, the ideological context had a crucial bearing on the way in which architecture was understood. There was a linguistic apparatus with which all social phenomena of any significance had to fit in.

The following article from a Romanian newspaper, published in 1952, is a commentary on the abovementioned resolution of the Central Committee and the Council of Ministers on the reform of Romanian building. The author, Ladislau Adler, was vice-president of the newly formed State Committee for Architecture and Buildings.

THE GREAT HONOR SHOWN TO CREATIVE WORK

In Socialist society, where there is no exploitation of one man by another, architecture is liberated, after the bourgeoisie have been deprived of power, from the fetters of bourgeois class interest, and is for the first time placed in the service of the true material and cultural needs of the entire people. The development of architecture is connected organically with the progress of science and technology and reflects the ideas and culture of the people during every epoch.

Socialist industrialization, the great tasks of our first five-year plan and of the electrification plan—which call for a tremendous volume of building for industrial and social-cultural purposes—confront our architects with completely new and outstandingly important qualitative and quantitative problems.

As Comrade Stalin teaches us in his ingenious work *The Economic Problems of Socialism in the USSR,* the economic constitution of socialism, in contradistinction to the capitalism of our time, anticipates maximum satisfaction of the constantly growing material and cultural needs of society. In order to raise work in the field of architecture, urban planning, and building to the level demanded by the construction of socialism, it is necessary to create buildings and cities that are capable of meeting the material and cultural needs of the workers laboring wholeheartedly for the prosperity of our beloved country.

After analyzing successes and, above all, shortcomings in this field, the Central Committee of the Romanian Workers' Party and the Council of Ministers adopted the resolutions of 13 November, resolutions that mark the beginning of a new phase of work for our architects.

These three resolutions—on the building and creation of cities and reorganization of activities in the field of architecture, on the general plan for the rebuilding of the capital of our native country, and on the construction of an underground railway in the capital—represent the concrete support given by the Party and Government to our planners.

These resolutions open up new perspectives for creative work. They express the confidence of our Party and the laboring people in the creative ability of our architects.

At the same time they also constitute a weapon in the struggle against bourgeois ideology and against fawning at the decadent art of the West, which is alien to our working people, the builders of socialism. As a supreme reflection of the desire of our people for peaceful construction, they are new blows against the imperialists who are trying to ferment a new world war.

To accomplish the magnificent tasks that these resolutions imply, we will need to learn from the glorious experience of the land of victorious socialism, to acquire the progressive, revolutionary Soviet technology, and, in the creation of new cities, to make fruitful use of the artistic traditions of the Romanian people.

The architects and builders of our socialist capital will have the honor of working under the direction of the most beloved son of our people, Comrade Gheorghe Gheorghiu-Dej. They are to transform the city of Bucharest into a new capital in a new state, reflecting the joy of living and the creative vigor of a people building up a happy and full life.

The transformation of the Dîmbovița into a large, navigable canal will create a magnificent traffic artery surrounded by palaces, monuments, and parks, at the same time as the climate of the capital will be greatly improved by the creation of a system of open spaces and woodlands.

By drawing on experience from the construction of the Moscow underground, which is a work of art of incomparable beauty, a convenient means of communication will be created which, on the one hand, will serve the workers in the best possible way and, on the other hand, will express the full beauty of the architecture of Socialist Realism.

The diversity of the artistic and technical requirements presented to us by the Party Central Committee and the Government obliges us to work with more determination and zeal than ever to elevate our ideological level and to achieve a high standard of professional mastery.

We, the architects of the Romanian People's Republic, are firmly intent on accomplishing the artistic and technical task with which the working class has presented us, and to devote all our strength and mastery to the prosperity of our beloved native land, the Romanian People's Republic.

(*Neuer Weg* 18/11 1952)

In the article, architecture and building are integrated with the ideological context and related to a number of key political concepts: class interest, the five-year plans, the working people, the native land, "the struggle against bourgeois ideology and against fawning at the decadent art of the West," imperialism, peaceful reconstruction, experience from the Soviet Union, national tradition, the "joy of living and the creative vigor of a people building up a happy and full life," and "the full beauty of the architecture of Socialist Realism." Most of all, this is explicit and overexplicit and, like the reference to Stalin and Gheorghiu-Dej, appeared to the contemporary readers as something of a formula reiterated in every context.

The heading, on the other hand, includes a more subtle point: In the people's democracies, tribute is paid to "creative work." Architecture there is *art.* Not so, by contrast, in the capitalist countries, where surplus value never accrues to the people, and architecture, consequently, is barren and artless.

The Soviet Union in 1932 versus the People's Democracies in 1949

Implementation of Socialist Realism in the Soviet Union was the necessary prerequisite of its implementation in the people's democracies. But this is not to say that its substance was identical in both cases, architecturally or ideologically.

In both cases, the political power had the last word. In the Soviet Union, however, it received no small measure of support from the professional establishment. The political leadership banished the extreme alternative and settled on that which came closest to the center. Modernism had an experimental, Utopian touch. Socialist Realism, on the other hand, was rooted in a long professional tradition. As S. Frederick Starr has aptly put it, the professionals took over after the avant-garde (*Architectural Association Quarterly,* 1979:2).

In the people's democracies, the opposite happened. The extreme alternative, Socialist Realism in its preformulated, thoroughly ideologized, and, on paper at least, dogmatic form, was elevated to the norm, at the expense of a more discreet architecture that received far more support from professional opinion. Resistance to Socialist Realism existed in both cases, but in the people's democracies it was fairly compact to begin with.

Neither alternative—Modernism or Socialist Realism—was the same in both situations. Modernism had grown less modern during the intervening years, while Socialist Realism had grown more grandiloquent and traditional.

There was also another important difference. In the Soviet Union, the establishment of Socialist Realism was part of a rigorous internal settlement of accounts that, on top of everything else, had nationalist overtones. In the people's democracies, on the other hand, Socialist Realism was something *extraneous,* looked on as part of an imminent threat, the threat to national sovereignty.

The new architectural ideals in the people's democracies were a challenge both to the professional self-esteem of the architects and to the national self-esteem of the various nations. The climate surrounding Socialist Realism there was much more negative than in the Soviet Union. But this is not to say that the architectural results are worthless, or that they are uninteresting.

So much for the differences of historic situation and significance. We will return to a consideration of the differences of architectural vocabulary in Chapter Six and in the concluding section.

Socialist Content

In all discussions concerning the relationship between architecture and politics, attention seems to focus on the question of *how* people built ("What style?"). Two other questions tend to be neglected: *What did they build?* and *How much of it?*

This chapter deals with the building assignments, that is, the question of what people built, or—in the more political terminology of the time—"the socialist content" of buildings. Something will also be said concerning the volume of building output.

Architectural treatises and the art academies of the nineteenth century had placed building assignments in ranking order, in terms of social prestige and symbolic pretensions. Public buildings ranked higher than housing. Buildings for education and culture outranked buildings for technical and industrial purposes. And a similar ranking order existed within each category: A university had to be seen as something different and superior to a secondary school, a secondary school superior to an elementary school.

An attempt to break or at least tone down this traditional hierarchy was already made by the early-twentieth-century Modernists Tony Garnier and Peter Behrens. To the Functionalists and Constructivists of the 1920s, this was a self-evident requirement. Buildings of all types were essentially equal. There was something dubious about symbolic pretensions; they were a kind of superstition that had actively contributed to the decline of architecture during the nineteenth century. The only symbolic form acceptable to the radical architects of the interwar years was that which was radically new or could be accommodated within a functionally or technically justified vocabulary. But the great international architecture competitions—for the *Chicago Tribune* building in 1922, the League of Nations headquarters in Geneva in 1927, and the Palace of the Soviets

V

in 1932—all showed that the big clients adhered to the old view of things.

For our purposes, of course, the competition for the Palace of the Soviets is of special interest. The result is referred to customarily as a victory for a traditional *vocabulary,* but it was no less a victory for the old view of the ranking order of buildings. The Palace of the Soviets was to be the most important building in a political system based on the principle of *the leading role of the Party,* a principle that could not be reconciled with the idea of equalization among buildings.

But the hierarchy of building types adopted in the Soviet Union during the 1930s was not just a reversion to the academic order of things. That old order was adapted to the new socialist content, and it was this revised hierarchy of building assignments that was to leave its imprint on building activities in the people's democracies.

Let us now consider, under three different headings, a sample of building assignments from the Stalin era and the Cold War era in the people's democracies.

The Great Construction Projects of Communism

Which types of buildings were most highly respected? Depending on the context, there were two possible answers to this question. The focus of attention in the architectural journals was on the traditional, representational briefs. Ideological and political journals, on the other hand, highlighted the building projects that symbolized the transformation of the economic base, that is, the great heavy-engineering projects: canals, power stations, dams, steelworks combined with newly founded cities, and underground railways. They were referred to as "the great construction projects of Communism," demonstrating as they did the superiority of the new social system over the old.

Similar projects had already been completed in the Soviet Union during the 1930s: the White Sea Canal, the Moscow–Volga Canal, the Dneproges power station, and the first phase of the Moscow underground. After the war, the projects grew bigger: the Volga–Don Canal, the big power stations at Kuibyshev and Stalingrad, immense irrigation, cultivation, and afforestation projects, and underground stations more magnificent than ever. There was a commensurate growth of rhetorical and ideological self-assertion.

A political brochure published in the DDR in 1953 was entitled "Die Bedeutung der Grossbauten des Kommunismus für die gesamte Menschheit" (The importance of the great construction projects of Communism for all mankind). Another, translated from Russian, was

58, 59 Two steelworks of the 1950s:
"J. W. Stalin," Stalinstadt, later
Eisenhüttenstadt; and "Klement
Gottwald," Ostrava.

called "Die Grossbauten der stalinschen Epoche" (The great construction projects of the Stalin era). Expressions like these, it is true, were reserved for the big Soviet projects, but the people's democracies followed suit, at a respectable distance and according to their ability. Or—as events were so often to prove—beyond their ability.

Heavy industry, represented by steelworks combined with new cities, occupied the main focus of attention, just as in the Soviet Union under the first five-year plan: the J. W. Stalin steelworks combine and Stalinstadt in the DDR (Fig. 58), Huta Lenina and Nowa Huta in Poland, the Klement Gottwald combine (Fig. 59) and (Nová) Ostrava in Czechoslovakia, the J. V. Stalin steelworks and Sztálinváros in Hungary, the V. I. Lenin iron and steelworks in the expanded city of Dimitrovo (Pernik) in Bulgaria. In the case of the DDR and Hungary, the projects defied the absence of both iron and coal deposits, so compelling was the example set by the Soviet Union. And it was the Soviet Union that provided the accompanying iconography: dramatic pictures of steelworks in clouds of steam and coal smoke. These themes blossomed forth in literature and political rhetoric into a *cult of steel,* having both symbolic and linguistic points of contact with the cult of Stalin, the man of steel.

The monumentalization of factory gates was also part of the architectural iconography. Work in heavy industry was arduous and dirty, but it was also heroic. We have already seen the entrance to the Stalin Chemicals Combine in Dimitrovgrad (see Fig. 39). The entrances to the Nowa Huta and Sztálinváros steelworks, like the workers' entrance at Casa Scînteii in Bucharest, are illustrated in the following section (see Figs. 90, 91, 174, 175, 144). But here we can see

60 Design for the entrance to the Stalinstadt steelworks. Competition entry by Hanns Hopp, 1953.

how Hanns Hopp—one of the leading DDR architects, who had previously practiced in Königsberg—illustrated, in his competition entry for the urban plan of Stalinstadt, the entrance to the steelworks (Fig. 60). It is monumental, quite overwhelming. The gateway arch achieves the same height as the roofs of the wings on either side of it.

Heavy industry called for both energy and better communications. Power stations and canals were planned and constructed. The biggest enterprise of this kind was the Danube–Black Sea Canal in Romania, construction of which began in 1949. The intention was to shorten the navigation route to the Black Sea, to pierce the mountain massif that forces the Danube in its lower reaches to describe a great northward loop.

The canal was to tie the Soviet Union and the people's democracies more closely together. Also part of the project was the enlargement of three nearby cities: Cernavodă, Medgidia, and Năvodari. A perspective by the architects Gustav Gusti and Cezar Lăzărescu shows the monumental facade presented by Năvodari to the canal (Fig. 61).

The canal project also played an important part in political propaganda, and it furnished the title for Petru Dumitriu's big Socialist-Realist novel *Drum fără pulbere* (Road without dust). But the project ran into difficulties that resulted in showpiece trials of "saboteurs and divergents" (*Neuer Weg*, 3–4/9 1952). Work on it was discontinued in 1953 and not resumed until the 1970s.

There were also plans for a Danube–Oder Canal through Czechoslovakia to link up the principal waterways of the new Eastern Europe. Among other things, this canal was to transform Ostrava into a major port, at the same time as the 120-meter-wide

expanse of water, the same size as the Moscow River, would beautify the urban scene (*Architectura ČSR* 1951:7–9; *Novoe Vremia* 1952:34).

More successful were the dam and hydropower projects: the "hydro-staircase" at Tiszalök in Hungary (Fig. 62), or the "V. I. Lenin hydroelectric center" at Bicaz in Romania, located, respectively, on two tributaries of the Danube—the Tisza and the Bistriţa. Located within the same network of waterways were the dam projects on the River Váh in Czechoslovakia and the Stalin Dam on the River Iskur in Bulgaria. Power stations, irrigation and flood control projects, and improved communications—the great construction projects were the beginning of a new, better life for the entire country. There was never any talk of risks or drawbacks. The new political system had also achieved mastery of nature. The old system had been neither willing nor able to do this.

61 Monumental facade presented by the city of Năvodari to the Danube–Black Sea Canal, as envisaged by Gustav Gusti and Cezar Lăzărescu, 1951.

62 Power station at Tiszalök, Hungary, on the Tisza, a tributary of the Danube, designed by István Nyiri and István Gergely. Model, 1955.

63 *The Lamp of Ilyich Will Burn for Us Too,* oil painting by the Romanian artist Anastase Anastasiu, early 1950s.

64 Sketch, 1951, for a station on the underground railway planned for Warsaw.

Petru Dumitriu presented the Bicaz project in the Cominform newspaper (*For a Lasting Peace,* 1953:3) under the heading "The light of Lenin in the mountains of Romania," and Anastase Anastasiu made it the subject of a heroic painting entitled "The Lamp of Ilyich Will Burn for Us Too" (Fig. 63), the reference in both cases being to Lenin's famous comment on the GOELRO plan in 1920: "Communism is Soviet power and nationwide electrification." New politics and new technology.

Among all these great construction projects, the underground railways were the only category with a direct bearing on the everyday lives of ordinary people. They were modeled on the Moscow underground, which had been expanding continuously ever since the first phase was commissioned in 1935. No other Soviet construction project achieved such fame, and before long, underground railway construction projects for capital cities were included in the programs of the people's democracies too (except for the DDR, where Berlin already had its U-Bahn). Work on the building of underground railways began in Warsaw in 1951 and in Budapest at about the same time (Fig. 64). Advanced plans of a similar kind existed in Prague and Bucharest (Figs. 65, 66), and were at least being prepared in Sofia.

During a discussion that took place in 1953 in the Polish architects' association (SARP), concerning the projects for the future underground stations of Warsaw, one of the participants character-

65, 66 River station and underground station for the future Bucharest. Perspective sketches from the early 1950s.

ized the task of the architects as follows: "The assignment from the community involves transforming long underground tunnels into cheerful and monumental palace halls. The stations must be given such an appearance that the passenger will have no sense of being belowground."

The first phase was to be opened officially in Warsaw in 1955 and in Budapest the year before that. By then, however, the project had come undone and the plans had already been shelved, as quietly and discreetly as possible.

Apart from the underground stations, the big Soviet construction projects included another spectacular assignment for the architects: the river station. The best-known example was the Chimki station at the Northern River Harbor in Moscow, built between 1932 and 1937 to a design inspired by both riverboats and the Leningrad Admiralty. A similar station was planned in Bucharest, conjointly with plans for a Bucharest–Danube Canal. Another, more modest effort was planned for Sztálinváros, on the Danube. Most of these projects, though, remained mere suggestions.

The underground construction projects and the Black Sea Canal were not the only projects to end in failure. The HUKO project in Czechoslovakia in 1951, a vast steelworks in the Košice region of Eastern Slovakia, also failed. This project was part of Stalin's plan for the rearmament of the Eastern Bloc, and it was intended to be one of the biggest steelworks in Europe. The project included an entirely new city, "the socialist city of Šaca," presented in detail in *Architektura ČSR* 1952 (nos. 3–4). Both steelworks and new city, however, were far beyond the strength of Czechoslovakia's economy, which was severely strained already.

Long afterward, when Nikita Khrushchev had fallen from power, he was to be accused of "project madness." The same could be said of the period when "the great construction projects of communism" occupied the center of politics. But the mechanism was not the same. Instead of Khrushchev's capricious improvisations there was perpetual overbidding. To have doubts about a big project was to doubt the system and its ability to excel itself. The same mechanism operated concerning tributes to Stalin. One exaggeration led to another. Restraint was impossible.

Concern for Mankind

In the West, "exploitation" continued, speeded by the Marshall Plan. In "the camp of peace and socialism," by contrast, it was "concern for humanity" that prevailed, sometimes also referred to as "Stalin's concern for mankind."

Housing production was important, not only in a practical sense but also ideologically. Gone were the days when workers only went home to eat and sleep. Now they also had leisure to spend in their homes, at the cultural center, and at the sports ground.

In this general connection there are two aspects of housing production that deserve special attention: How much was built, and to what standard?

There are at least two ways of gauging the volume of housing production. We have the planning targets that were set, then we have the picture of housing production during the 1950s with which the output of the sixties and seventies was compared contrastingly and favorably.

The Polish six-year plan, extending from 1950 to 1955, provided for 723,000 rooms (kitchens included), that is, 120,500 new rooms per annum (Garliński). This meant 4.82 new rooms for every 1,000 inhabitants according to the 1950 census, or between two and three new *dwelling units* per annum and per 1,000 inhabitants in a country with severe overcrowding and a big housing shortage.

In Sofia at the end of the 1970s, annual output was 15,000 dwelling units with an average floor space of 40 m². To highlight these figures, they have been compared with the modest level of housing production in the same city between 1949 and 1952: 831 dwelling units annually, with an average floor space of 27 m² (Labov). Expressed in square meters, housing production at the beginning of the 1950s was less than one-twenty-fifth of output at the end of the 1970s.

To this we may add a comparative table from Romanian official statistics.

In other words, housing production in the people's democra-

New Housing Units per 1,000 Inhabitants		
	1950	1955
DDR	1.7	2.0
Poland	2.7	3.3
Czechoslovakia	3.1	3.9
Hungary	2.6	3.2
Romania	3.0 (1951)	3.2
Bulgaria	-	5.8
Soviet Union	-	7.7
Finland	6.5	7.8
Sweden	6.4	7.9
West Germany	7.5	10.7
Austria	6.7	6.0

Source: *Anuarul Statistic al R.P.R. 1961*, Bucharest 1961.

cies during the Cold War was low, decidedly lower than in the West, in spite of repeated claims to the contrary. After the rapid recovery of the earliest postwar years, housing standards improved remarkably slowly. The same pattern applied to private consumption generally. Other sectors and other purposes had priority, in particular heavy industry, the central administration, and the military sector.

So what about housing standards? Here we will take as our starting point a supposition commonly entertained by Modernist architects in both East and West: that the traditional vocabulary of architecture was implacably opposed to a necessary improvement of material standards for the population. Was this true in practice? Let us consider a couple of housing designs.

Our first example, from Bulgaria, shows the second story of a four-story block in Dimitrovgrad, built in 1953 (Figs. 67, 68). There are four apartments, three comprising two rooms and a kitchen each (68 m^2), one consisting of three rooms and a kitchen (83 m^2). The rooms line a corridor and the toilets, bathrooms, and kitchens are at the ends of the corridor. All the apartments are single-sided, but the kitchens also have windows at the end of the building. Two of the apartments have a balcony, one of them has two balconies, and the three-room apartment actually has three. Three floors up, however, there are no balconies at all. Distribution of the balconies has been governed by considerations of architectural effect.

Our second example comes from Stalinallee in Berlin and

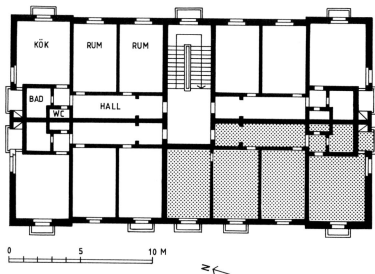

67, 68 Apartment blocks in the Tolbukhin district of Dimitrovgrad, built in 1953. Exterior and ground plan of four apartments. Compare perspective of the same district, Figure 180.

shows a stairwell section, with three apartments grouped around it (Fig. 69). One of these three apartments is single-sided (63 m²) and two of them (62 m²) run the full width of the building. All three have two rooms and a kitchen, a hall, and a bathroom. The kitchens are small, with a sink and running water as their only fixture. The bathrooms adjoin the outer wall and have windows. The hall includes a storeroom. The living rooms of the flats running the full breadth of the building have a loggia. The stairwell is fitted with a lift and a refuse chute.

In both these designs the apartments are large compared with current standards, and all of them have bathrooms. There were hard-

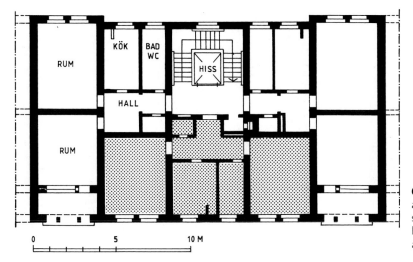

69 Detail from ground plan of an apartment block on Stalinallee, stairwell with three apartments. The long building volume is on an east-west axis.

ly any new flats that did not have bathrooms. The lift and rubbish chute in Stalinallee, however, were unusual features. In both instances the external architecture has influenced layout, but to very different extents. The Dimitrovgrad ground plan harks back to the tenement buildings of the nineteenth century. The Stalinallee ground plan, by contrast, in spite of all castigation of "formalism," belongs to the tradition of the radical twenties. The massive blocks of Stalinallee are 2 meters narrower than the small tenement buildings of Dimitrovgrad and, surprisingly, there are small flats with windows on two sides.

Behind the facades of Socialist Realism, there was a great deal of variation with regard to layout and housing standards. Too few apartments were built and their quality varied. But the cost of a flat, when allocated, was very small.

Just as important, ideologically, as the new housing was "the House of Culture." Unlike the housing, however, it was widely realized in all six countries: *Kulturhaus* in the DDR, *dom kultury* in Poland, *kulturný dům* in Czechoslovakia, *kulturház* in Hungary, *casa de cultură* in Romania, *kulturen dom* in Bulgaria. "The House of Culture is Socialism's gift to working people," said *Deutsche Architektur* (1954:3).

During the Modernist twenties in the Soviet Union, the "workers' club" had been a new, widely publicized building type. But roughly simultaneous with the transition to Socialist Realism, it acquired a different, more dignified name, that of *House of Culture,* and to some extent it also acquired a different, more official content.

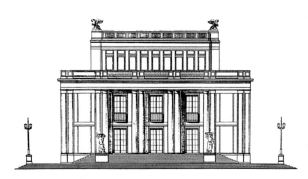

70, 71 House of Culture in Rzeszów, Poland, designed by Jósef Polak, early 1950s. Facade and foyer.

Houses of culture could be set up in old palaces or other historic buildings, but the most conspicuous of them were new buildings (Figs. 70–73). The main facility was a large assembly hall (complete with stage and foyer) for theatrical performances, film shows, and political meetings. There would also be a club room, reading rooms, and perhaps a cafe. Judging from the plans, the stocks of books were small in relation to the size of the reading rooms. The books could hardly ever be taken home by borrowers; they had to be read on the spot. The exterior had to be dignified, preferably Classical. And, if possible, the house of culture should occupy a monumental position in the townscape, that of a temple of culture, as for example in the Tolbukhin district of Dimitrovgrad (see Fig. 180).

An article in *Deutsche Architektur* (1954:3) declared:

People come to the house of culture after work. They walk into the brightly lit, spacious premises, they see a painting, a sculpture, they read a book. In the auditorium and study circle they broaden their field of vision and consolidate their conviction and vocational skill. . . . They behold the world as it was and as it will be. With dignity they celebrate the national festivals.

The same article referred to the houses of culture as the workers' *own* institutions, but at the same time they had a very official look about them. Above the proscenium in the Nowy Port house of culture in Gdańsk, the audience could read the section of the constitution of the People's Republic of Poland in which the state guaranteed citizens access to culture.

A big factory was supposed to have its own house of culture, for its own workers, but the usual practice was for the house of culture to belong to the city or district. The *palace of culture* was bigger than the house of culture, the *club* was smaller, and the *red corner* was smallest of all.

Socialist content also included reading rooms for the perusal of newspapers and magazines, kindergartens and nursery schools to educate the children and enable their mothers to go out to work, sports centers and stadium facilities marking the new role of sport in the life of the community, and rest homes for deserving workers, often located in special spas like Stalin (Varna) on the Black Sea, the people's democracies' counterpart of Sochi in the Crimea.

The schools were less prominent and the role allotted to hospitals and other types of caring institutions was fairly insignificant. In the socialist world, people were healthy and nearly all of them seemed to be in the prime of life. In the architectural journals of the people's democracies, one looks in vain for old people's homes and mental hospitals. Buildings of this kind received no priority and could really be discounted, now that "man's exploitation of man" had ceased.

Ostentation and Monumentality

The monuments became numerous, from the Baltic to the Black Sea, and not only in the capitals but in small towns and the countryside as well. They paid tribute to the Soviet Army, the communist resistance, and the socialist pioneers. They indicated the foundations of the new order.

That order meant not only a new political system but also a new political *style*. Among other things, the style called for a tribune for the top political leaders, a place where the people could march past on the national day and on May Day, in short, a venue for mass meetings, state ceremonies, and military parades, where the legitimacy of the political system could receive regularly recurring ceremonial confirmation. The great exemplar here was the Lenin Mausoleum and Red Square in Moscow.

The Bulgarians came close to the example thus set. The Dimitrov Mausoleum in Sofia, completed in 1949, also presented a combination of place of remembrance for the embalmed leader and ceremonial tribune for the national leaders. And the new ceremonial square, Ploshtad 9 septemvri, emulated Red Square by being located near the palace of the deposed tsar.

Similar tribunes were built in Bucharest and Budapest, close to newly erected statues of Stalin, in big open squares bearing his name (but today called Piaţa aviatorilor and Dózsa György út, respectively). In Budapest, the base of the monument served as a tribune. In a photograph from the eleventh anniversary of liberation from fascism, 4 April 1956 (see Fig. 200), we see the monument in use and the state and Party leaders assembled at Stalin's feet. The parapet in front of the tribune is decorated with reliefs depicting scenes from the liberation. The side galleries are adorned with large portraits of the national leaders (Rákosi et al.) and of the leaders of the foreign parties (Khrushchev and Mao Zedong). Troops parade on the square, forming perfect, closed squares of their own. ZIM cars are waiting in the background. This was one of the last manifestations to take place at the monument, which had been built only five years before. Just six months later, Stalin was to be pulled off his pedestal by the rebellious crowds (see Figs. 201–206).

Warsaw did not have a Stalin monument, but the same purpose was more than adequately served by the Palace of Culture and, while that palace was still being built, a tribune for the leaders was erected at its foot in Plac Stalina (now Plac Defilad).

In East Berlin, the tribune was erected at the Lustgarten, which on May Day 1951 was renamed Marx-Engels-Platz. Mass political

meetings took place in the lee of the bomb-damaged former royal palace and the ruins of the Prussian government buildings. Plans existed to replace them, for example, with a high-rise building for the new leaders of state, comparable in size and proportions to the Palace of Culture in Warsaw, while out on the square there was to be a monument to Marx and Engels (Fig. 74).

Prague, left comparatively undamaged by the war, was the only city to refrain from a new order of things. Václavské náměstí was not only the center of modern Prague but, ever since the revolutionary year of 1848, had also been the appointed place for political manifestations. Plans existed for a demonstration and parade square on the Letná Mountain behind the Stalin Monument, but nothing came of them. It is true that when Klement Gottwald died in 1953 he was embalmed like Lenin, Dimitrov, and Stalin, but no mausoleum with a tribune for the political leaders was built for the masses to file past. Instead, the national monument on Žižkov Mountain, dating from the 1930s, was turned into a pantheon for the new regime.

74 Model of the 1951 scheme for the center of Berlin by Planungsgruppe Berlin, headed by Edmund Collein. In the background of the big square, renamed Marx-Engels-Platz, is a high-rise building "expressing the grandeur and significance of the victory of socialism in Germany." The Palast der Republik was built on approximately the same site in the 1970s.

Socialist monumentality could assume many different guises. The great building projects of the capital cities are treated separately in Chapter Seven of this book, and so for the present we will concentrate on one type of building to which particular importance was attached: the *high-rise building*. All through history, tall buildings had been "the most ample expression of technical progress and of man's victory over the forces of nature" (*Architektura*, 1954:5). This was still true, but not all high-rise buildings were equal. They were subject to ideology. The high-rise building as conceived by Socialist Realism was a different thing altogether from the skyscraper of the capitalist world.

The skyscraper was an office block built on an ordinary precinct site. The plot was a small one and the building took the form of a tower occupying the full area. The high-rise building, by contrast, could have a variety of functions: government offices, hotel, or apartment building. Position and height were geared to the townscape. The site was spacious and a proper high-rise building would ascend out of a wide base several stories high.

Skyscrapers were an expression of exploitation in the West. The Soviet high-rise buildings, by contrast, embodied "the magnificent, upward force of Soviet society, the onward-forging lifestyle of Soviet people and their abundant, many-sided joy of living" (*Deutsche Architektur*, 1952:1).

The corresponding social ethos in the people's democracies demanded similar expression, in the name of consistency; furthermore, the high-rise buildings fitted in with the type of urban planning introduced with Socialist Realism, as vertical accents to punctuate the skyline, indicating what was ideologically important.

There were high-rise buildings of different sizes. The people's democracies produced only one on a really grand scale, comparable with the originals in Moscow: the Palace of Culture in Warsaw (see Chapter Seven). But the ideologist Edmund Goldzamt planned another two such buildings in the same city, one at Plac Unii Lubelskiej and another at Plac Zamkowy. There were eight high-rise buildings in Moscow. In that case, three in Warsaw would not be too many. The high-rise building in Marx-Engels-Platz in East Berlin, already referred to, was also intended for this category. It would have been more than 100 meters high and it was intended for the reunited German government that was the official objective of the Soviet Union's German policy.

Prague's Hotel International is of somewhat more modest proportions (Fig. 75). Built in the Dejvice district at the initiative of the Minister of Defense Alexej Čepička as part of a large military com-

75 Hotel International, Prague, designed in 1951 by František Jeřábek and his collective, completed 1956.

plex, it was, accordingly, designed by a military planning bureau. There is no mistaking the dependence on Soviet examples, at the same time as the sgraffito decor is deliberately national.

The high-rise building planned for Altmarkt in Dresden also was modeled on Soviet lines. The first version was criticized for excessively dominating the remains of the historic city center (*Deutsche Architektur,* 1953:1) . The second version, illustrated here, is not only more graceful but is more compliant with the Soviet exem-

76, 77 Left: High-rise design for
Altmarkt, Dresden, by Herbert
Schneider, 1953. Viewed from the east
(see also Figs. 237, 238).
Right: High-rise building by Tibor
Weiner, Béla Bakos, and József
Tiefenbeck, on the main street of
Sztálinváros, now Dunaújváros.

plars, with their wealth of detail and their stepped construction (Fig. 76, see Figs. 88, 237).

Another kind of high-rise building, instead of standing alone, formed part of a larger composition. Well-known examples of this kind are the high-rise buildings of Strausberger Platz in East Berlin and the large gabled building in Lange Strasse, Rostock (see Fig. 86). Then there is the high-rise building on the main street of Sztálinváros, typical of many such accents on newly laid-out streets and newly developed housing areas all over Eastern Europe (Fig. 77). Although it is only three stories higher than the surrounding buildings, it imparts to the street the variety and monumentality that high-rise buildings were meant to provide. The facade is divided into three parts, in the Classical manner, and the balconies are decoratively positioned without any consideration for the flats inside. As is so often the case in Hungary, however, the architectural idiom is too plain to meet the requirements of Socialist Realism. If anything, it reminds one of the 1920s.

There was no hard and fast boundary between high-rise buildings proper and buildings with towers. Both had the same architectural function and ideological content, and the terminology was unclear. Towered buildings, again, derived their inspiration from the Soviet Union, but they could also refer to historical tradition, as for example in the case of buildings for city authorities; this is true of the projects for Nowa Huta, Dimitrovgrad, and Sofia.

78 Twin towers of Frankfurter Tor, Stalinallee, East Berlin, viewed from the east, looking toward the center. Architect: Hermann Henselmann. This section of Stalinallee was begun in 1953 and completed in 1956.

High-rise buildings and towered buildings were part of the ideological face of the city. They were architecture's foremost contribution to monumental propaganda and, as building assignments, they carried great prestige. They were incorporated in city development plans in large numbers, and, in the forms we have now studied, they were included in models of the future city, from Magdeburg and Gdańsk to Oraşul Stalin (Braşov) and Dimitrovgrad. Most of them, however, never got any further than this, and an even larger number probably died on the drawing board.

When policy changed in the mid-1950s and architecture was given new objectives, the high-rise buildings were the main target of criticism. They made a perfect butt for irony. Instead of ideology and the new social order, they now stood for futility and waste. The same reproach was incurred by Hermann Henselmann's twin towers at the Frankfurter Tor end of Stalinallee (Fig. 78). What a waste! Consider the cost of these unnecessary ornaments! Henselmann curtly replied that the two towers together had cost the same amount as a DEFA film (an ordinary feature film). It was an ingenious riposte, fending off both the economic and the ideological criticism subsequently leveled at Socialist Realism.

No such questions were asked, however, at the beginning of the 1950s. The architects' big problem then was not economics, and not even ideological content. Their problem, at the drawing boards of the state planning bureaus, was that of *national form*.

National Form

The definition of Socialist Realism indicated that form had to be *national*. But what did this mean in terms of practical building, in the Soviet Union and above all in the people's democracies in the early years of the 1950s?

To answer this we need examples, and in order to understand the examples we also need a background. What were the national architectural traditions of the various countries? And what about national identity in the political sense? Was it self-evident or did it present anything of a problem?

Then there is another question to be asked. How does the national form of Socialist Realism relate to other national forms in the architectural history of the twentieth century? Is it a thing apart? Or is it part of a wider context?

The term "Socialist Realism" as first used, in the Soviet Union in 1934, referred to literature. In that field it was easy to understand what was meant by *realism*, but *national form* was less clear.

In architecture, the opposite was true. *Realism* there was a difficult concept and would remain so. *National form*, on the other hand, was easy to understand.

The idea of national form is an old one. It was part of the *raison d'être* of the Gothic Revival, which in Germany, England, and France alike was looked on as something national. Demands on national form were then refined as the nineteenth century wore on. There were many motivating forces involved: political and ideological constellations, pictorial art, music and literature, expanding knowledge of the national heritage, and, not least, a striving by the architect to renew the eclectic repertoire. Norway acquired a national architecture rooted in the building of its stave churches; Russia acquired its own national architecture, founded on native Byzantine traditions, and so on. These refined canons could also lead on to the develop-

VI

ment of regional architectural themes, as soon happened in both Germany and France.

This pursuit of national form is well known to us as far as the nineteenth century is concerned. It was observed not only by contemporaries but also by posterity. It tallied with the architectural historians' image of the nineteenth century. But where the twentieth century is concerned, those same architectural historians, following in the footsteps of Pevsner and Giedion, have treated the pursuit of national form as a curiosity, a relic of the past, essentially unconnected with the new century. It has been observed and taken seriously only in certain countries, for example, Sweden or Finland, but it has never been viewed as a whole, as an international current in the history of twentieth-century architecture. That history, then, includes not only Classicism and Modernism—the Latin and Esperanto of architecture—but also the national languages and dialects.

The following figure will serve to show, schematically, how this pursuit of national form relates to Classicism and Modernism (Diagram B):

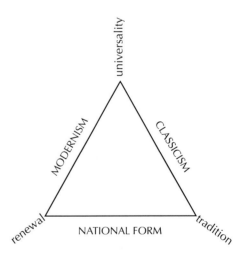

Diagram B

Here we have not just "groups of architectural motifs" (three languages) but also three concepts suggesting ways in which they can be paired off: *tradition* is the common foundation of Classicism and national form; *renewal* is the objective both of national form and of Modernism; *universality* is pursued by Classicism and Modernism alike.

Already in the 1920s, though, we can draw another schematic diagram, a simplification in that it recognizes only two main tendencies—Traditionalism and Modernism—but complicated in that it also includes the ideological and political dimension. That figure (Diagram A) has already been presented in our introduction and will be discussed at greater length in the concluding chapter.

The 1900 World Exposition in Paris included a Rue des nations, a Street of Nations, in which the participating countries presented themselves in national pavilions (Fig. 79). Nearly all the pavilions were designed so as to be immediately identifiable from their style of architecture. That, at any rate, was the intention of the clients and architects. But there was a big difference between direct imitations (Hungary, Britain, Belgium) and free interpretations (Finland, Sweden). The 1900 exposition was a tremendous manifestation of "national form" and there was virtually nothing to suggest that completely different ideals were in the offing.

At the 1937 World Exposition in Paris, national and regional forms did not play the same part as in 1900, but what is more remarkable is that they were still there at all. Striking examples in this respect were the Bulgarian, Romanian, South African, Iraqi, and Siamese pavilions and practically all of the many pavilions representing the provinces and colonies of France. And indeed, the exhibition as a whole, seen in an Eastern European perspective by the Polish architectural historian Andrzej K. Olszewski, has been amply characterized as a hybrid of Functionalism and Socialist Realism! This excellent turn of phrase shows quite clearly that the *architectural* ingredients of Socialist Realism were present in many quarters.

80-82 The permanent agricultural exposition in Moscow in 1939. The pavilions for the Soviet republics of Azerbaijan (left) and Georgia (right). Architects, respectively: Artshil Kurdiani and Georgi Lezhava, and Sadykh Dadashev and Mikael Useinov. Below: Detail of the facade of the Georgian pavilion.

Two years later, on 1 August 1939, came the opening of the big, permanent agricultural exposition in Moscow, VSKhV. This included pavilions for all the Soviet republics—Azerbaijan, Georgia, Ukraine, and so on (Figs. 80–82). And there were special pavilions for different parts of the great Russian Soviet Republic—Leningrad, Siberia, and the Volga regions, for example.

These pavilions had three distinctive characteristics. First, a monumental, Classical composition. Second, an aura of wealth and exuberance, conveyed by ornamentation and iconography (sheaves of corn, grape vines, cornucopias). Third, national form: Notable features of the Azerbaijan pavilion were stalactite vaulting and other features of the Islamic tradition of architecture; the Leningrad pavilion was a modern application of Petersburg Classicism; the Georgian and Armenian pavilions incorporated elements of local, Byzantine-inspired traditions. But there was one tradition that had not yet been enlisted. There were no towers and spires, no allusions to the Kremlin tradition. That tradition had formed the basis of the late-nineteenth-century Neo-Russian style (the Moscow Historical Museum, the Church of the Resurrection in St. Petersburg), which was closely associated with the tsars and the Church. Iofan's design for the Palace of the Soviets (see Fig. 46), admittedly, was an attempt to merge the Kremlin tradition with communism, but the idea went virtually unregarded until after World War II (the high-rise buildings of Moscow).

National traditions had been tried earlier, during the 1920s or as early as the nineteenth century. The new thing about VSKhV was not its vocabulary but the ideological setting. The exposition marked the breakthrough of the national form of Socialist Realism. A new tradition was established, and it was this tradition, evolving further during the 1940s, which the architects of the people's democracies had to adjust to in the early years of the 1950s.

Let us now consider the six countries individually, before summing up and trying to answer the questions with which we began.

DDR

In Germany, the prospects of a national architecture could not have been worse. The Nazis had poisoned the national question from every point of view and, as it seemed, for all time. Modernism had recovered its authority; above all, the cities were in ruins and concerns about style came well down on the agenda.

But the campaign against Cosmopolitanism also confronted the DDR with the demand for a culture having a "national form." The nation thus referred to, however, was not the DDR but Germany as a whole, the objective of the Soviet Union being a Germany reunited in accordance with Soviet principles. Stalin was often said to be "the German people's best friend"—not the DDR's. And architecture with consequences extending far into the future must focus on the great objective. Zonal and sectorial boundaries would pass away. But the buildings would not.

In November 1951, as "the national program of reconstruction" was about to begin, Kurt Liebknecht presented a definition of terms in a lecture entitled "Das grosse Vorbild" (The great model). What was Socialist Realism? In the Soviet Union and in Germany? What were the points of departure for a new *German* architecture? The answer was that there were two kinds of positive national tradition, *local* and *pan-German*. In the former instance there was a wide register, ranging from the Late Middle Ages to the nineteenth century, from the Baltic to southern Germany. But in the latter instance there was only one answer, *Classicism*, referring above all to Berlin Classicism from Langhans to Schinkel. Classicism was the last *progressive* architecture. Liebknecht also quoted examples of new buildings in the Classical spirit: the House of Culture at Maxhütte in Unterwellenborn, by architects Hanns Hopp and Josef Kaiser (Fig. 83), and the high-rise building at Weberwiese, Berlin, by Hermann Henselmann (Fig. 84, see Fig. 122). The House of Culture, still in the planning stage, would when completed be reminiscent of both the rebuilt opera house in Unter den Linden (the central section) and of the Brandenburg Gate (the projecting wings). The high-rise building, work on which had already begun, bore some resemblance (windows) to Schinkel's house for the tile manufacturer Feilner, destroyed

83 Design for House of Culture at the Maxhütte steelworks, Unterwellenborn, in the southern DDR, by Hanns Hopp and Josef Kaiser; built 1952–54.

84, 85 Left: Facade drawing, 1951, for Hochhaus Weberwiese, just south of Stalinallee. Architect: Hermann Henselmann; built 1952. Right: Facade detailing for Feilnerhaus, Berlin, by Karl Friedrich Schinkel, 1829.

in the war (Fig. 85), and, since it was one of the starting points for the planning of Stalinallee, the affinity would be invoked on further occasions. What was more striking, Henselmann's towers at Frankfurter Tor (see Fig. 78) had precursors in both Karl von Gontard's two church towers at Gendarmenmarkt (1780–85) and in Ludwig Hoffmann's City Hall (1902–10).

Speaking in Rostock in 1953, East German leader Walter Ulbricht declared that West Germans visiting Berlin and Stalinallee would see that *a new German architecture* was being developed there, as opposed to "imitating American crates and boxes." Modifying the influence of the great "magistrals" in Moscow were national architectural themes and political pedagogics.

Stalinallee was the great pan-German manifestation. The most

widely observed examples of the local tradition being implemented were Lange Strasse in Rostock and Altmarkt in Dresden, both started in 1953 as important parts of *das nationale Aufbauprogramm*. Here, quite contrary to contemporary practice in West Germany, the aim was for new buildings to restore to the ruined cities some of the historical identity they had lost. In Rostock, one of the points of departure was the Kerkhofhaus of 1470, (Figs. 86, 87). In Dresden there was a house by Pöppelmann, the Haus am Jüdenhof from 1716 (Figs. 88, 89), both buildings representing bourgeois architecture that, in its historical context, could be termed *progressive*—Gothic and Baroque, but not ecclesiastical Gothic and not royal Baroque. In the case of

86, 87 Left: Lange Strasse, the main street in Rostock, designed by Joachim Näther and his collective, built 1953-59. Right: Kerkhofhaus in the same city, a burgher's residence of the late Middle Ages.

88, 89 Left: East side of the restored Altmarkt, Dresden. Architect: Herbert Schneider; built 1954–55. Right: Haus am Jüdenhof designed by M. D. Pöppelmann, the architect of the Zwinger, destroyed during World War II.

Dresden, Hermann Henselmann had defined the objective in dialectical rhetoric: "to amalgamate the noble tradition of this city with the great ideas of our age and to embody them in buildings of artistic and social worth" (*Deutsche Architektur*, 1952:3).

Poland

There was a crucial difference between German and Polish misery at the end of the war: The Polish nation was not morally compromised. But there was another complication in that postwar Poland was a state within new boundaries. A great deal of territory in the east had been lost to the Soviet Union and, by way of compensation, the Poles had been allotted Silesia, Pomerania, Danzig, and part of East Prussia. The new Poland tallied quite well with the Poland of the Piast dynasty, and in this way the Middle Ages took on a new significance. The earliest Polish state conferred legitimacy on People's Poland. More important, though, not least where architecture was concerned, was the period of political and cultural greatness in the sixteenth and seventeenth centuries.

In spite of fierce disagreements during the early postwar years, there was a consensus on the reconstruction of the ruined historic monuments—the old parts of Warsaw and Gdańsk, the castles of Wilanów and Łazienki, and so on. This was the great national building issue, even after 1949. It could be incorporated unchanged in the Communist rhetoric, but it did not excuse the Poles from giving a national form to new buildings as well.

How, then, was national form manifested, for example at Nowa Huta, the biggest and most prestigious construction project in postwar Poland (Figs. 90, 91)? The buildings in the city center were given decorative detailing—balustrades, window pediments, portals—derived from Wawel, the castle of the kings of Poland in nearby

90, 91 Nowa Huta. Left: One of the two administrative buildings flanking the entrance to the steelworks, designed by Janusz and Marta Ingarden. Right: Site plan.

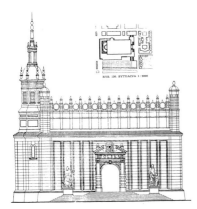

92, 93 Left: Design for a Polish pavilion at the permanent agricultural exposition, Moscow, by Zygmunt Stępiński, 1951. Right: Polish students studying the model on display in Warsaw.

Cracow. Still more striking, however, were the two administrative buildings at the entrance to the steelworks, surmounted by the Renaissance motif known as "Polish parapet." It occurred in many different variants during the second half of the sixteenth century, on town halls (Chełmno, Sandomierz), on castles (Baranów, Krasiczyn), on the Cloth Hall at Cracow. At the beginning of the twentieth century it was used by Stefan Szyller for the entrance pavilions of the Poniatowski Bridge in Warsaw (1907–13, reopened 1946). Polish parapet was the most articulate of all national motifs. And yet, like the Renaissance generally, it was used quite sparingly during the era of Socialist Realism, except where national form was an inescapable demand: in the Palace of Culture in Warsaw, designed by Soviet architects (see Figs. 127–130, 133–138), and in schemes for a Polish pavilion at the Moscow Agricultural Exposition in 1951 (Figs. 92, 93).

Thus there was a certain amount of resistance to the excessively pronounced national form, and as far as possible architects took another path—that of Classicism, not the Renaissance. But there were several reasons for this. One of them was that Classicism, by virtue of its strong position in the Soviet Union, was always a possible alternative. Another was the great importance of Classicism in the architectural history of Warsaw (Corazzi, Aigner et al.). A third cause was the experience and knowledge possessed by the generation of architects that had been trained during the interwar years: Classicism was familiar, while the Renaissance on the other hand was rather unfamiliar.

94, 95 Left: Section of MDM, Warsaw. Architects: Jankowski, Knothe, Sigalin, and Stępiński (see also Fig. 55). Right: Apartment block in the same city, designed by Jan Heurich and built 1910.

Ideologically speaking, however, the Classical architecture that in reality became Poland's "national form" was inadequately rooted in history. The main focus of discussion was on the central housing blocks in Warsaw, which were officially called Marszałkowska Dzielnica Mieszkaniowa (the Marszałkowska area) but always referred to as MDM (Fig. 94, see also Fig. 55). The facades of MDM echoed a large apartment building at Plac Małachowskiego, built in 1907–10, designed by Jan Heurich and reinstated after the war by Bohdan Pniewski (Fig. 95). This is one of the few residential buildings in old Warsaw having both the monumental stature and the dimensions that were wanted. It was a practical choice of starting point, but in the mind of Edmund Goldzamt, ideological leader of the Polish architects, it was wrong all the same: Tradition should be taken straight from the source and should not be viewed "through the spectacles of the Polish bourgeoisie" (*Architektura,* 1953:1). The architects *ought* to have made the Renaissance their starting point.

When the editors of *Architektura* summed up discussions of MDM, they particularly emphasized that Polish architecture of the early twentieth century presented an alternative to Heurich, one that met the requirement of "realism": Adolf Szyszko-Bohusz. Like his compatriots Marian Lalewicz and Paweł Wędziagolski, he had studied at the St. Petersburg Academy of Art and, like them, he could now be launched as a native forerunner of the academic aesthetic that was the nucleus of Socialist Realism. That too emanated originally from the St. Petersburg Academy.

Czechoslovakia

Modernism occupied a strong position in Czechoslovakia during the interwar years, and the 1937 Paris Exposition showed as much. The official catalogue described the Czech pavilion as "une création modèle de l'architecture de l'avenir." National form occupied a correspondingly weaker position compared with the surrounding countries. The same was true during the early postwar years, and after February 1948 this was a drawback: There was no national form available.

What, then, was brought out of the Czechoslovak past as a starting point for a new architecture in the spirit of Socialist Realism? Answer: "The revolutionary Hussite tradition," the Renaissance, traditional architecture, and the National Theater in Prague (*Architektura ČSR*, 1951:1–2). By contrast, everything associated with the period between the collapse of Bohemian independence in 1620 (at the battle of the White Mountain) and the revolutionary year of 1848 was passed over in silence. That was the period of the Hapsburgs, the Counter-Reformation, and Germanization, and so the Baroque was ruled out, at all events for official purposes. For the Baroque was "the style of power-hungry individualism."

So much for the principles. In practice there were few monumental assignments and the need was for forms that could impart a national imprint on the fairly heavy output of housing. And so it was the bourgeois architectural tradition that had something to offer, with its richly decorated gables, its ornamental parapets, and its sgraffito embellishments. Not only was it national, it was—readers were told—optimistic (*Tvorba*, 1950:50).

One example of the newly launched national tradition could be seen in the facade drawing reproduced here (type T20/52 apartment block), dating from 1951 (Fig. 96). The triangular grouping of arches surmounting the center of the facade occurs widely in native tradition, but it is also to be seen in Tábor, the fortified city of the Hussites (Fig. 97). The symbolic intention is clear enough, but as so often in the history of art and architecture, it is anybody's guess whether or not the message went home.

Gables of different kinds were one group of national motif. The other was facade decoration using sgraffito technique, either with traditional ornaments or with a new, socialist iconography (Figs. 98, 99). In Czechoslovakia there was a link with folk art that had no counterpart in the DDR, Poland, or Hungary.

It was always the Bohemian that predominated in the interpre-

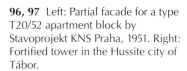

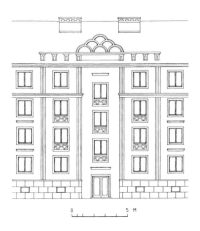

96, 97 Left: Partial facade for a type T20/52 apartment block by Stavoprojekt KNS Praha, 1951. Right: Fortified tower in the Hussite city of Tábor.

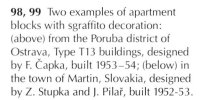

98, 99 Two examples of apartment blocks with sgraffito decoration: (above) from the Poruba district of Ostrava, Type T13 buildings, designed by F. Čapka, built 1953–54; (below) in the town of Martin, Slovakia, designed by Z. Stupka and J. Pilař, built 1952-53.

100 Entrance to the Mladá Garda student city in Bratislava. Gray-rendered facade, reddish-brown and white decoration. Architect: Emil Belluš; built 1953.

tation of national tradition, just as Bohemia was politically dominant, above all at the expense of Slovakia. But Slovakia had a different history and for centuries had been part of Hungary. The Slovak name of its capital, Bratislava, was a new formation from 1918. Historically the city was known by its Hungarian and German names, Pozsony and Pressburg, respectively.

The most widely observed building project in Bratislava during the early 1950s was the Mladá Garda student city, a large complex of interconnected residential enfilades with an entrance and dining hall in the middle (Fig. 100). The singular facade incorporates nothing from the city's own wealth of architectural traditions. The coping and the square tower come from Eastern Slovakia and the sgraffito decoration is a Bohemian touch. The name, finally, is the title of a famous Soviet novel, *The Young Guard,* by Alexander Fadeyev, published in 1946.

Hungary

The Hungarian pavilion for the 1900 World Exposition in Paris had been designed in close conformity with the fortress in Transylvania (Vajda-Hunyad) of the national hero János Hunyadi. Transylvania meant even more to Hungarian national feeling than Karelia meant to the Finns. During a critical phase of Hungarian national history, Transylvania alone preserved a measure of political independence (1541–1686). After World War I, however, Transylvania had to be ceded to Romania, and after World War II—following Horthy's attempt, supported by Hitler, to revise the Treaty of Trianon—it was

101 Staircase of the National Museum in Budapest, the principal work of nineteenth-century Hungarian Classicism, designed by Mihály Pollack and built 1837–47.

102 Budapest School of Industrial Design, by Zoltán Farkasdy et al., built 1953.

ceded again. Reminiscing about the Hungarian cultural heritage of Transylvania was politically impossible. That sort of thing was "bourgeois nationalism" and a provocation to both Romania and the Soviet Union. For the same reason, Hungary's period of greatness under Matthias Corvinus (Hunyadi), the Hungarian Renaissance of the fifteenth century, was also ruled out.

Fortunately there was another prestigious period that could be highlighted as an example, namely, the so-called Reform era, the first half of the nineteenth century. That was the time of the rebirth of the Hungarian language and of opposition to the Hapsburgs, a time not least of social and economic reform, culminating dramatically in the Hungarian Rising of 1848–49. In architecture it was the period of Classicism, with Mihály Pollack (1773–1855) as its leading name and his National Museum in Budapest as the best-known building (Fig. 101). Another building, also by Pollack, was the Assembly Room (Hung. *vigadó*) overlooking the Danube in Budapest, destroyed in 1849 during the suppression of the Hungarian Revolt. A third building from the same period was the suspension bridge over the Danube (Lánchíd, "Chain Bridge"), the first permanent link between Buda and Pest. All three were buildings with a positive symbolic content (at least, disregarding the fact that the Hapsburgs had put the Hungarians in their place with Russian help, while the bridge had been built by English specialists). In a book published in 1951 with the illuminating title *The Progressive Tradition in Hungarian Architecture*, half the examples quoted come from this relatively brief period.

Monumental instances of this tradition being applied are the School of Industrial Design in Budapest (Zoltán Farkasdy et al.; Fig. 102), the Party building in the Second District of Budapest (József Körner), and the House of Culture in Tolna (Béla Pintér). Then there is the design for a Party building in Sztálinváros, somewhat changed in the event and now a museum (Tibor Weiner; Fig. 103).

More common, however, was a free Classicism that if anything put one in mind of the interwar years—both in Hungary itself and, to some extent, in Scandinavia—rather than of the early nineteenth century. This is true of those parts of the Institute of Technology in Budapest built during the years of Socialist Realism (Gyula Rimanóczy and János Kleineisel; Figs. 104, 105), and of the vocational school for miners (*vájáriskola*) in Várpalota, presented earlier (see Fig. 56), which was also by Rimanóczy.

The national tradition was clearly defined, but it was less emulated than in the other people's democracies. And the period of strict adherence to Socialist Realism was briefer than elsewhere.

103 Party building in Sztálinváros, designed by Tibor Weiner and built c. 1953.

Romania

Next to Poland, Romania was the most populous state in Eastern Europe. Greater Romania had been formed in 1919–20, when the country doubled both its area and its population. In 1945, it had the only sizable national minority remaining in Eastern Europe, the Hungarians of Transylvania. Unlike the other people's democracies, Romania was a state without a great national past; at least, none could be readily identified. Its nucleus was the old princedoms of Moldova (Moldavia/Moldau) and Valahia (Walachia). Their architectural tradition was Byzantine, with certain Turkish elements. Western

104, 105 Two interiors from the Budapest Institute of Technology, by Gyula Rimanóczy and János Kleineisel, 1954.

106 Casa Scînteii polygraphic combine, Bucharest, Horia Maicu et al. Perspective from the beginning of the 1950s. Later the exterior was simplified somewhat; for example, the porticos of the side facades were dispensed with.

107, 108 Left: The Church of the Patriarch, Bucharest, 1650s; in the foreground, gateway building and bell tower from 1698. Right: Casa Scînteii, detail of main facade.

European influence grew strong during the nineteenth century, but from the beginning of the twentieth century onward a bid was also made to create a *Romanian* architecture (Mincu, Antonescu et al.). That endeavor now became the norm. The old architecture and the new were presented together.

The main building project in postwar Romania was the polygraphic combine Casa Scînteii in Bucharest (Horia Maicu et al.), work on which began in 1949 (Figs. 106–110, see Figs. 139–150). After several designs had been rejected, a "national form" had finally been

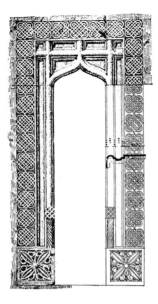

109, 110 Left: Casa Scînteii, entrance to the editorial offices of the Party newspaper *Scînteia* (Spark). Right: Window surround from the seventeenth-century church of the Plumbuita Monastery, Bucharest.

arrived at. This had the tall, closely spaced arches, without capitals, of the Byzantine tradition, arcades at ground-floor level, open galleries high up under the eaves, portals with Byzantine ornamentation, and spiral columns for the porticos of the side facades. But the columns were to remain on paper. They represented the unduly picturesque side of national tradition, in common with painted church facades and richly decorated trefoil arches. The decorative domes were also out of the question, with or without the peculiar spiral drum. The domes were too ecclesiastical. But the towers of Casa Scînteii should be thought of as an attempted modern counterpart.

A stylized Byzantine architecture, then, was launched as Romania's national form. It was stressed, though, that this architecture had been influenced not only from the south but also from the east, from Armenia, Georgia, and also, in the seventeenth century, Russia. This idea fitted in admirably with the endeavor of the 1950s to stress Romania's dependence on the Soviet Union in every possible context. But the idea, although opportune, was not a new one. Ultimately it stemmed from the Austrian art historian Joseph Strzygowski and his theory of powerful Eastern influence on European architecture. Accordingly, the Armenian version of Socialist Realism—Aleksander Tamanian's buildings in Yerevan—appears to have been of some importance to the Romanians, being looked on as the nearest "example from the Soviet Union."

The regional, Transylvanian style was represented in published surveys of the Steagul Roşu (Red Flag) housing area in Braşov/Oraşul

111, 112 Left: Steagul Roşu housing area, built for workers at the tractor factory of the same name in Braşov, known as "Stalin City" in the 1950s. Designed by Nicolae Nedelescu. Right: The Steaua housing area, Bucharest, built primarily for employees in the railway workshops.

Stalin, which, with its eaves, lucarnes, shutters, and half-timbered gables, belongs to a tradition common to the Alps and Carpathians (Fig. 111). This area was designed and to a great extent built *before* the proclamation of Socialist Realism, hence the "formalist" layout with its parallel three-story blocks. Clearly, then, this architecture fitted the bill all the same. The Steaua (Star) housing area in Bucharest, built two years later, shows how the same assignment was tackled in the Romanian heartland (Valahia) (Fig. 112).

Regional variation was also utilized in the preparation of standard projects, as in the designs reproduced here for houses of cul-

113, 114 Standard drawings for houses of culture in the People's Republic of Romania. Three regional facade variants for (a) Moldova and Valahia, (b) Transylvania, and (c) Dobrogea. The basic plan is the same for all three.

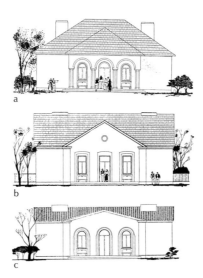 

ture for Moldova and Valahia, for Transylvania, and for Dobrogea on the Black Sea; the main difference here is in roof geometry, specifically, the hipped roofs and high/low saddleback roofs (Figs. 113, 114).

Bulgaria

Bulgaria, like Romania, had the typical Balkan combination of Byzantine and Turkish traditions, but here the Turkish element was stronger, even though it was not always referred to by its proper name.

This architectural tradition acquired its national content during the so-called Bulgarian Renaissance *(vuzrazhdane)*, the century preceding liberation from the Turks (c. 1750–1878), a period that is particularly well represented in Tărnovo, Koprivshtitsa, and the old city of Plovdiv. There we see timber buildings with eaves and cantilevered upper stories, verandas, bay windows, yoke-shaped arch-

115, 116 Left: An example of National Bulgarian architecture is this apartment block in Plovdiv, 1954, overlooking the River Maritsa. Right: Georgiadi House in the same city built 1846–48.

es, and, on the inside, decoratively designed ceilings. Another aspect of this tradition is represented by the famous Rila Monastery.

National tradition was very much alive during the interwar years, one picturesque example being the Bulgarian pavilion at the Paris Exposition of 1937 (Iordanov and Sugarev). More austere and Classical were the government offices and other public buildings erected in Sofia during the 1930s and well into the 1940s.

Thus, at the proclamation of Socialist Realism, an established national form was already available. Its content was unassailable. The Bulgarian Renaissance evoked thoughts of the liberation from the Turks. That had been accomplished with Russian assistance and was now presented as a historic parallel to "liberation from fascism" in 1944. The implementation, however, was too Formalistic, and when Bulgarian tradition came to be incorporated in Socialist Realism, it acquired, under the powerful influence of the Soviet Union, a different character from that of the interwar period.

First, though, a comparison of the same kind as before: the new national form, juxtaposed with ancient tradition. In other words: the corner of a large housing complex in the center of Plovdiv, dating from 1954, and the so-called Georgiadi House in old Plovdiv, built in 1848 (Figs. 115, 116). The similarities are clear, despite the difference in building materials and scale: the eaves, the yokeshaped arch, the fenestration.

Now a comparison of Socialist Realism with the interwar period's interpretation of national tradition: The National Bank (1934–37), in the new center of Sofia, contrasted with the nearby Grand Hotel Balkan (1954-57; Figs. 117, 118). This is a reasonable comparison, all the more so as one architect, Dimitur Tsolov, was involved in both projects. The later building retains little of the fluency inherited by the early one from the native tradition of timber architecture. Instead it has the ponderous quality of Soviet Classicism. The national quality lies in the motifs.

Close by is the Ministry for Heavy Industry, the splendid interior of which is one of the most remarkable examples of national form in the people's democracies (Fig. 119). In this government office from the 1950s we find unmistakable touches of the Byzantine palace.

National Form: Practice and Implications

The six people's democracies had very different historical backgrounds, hence the differences occurring when they came to point out *progressive* national tradition. But there were also striking similarities in the ideological arguments and in practical implementation.

117 Bulgarian architecture of the 1930s: National Bank in Sofia, by Ivan Vasilov and Dimitur Tsolov.

Tradition was not molded by the past. Instead, it was the present that chose and rejected.

Gothic and *Baroque* were the styles of the Church and royal power and were inconceivable on any occasion connected with the State and the capital city. They could be accepted, on the other hand, as expressions of a local or regional tradition, on the Baltic or in Saxony.

Both in Poland and in Czechoslovakia, the Renaissance was held out as an expression of national independence, while in Czechoslovakia it was also bound up with "the revolutionary Hussite tradition."

In the DDR and Hungary, on the other hand, *Neo-Classicism* was the progressive style, associated with periods of cultural greatness and revival. More explicitly national, at all events from a Western European point of view, were the *Byzantine and Turkish traditions,* which, on various grounds, were launched as the national form of Romania and Bulgaria.

The relationship to *eclecticism* and the architecture of the past few decades was a complicated one. The general verdict was negative, but exceptions were made. These were prompted partly by ideological considerations (the high value put on the National Theater in Prague) and by practical ones (Heurich's architecture as a starting point for MDM). It was common for tradition to be passed on through the national architecture of the late nineteenth and early twentieth centuries. The House of Culture in Unterwellenborn (see Fig. 85) puts one in mind not only of German Classicism "um 1800" but also, to no less an extent, of Heinrich Tessenow. Lange Strasse in

118, 119 Left: Grand Hotel Balkan, Sofia, designed by Dimitur Tsolov and his collective, built 1954–57. Photograph was taken in 1982, when the sign on the roof still read: Proletarians in all countries, unite! Today it reads: Sheraton Sofia—Hotel Balkan. Right: Vestibule of the Ministry for Heavy Industry, Sofia, designed by Kosta Nikolov and his collective and built 1954–56.

Rostock (see Fig. 86) evokes not only the Middle Ages but also the brick architecture of Fritz Schumacher and Fritz Höger.

It was never the intention that the architecture of the progressive periods should be revived in its entirety. Socialist Realism looked to history, not for styles but for telling *motifs,* motifs whose prestige would be further elevated by the new use made of them. So it was not the intention for the new buildings to make an antiquated impression. Only exceptionally did the architects resort to such well-known dodges as the use of small window lights to give their buildings a traditional look. Socialist Realism was neither romantic nor evocative.

Still less was there any question of buildings being constructed by traditional methods and with ancient materials. Insofar as this did happen, it was not due to any principle but to the fact that all technical development was concentrated on heavy industry or reserved for military purposes.

There is a continuity between the national architecture of the nineteenth and twentieth centuries, but there is also an important difference between these periods. Somewhat drastically, one can put it like this: The national form of the nineteenth century, like the Gothic revival, was opposed to the Classical tradition. After World War I, however, a different situation prevailed. National architecture was now on the same side as Classicism. Both represented tradition—different aspects of tradition—as opposed to the emergent Modernism. During the interwar period, Classicism was the overriding concept. In postwar Eastern Europe, it was the national form. This means, as we have already seen, that national form could very well be strictly Classical.

In one way, the pursuit of national form was paradoxical. During the nineteenth century or the early twentieth, an endeavor of this kind had always been united with a wave of political or cultural nationalism. But this time it was different. National self-consciousness was brought up short. Things national were always inferior to things coming from the Soviet Union. A country's own flag ought preferably to occur only in combination with that of the Soviet Union. To a large part of the population—and not only to those who, one way or another, could be called "bourgeois nationalists"—national sovereignty seemed to be challenged.

Thus we have national form, but not much nationalism in the ordinary sense. The kind of nationalism that did exist and was encouraged was strictly formalized, reserved for special occasions. Perhaps one might even say that, like popular and regional culture, it was stage-managed. It was no longer spontaneous and it was innocuous. It could be compared with nationalism in the Soviet republics—Armenia or Uzbekistan.

And just as the Soviet republics in 1939 had been allotted pavilions of their own at the big agricultural exposition in Moscow, now in the early l950s it was the turn of the people's democracies. During 1951, Polish, Hungarian, and Bulgarian architects competed to design pavilions for their several countries, and presumably the same invitation had also been sent to architects in the DDR, Czechoslovakia, and Romania.

There is nothing to confirm the very widespread supposition that the people's democracies in the long run were in danger of being demoted to Soviet republics. Only one thing was certain: If this did happen, then the architecture suitable for the People's Republic of Poland would be equally suitable for the Soviet republic of Poland.

To understand the word *national* as used in *national form,* we have to appreciate that the word is the antithesis of *cosmopolitan,* and that the latter word, in the official usage of the Soviet Union and the people's democracies, led nearly automatically to the use of other words: *imperialist, capitalist,* "the Anglo-American warmongers," and so on. The national form of Eastern European architecture was part of the ideological-political front.

This special significance of the word *national* can be traced back to the period immediately following the death of Lenin, when Stalin, denouncing Trotsky and his idea of permanent revolution, launched the concept of "socialism in one country." That concept engendered a doctrine with tremendous repercussions, the starting point among other things for the rejection of Modernism, for Socialist Realism, and for national form—in architecture as in other fields. What then happened, after World War II, was paradoxical: The doctrine of "socialism in one country," created for domestic use, was now also to be applied abroad.

It is possible, however, to go further back. Already in Stalin's *Marxism and the National Question,* published in 1913 and written at Lenin's suggestion to set out the Bolshevik standpoint, there are many turns of phrase that foreshadow subsequent developments: national culture, but without national independence.

Prospects and retrospects of this kind hardly explain architecture as a formal language, but they do explain the context that, during the Stalin era and in the thoroughly ideologized climate of the Cold War, gave architecture its meaning.

Monumental Buildings in the Capital Cities

It was important for the new political order to be manifested by representational buildings, especially in the capital cities.

In bombed-out Berlin, Stalinallee was the great manifestation. Another big project, the government palace in Marx-Engels-Platz, remained on paper. In Warsaw, where the destruction was if anything even worse, a similar role was first played by MDM, and also to some extent by the reconstructed Old City, Stare Miasto, which however was associated more with the nation than with the regime. Instead it was the Palace of Culture that came to symbolize the new order.

In Prague and Budapest, on the other hand, this task was performed by the Stalin Monuments, to be dealt with in Chapter Ten. In Bucharest it was the printing combine Casa Scînteii, and in Sofia it was the new center at Ploshtad Lenin and Ploshtad 9 septemvri.

Stalinallee in East Berlin

One of the worst-bombed districts of Berlin was Friedrichshain in the Russian sector. Frankfurter Allee, the old main street traversing this district of tenement buildings, now passed through a desert landscape.

Hans Scharoun led the work of urban planning in the as-yet undivided city. Following the administrative partition he stayed on in East Berlin for a while. What he and his associates intended was not reconstruction in the true sense but a new type of city, an open city of *Stadtlandschaft*. The plan for Nachbarschaft Friedrichshain has already been presented, in the section dealing with the early postwar years (see Chapter One).

Construction in Friedrichshain began soon after the DDR was proclaimed a separate state on 7 October 1949. Next to Frankfurter

VII

120 The first new building on Stalinallee: galleried apartment block on the south side of the street, by Ludmilla Herzenstein, 1949–50.

Allee, on the south side of the street, work began with a couple of gallery apartment blocks in the Bauhaus tradition, designed by Ludmilla Herzenstein, a member of Scharoun's circle (Fig. 120).

Stalin's seventieth birthday came on 21 December and in the newly founded DDR, as elsewhere, the tributes paid achieved heights of improbability. Frankfurter Allee was renamed Stalinallee. Aspirations for the street were elevated accordingly, but another two years were to pass before the project caught up with the new name.

The campaign against Formalism and Cosmopolitanism culminated in 1950–51. On 27 July 1950 the DDR government adopted sixteen "principles of urbanism," which not only stated the functional requirements but referred to "the face of the city, its artistic individuality." The gallery buildings on the south side of Stalinallee, now completed, were dismissed by Walter Ulbricht, the strong man of the Party, as "sanatoria" (*Lungenheilanstalten) (Deutsche Architektur*, 1953:4).

Two buildings marked the breach with Modernism and pointed out a new way.

The first was the Deutsche Sporthalle, completed in 119 days during 1951, in time for the Third World Youth Festival, which took place in East Berlin that August (Fig. 121). The sports center was the first essay in Socialist Realism and the first Classical facade in Berlin since the war—or, more precisely, since Albert Speer. It did not have a proper columned facade, though, and Walter Ulbricht advocated the addition of bases and capitals (*Deutsche Architektur*, 1953:4).

121 The first example of a new architecture in the DDR: Deutsche Sporthalle by Richard Paulick, on the north side of Stalinallee, built 1950–51 and demolished twenty years later.

The architect, Richard Paulick, had as a young man been one of Walter Gropius's assistants in Dessau, and had now been recalled from exile in China, where he had practiced in Shanghai between 1933 and 1949. *Der Spiegel* (14/5 1952) presented Paulick as "der rote Schlüter" (the red Schlüter), alluding to the famous author of the Royal Palace in Berlin.

The allusion was not altogether out of place. The athletic figures that Paulick erected in front of the building had previously decorated the balustrade of the recently demolished palace. But the large relief over the colonnade, with its boxers, relay runners, and young men and women carrying garlands, was, of course, a new composition—a companion piece to a statue of Stalin across the street.

The second building, which we have already mentioned, was Hochhaus Weberwiese (Fig. 122, see Fig. 84). On 29 July 1951, with the sports center approaching completion, *Neues Deutschland* had fiercely attacked the residues of Functionalism, and more specifically the architect Hermann Henselmann. Five days later the newspaper was able to announce that Henselmann had mended his ways and put forward a new housing development project for Weberwiese, immediately adjoining Stalinallee. Formalism was left behind. A new architecture was in the making, based on progressive German tradition, that is, primarily on Schinkel (window shapes, proportions). With the wisdom of hindsight, we can see that Hochhaus Weberwiese was a pilot study for Henselmann's two high-rise buildings at Strausberger Platz (see Fig. 124).

122 The second example of new architecture in the DDR: Hochhaus Weberwiese by Hermann Henselmann, 1951–52.

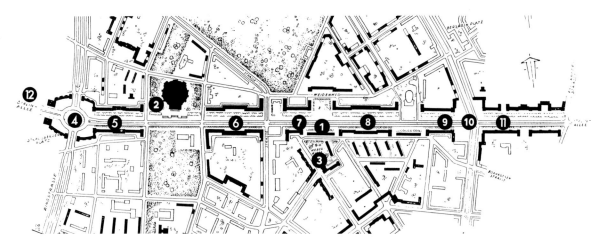

123 Stalinallee (renamed Karl-Marx-Allee in 1961) at the end of the 1950s. All subsections included buildings on both sides of the street. Facing buildings were treated as one unit.

1 Gallery apartment building (Herzenstein)
2 Deutsche Sporthalle (Paulick)
3 Weberwiese (Henselmann)
4 Strausberger Platz (Henselmann)
5 Block B (Hartmann)
6 Block C (Paulick)
7 Block D (Leucht)
8 Block E (Hopp)
9 Block F (Souradny)
10 Frankfurter Tor (Henselmann)
11 Block G, late 1950s (Hopp)
12 Phase II, 1959–64 (Collein et al.)

Meantime, work was proceeding apace on the planning of Stalinallee, starting with the eastern part of it. This in turn was divided up into six sections, allotted to the same number of architectural collectives, each of which was named after a senior architect: Hermann Henselmann, Egon Hartmann, Richard Paulick, Kurt W. Leucht, Hanns Hopp, and Karl Souradny, enumerated here in the order of their several sections, from west to east (Fig. 123). Henselmann, then, was not alone, though sometimes posterity was to think of him as the architect of the entire street. In addition to his own section (Strausberger Platz, see Fig. 124), however, he also designed the two towers marking the eastern end of Stalinallee, at Frankfurter Tor (see Fig. 78). These followed on from earlier Berlin architecture, the church towers at Gendarmenmarkt and Ludwig Hoffmann's City Hall.

Toward the end of 1951, the architects were visited by two eminent Soviet experts: Alexander Vlasov, city architect of Moscow, and Sergei Chernyshev, one of the authors of the new Moscow University. They had had experience with the great magisterial building projects in Moscow, but they also emphasized the need to find the national, German tradition (*Neues Deutschland*, 23/12 1951).

Otto Grotewohl, the head of the government, laid the foundation stone of Stalinallee on 3 February 1952, the anniversary of the devastating Anglo-American bombing raids on Berlin seven years earlier. The British and Americans had wreaked destruction. The German Democratic Republic, under the leadership of the United Socialist Party, was building things up again. Grotewohl also remarked that the street was the first stage of the road from Alexanderplatz, the center of old Berlin, to Moscow, heart of the socialist world.

Let us, however, disregard the rhetoric in Grotewohl's speech and the fact that hardly any other building project in European history has been shrouded in so much political propaganda—and counterpropaganda. Instead, let us consider the finished result, as it began to appear toward the end of 1953.

Stalinallee is a street in the same Classical sense as Unter den Linden or the Champs Élysées. All three, as *Handbuch für Architekten* pointed out, are just over twenty times as long as they are wide. They have a beginning and an end and a clearly defined street space. In the case of Stalinallee, the width is about two and a half times the facade height. Stalinallee is also a Classical street in the sense that the buildings have a pronounced rear elevation.

The main thing is the street, not the apartments—which is not to say that the latter were neglected. Two thousand apartments could have been obtained far more cheaply, but there was more involved

124 Stalinallee, Block B South by Egon Hartmann. In the background is Strausberger Platz by Hermann Henselmann, showing one of the two tower buildings that form the entrance to Stalinallee at the west end and match the tower buildings of Frankfurter Tor at the east end (see Fig. 78).

125, 126 Stalinallee Block C, North (above) and South (below), both by Richard Paulick and his *Meisterwerkstatt.*

here than "Die Wohnung für das Existenzminimum" (housing for a living wage). Many of the apartments (57 percent) comprise two rooms and a kitchen and have a floor space of about 67 square meters. All of them have bathrooms, but they only have balconies (loggias) insofar as the facade design allows. All stairwells have lifts, refuse chutes, and storage rooms for bicycles and prams. The buildings are surprisingly narrow (about 12 meters) in relation to their enormous length, and many of them have three flats per staircase and story (see Figs. 69, 123).

The brick walls, which climb rapidly in a spirit of "socialist competition"—rather reminiscent of *The Marble Man* (see Chapter Ten)—are clad with square ceramic tiles made in Meissen. These were almost white to begin with. Today they have darkened and in many places fallen off. The contrast is striking between the present decay and the street as it looked in the fifties.

The tremendous volumes of these buildings are richly articulated. The facades are divided in three, and the Classical motifs of architecture are to be found here in superabundance, sometimes ingeniously and sometimes more glibly treated (Figs. 124–126). Grand and solid, but not exactly elegant. And national form notwithstanding, more associations are evoked with Soviet architecture than with Schinkel.

Stalinallee differs from the Champs Élysées and Unter den Linden in that opposing facades make up architectural ensembles, designed in a single context and by one and the same architect. It also differs in the exceptional length of the blocks—about 200 meters. This cannot be ascribed to the program (apartments, shops, and one or two restaurants), nor is it really explained by there being only one land owner and one client. The explanation is the client's very determined pursuit of the effect of mass and monumentality. Stalinallee was built primarily not for the capital of the DDR but for the capital of a Germany reunited on Soviet guidelines, a nation that, second to the Soviet Union, would be the most powerful in Europe.

The Palace of Culture in Warsaw

The most despised and the most lauded buildings in Europe during the 1950s were both in Warsaw. Nothing was so greatly appreciated as the reconstruction of the Old City (Stare Miasto). And nothing incurred so much criticism, inspired so much revulsion, as the Palace of Culture (see Figs. 127–130, 133–138). The Old City represented the tenacious adherence of the Poles to their own historical identity. The

Palace of Culture represented their enforced alliance with the Soviet Union.

The architectural and aesthetic verdict was just as unequivocal as the political: In one instance it was legitimate and praiseworthy to build historically, while in the other it was misguided or even reprehensible.

Over the years the Old City has attracted, and rightly so, a great deal of attention. The Palace of Culture has seldom inspired more than a few words in passing (though, on the other hand, they are obligatory in even the briefest of articles on Warsaw).

Before the war, the part of Warsaw where the Palace of Culture is now located had been completely different in character—a lively but rather disorderly district with a medley of buildings, mostly residential with shops at ground-floor level (Fig. 127). Close by was the central station, and Ulica Marszałkowska, still quite narrow in those days, was a very busy street indeed.

By the end of the war, however, here as in so many other parts of Warsaw, practically everything had been burned down and shot to pieces. After the ruins had been cleared up, all that really remained were the two main streets: Aleje Jerozolimskie running from east to west, and Ulica Marszałkowska from north to south. Otherwise there was little but vacant lots.

The future planning of the area came up for public scrutiny through an architects' competition decided in 1948 (see Fig. 17). To understand the outcome, one needs to know that urban planning in Warsaw during the first few years after the war was profoundly inspired by Le Corbusier. His ideas had been transmitted to Poland during the thirties by Szymon Syrkus. They had never caught on at the time, but now they were represented by many young architects in strategic positions. One of these was Maciej Nowicki, who was to become well known in the USA a couple of years later. The competition brief proposed high-rise development. Potential developers were the PZUW state insurance company and the Społem cooperative.

Both the winning entries were radically Modernist. One of them was reminiscent of the UN headquarters in New York, on which work was now in progress. The other featured four cylindrical high-rise buildings. A couple of years later, projects like these would be a butt of ridicule, the standard crack being that they were wastepaper baskets and chimneys, not architecture.

The year 1949 was a turning point in the history of People's Poland. The journey from people's front politics to Party dictatorship had now been completed, the phase referred to by Karel Kaplan as "the Short March."

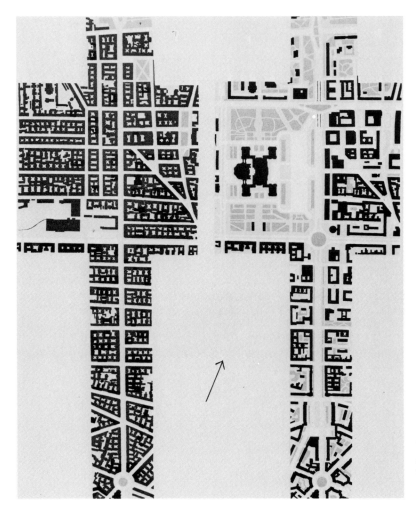

127 Warsaw, section of Marszałkowska Street. Left, before the war; at right, after the building of the Palace of Culture. MDM and Plac Konstytucji are at the far southern end.

The impact on architecture can be summarized under three heads: (1) All building was subordinate to the six-year plan; (2) the architects were organized into big state planning offices; (3) Socialist Realism became the official yardstick. The first two of these points were consequences of socialization, while the third resulted from the campaign against Cosmopolitanism.

Socialist Realism was promoted in every way. The architects themselves referred to it, in everyday speech, as "socrealism" or sometimes, more disrespectfully, as "soc."

A presentation volume published in 1950 in the name of President Bolesław Bierut included twenty-five perspective drawings to show what Warsaw would look like in 1955. One of them showed the plot that had formed the subject of the recent competi-

128 The future "Central House of Culture" in Warsaw, drawing by Kazimierz Marczewski, 1950.

tion. This perspective was drawn in an Expressionist manner by the architect Kazimierz Marczewski, and it showed the Central House of Culture, a project in the spirit of Socialist Realism, with a touch of the stepped pyramids (Fig. 128). The idea of high-rise development lived on from 1948, but otherwise the earlier scheme was worlds away. On the other hand, there was a good deal of similarity with future Soviet schemes, which presumably were already in preparation.

The Soviet government approached the government of Poland, offering to build a high-rise block in Warsaw. On 5 April 1952 the two governments signed an agreement whereby the Soviet Union was to make Poland a gift of a Palace of Culture and Science.

Two days later Bolesław Bierut wrote Stalin a letter of thanks, the wording of which indicates the ideological framework intended for the gift. The letter was published in the Cominform weekly (*For a*

Lasting Peace, 1952:24), which at that time was appearing in seventeen different languages.

> The beautiful high-rise building which people from the Soviet Union—workers, technicians, engineers, and architects—are building right in the heart of a Warsaw devastated by fascist vandals will be a perpetual memorial to the brotherly concern for other peoples which, for the first time in human history, has been displayed by the Soviet peoples, will be an embodiment of the unshakable, eternally sealed friendship between the Polish people and the Soviet peoples. It will be a monument to the noble-mindedness and greatness of the Russian people and to the entire united family of the Soviet peoples. It will be a monument to the Stalin epoch, its inexhaustible strength and victorious ideas.

There were many possible variations on this theme. One poster shows Stalin and Bierut side by side (Fig. 129). In the background are the flags of the Soviet Union and Poland, with the Palace of Culture standing out against a light blue sky. The caption reads: POLISH-SOVIET FRIENDSHIP MEANS PEACE, INDEPENDENCE AND A HAPPY TOMORROW FOR OUR FATHERLAND.

The symbolic pretensions were enormous, but in reality Soviet-Polish friendship was a touchy subject. There were many deficit items on the balance sheet, all throughout history. Even disregarding everything that could in a sense be classed as "bourgeois nationalism," there remained the fact that in 1937–38 Stalin had carried out a brutal purge of Polish Communists, thereby causing the dissolution of the Party as it then was.

Media coverage of the Palace of Culture was intensive, from the moment the Soviet excavators first dug into the soil right up to the official opening on 22 July 1955, on Poland's new national day. This coincided with the holding of the Fifth World Youth Festival in Warsaw.

The official name of the newly opened building was Pałac Kultury i Nauki Imienia Józefa Stalina (The Palace of Culture and Science named after Joseph Stalin). That name was displayed, in letters of bronze, above the main entrance overlooking Plac Stalina (now Plac Defilad).

The intention was for the work to continue with a monumentalization of the immediate surroundings. A competition in this spirit had already been decided the previous year (*Arkhitektura,* 1954:7–8), but the result did not get any further than a detailed

129 Poster by Maciej Nehring, 1952.

130 Warsaw, Palace of Culture. Facade drawing by the Soviet architects' collective. Pilot study for the final project.

model. Already by about 1960 the main concern was to be the opposite: toning down the effect of the Palace of Culture if possible.

Let us dispel a widespread misunderstanding: The Palace of Culture is no more typical of Poland than it is of the rest of Eastern Europe. It is unique of its kind outside the Soviet Union, and it is an offshoot of the seven high-rise buildings constructed in Moscow, both technically and aesthetically speaking.

Three members of the Soviet five-man collective that designed the Palace of Culture came straight from working on Moscow University (Fig. 130). Apart from Lev Rudnev, who headed the collective in both instances, the team also included Alexander Khriakov and the structural engineer Vsevolod Nasonov. Work on Moscow University began in 1949, and planning work on the Palace of Culture must have started soon after that. Rudnev and his associates visited Poland at an early stage of things, and together with Polish colleagues they visited Cracow, Sandomierz, Toruń, and Chełmno, collecting motifs to meet the demand of Socialist Realism for national form. In the finished building, the results are to be seen above all in the typical coping, known as "Polish parapet" and most easily described as decorative crenellation (see Figs. 92, 93).

A much stronger impression conveyed by the Palace of Culture, however, is that of Soviet architecture and Russian architecture, *academic architecture on Byzantine foundations.* It merits comparison not only with the contemporary high-rise buildings in Moscow but also with St. Basil's Cathedral on Red Square (1555–60; Fig. 131) and with the Admiralty in Leningrad (1806–20; Fig. 132). The vocabularies dif-

131, 132 Two examples of the Russian tradition: St. Basil's Cathedral in Moscow (left), and the Admiralty, Leningrad (right), as rebuilt by A. D. Zakharov, 1806–23.

fer, but the principle of composition is the same in all three instances. The volumes of the buildings rise by stages from a broad base, until finally the building points straight up into the sky—a kind of architectural three-stage rocket.

So much for the pedigree of the architectural style. But what exactly did the Palace of Culture express? The fact is, we have an authorized answer to this question.

When the exterior was complete, a year before the official opening, one could read the following in the journal *Architektura* (1954:5): "The monumental, tremendous building expresses joy. It is full of cheerfulness and optimism. It is human." The journal also remarked that, in spite of its colossal dimensions, the building did not bear down on people or on other buildings in the vicinity. And it gave Warsaw's skyline an element of pleasantness and lightness.

The programmatic element is unmistakable here: Joy and optimism are a direct consequence of the building representing the Soviet Union. And there is probably also an ideological undertone in the reference made to the good relations of the Palace of Culture with its surroundings: The Soviet Union is immense, but it is not the ruling power oppressing its neighbors.

Most people, however—the great majority of Poles and practically all visitors from the West—were to see the building in a completely different light. One of the many was the Swedish poet Folke Isaksson, who in a book about Warsaw published in 1964 wrote that the Palace of Culture "radiates coldness and represents emptiness."

Hardly any of the people commenting on the Palace of Culture did more than project onto the building their opinion of the regime that commissioned it. Is there an open-minded description? There are at all events certain properties of the building that are beyond dispute (Figs. 133–138).

The most important quality of the Palace of Culture is its large scale. It expresses power, because it presupposes the client's tremendous concentration of resources. Next in order of importance are symmetry and centrality (see Figs. 135, 136). Superiority/subordination is the principle by which the volumes of the building are organized.

The historic forms incorporate the building in a long tradition. Their significance has varied, but here—combined with the tremendous scale of things—they have their most common significance, reinforcing the impression of power. One is also struck by the abundance of detail, common in earlier monumental architecture but fairly uncommon during the twentieth century. This building is also meant to be seen at close quarters.

133 The Palace of Culture under construction, Warsaw, October 1953.

134 Palace of Culture: three examples of light fixtures.

The Palace of Culture is lavish but not elegant, elaborate but not tasteful, solid but without perfection. There is no parading of its technical and structural properties (that sort of thing was called "technical fetishism" in the critical language of Socialist Realism). The interior, which really deserves a chapter to itself, is to a great extent grandiloquent and costly, until suddenly the costliness comes to an end and expensive materials and carefully worked out forms are starkly contrasted with simple, everyday features.

While construction was in progress and for the first few years thereafter, the Palace of Culture was always presented in figures. It was thirty stories high (not including the tower stories) and its highest point was 230 meters above the ground. The area of land it occupied measured 254 by 212 meters. It was 817,000 m³ in volume and its total floor space was 66,000 m². The ten elevators moved at a speed of 3.5 meters per second. Other figures showed the number of bricks used or the measurements and weights of steel girders and concrete bases.

If all the officials of the Academy of Science were on duty at once and all other work stations were manned; if the wintergarden, the museums, and the youth facilities were properly subscribed; if theaters, cinemas, auditoria, and restaurants were filled; if there was swimming in the swimming pools, gymnastics in the gymnasium, and a congress in the main congress hall, then altogether the building would be occupied by twelve thousand people. Yes indeed, the Palace of Culture was a building that, quantitatively speaking, surpassed everything previously built in Poland, and not only there.

135 Air photograph of the completed Palace of Culture, from the southwest.

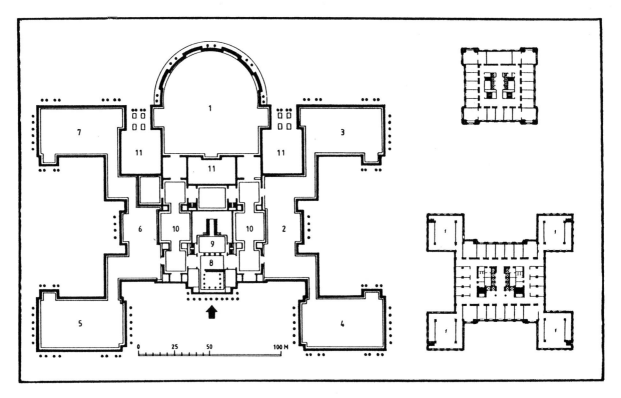

136 Schematic ground plans for the Palace of Culture on three different levels—ground floor and floors 8 and 15.

Ground floor:
  1 Congress Hall
  2 Palace of Youth
  3 Swimming pools, gymnasium, etc.
  4 Youth theater
  5 Dramatic theater
  6 Films, music, lectures
  7 Technical museum
  8 Entrance hall
  9 Elevators
 10 Exhibitions
 11 Courtyards

But how would we characterize it if we knew nothing about the historical and political context? With its tremendous dimensions, its immense variety of functions inside an envelope of eclectic architecture, the Palace of Culture resembles something from a novel by Jules Verne, built by one of his superman heroes, a philanthropic multimillionaire, confident of knowing what is best for his subjects. The Palace of Culture has a remarkable air of patriarchal nineteenth-century Utopia put into practice.

But it also evokes thoughts of the Roman Empire. The Thermae of Caracalla and Diocletian were not just public baths, they were also a kind of cultural center. They were gifts from the emperors to the people and they were the most spectacular building enterprises of their age.

Although the Palace of Culture took little more than three years to build, it was still finished too late. By then Stalin had been dead for two years and completely different architectural ideals were beginning to come from the Soviet Union. While the interiors were being finished and richly adorned in marble, bronze, and crystal, *Arkhitektura SSSR* (1954:11) carried an article by Rudnev, the senior

137, 138 Two interiors of the Palace of Culture: swimming pool and Congress Hall.

architect for the project, condemning the exaggerated, wasteful use of ornament in architecture.

Plans had existed for a sumptuous publication of the Palace of Culture in four volumes, but they came undone and the fairly plain volume actually published in 1957 was remarkable for three reasons. There was no trace of the previous rhetoric. The book dealt almost entirely with the technical qualities of the building. And the edition ran to 720 copies.

To take another side of the verdict, for a short time there was a brand of cigarettes with a picture of the Palace of Culture on the packet. The brand was called DAR, meaning *the gift,* but it never became very popular. The saying went, "The gift was bad and expensive." This was a way of expressing not only general aversion to the Palace of Culture but also the popular conviction that the gift had by no means been free of charge but had been paid for dearly by the Polish people.

The DAR brand of cigarettes was discontinued. But the Palace of Culture remained where it stood.

Casa Scînteii in Bucharest

The approach to Casa Scînteii is a lesson in Romanian history as officially interpreted (Fig. 139). Moving north from Calea Victoriei and

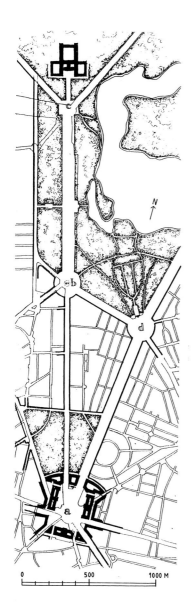

139 The road to Casa Scînteii, through the northern districts of Bucharest.

(a) Piaţa Victoriei
(b) Triumphal arch
(c) Piaţa Scînteii in front of Casa Scînteii
(d) Piaţa Stalin (now Piaţa aviatorilor) with ceremonial tribune and statue of Stalin. North of this the J. V. Stalin Cultural and Recreational Park (now the Herăstrău Park).

Piaţa Victoriei (Victory Street and Victory Square, respectively), named after the victory over the Turks in 1877 that settled Romanian independence, one soon comes to a large triumphal arch, erected in the 1930s and dedicated to the Romanians who fell in World War I, a war that ended in big territorial gains for Romania. Looking through the triumphal arch one sees, far away, the enormous Casa Scînteii, built as a manifestation of the new, socialist Romania (Figs. 140–150; see Figs. 106, 108, 109). Casa Scînteii is a view-stopper. Nothing behind it can be of any interest. And so we have 1877, 1918, and 1944, and the greatest of them all—on the urban scene as in every other context—is 1944. Or so it was until 1989.

The need for a visual manifestation of the new political order was the same in Bucharest as in Berlin and Warsaw, but the assignment here was a different one: The building had to indicate, in a backward agrarian country, the leading role of industry and the great importance of political propaganda.

Casa Scînteii is named after the newspaper of the Central Committee, *Scînteia* (The Spark), but it is more than an ordinary newspaper building. It houses a printing and publishing combine; in fact, it contains everything relating to the printed word: a big printing works, editorial offices of newspapers and magazines, publishing firms, libraries, and a large banquet hall.

The foundations were laid in 1950 and the first phase, part of the printing works, was ready for commissioning by 8 May the following year, the thirtieth anniversary of the foundation of the Romanian Communist Party. When completed, the building would produce 3 million newspapers a day, 100,000 books, and 160,000 brochures. It would provide 98 percent of the country's schoolbooks. There were 5,000 men employed on the construction project, which would take six years to complete. The finished building would have a volume of 0.75 million m^3, would occupy an area of 25,000 m^2, and would have a maximum height of 85 meters—101 meters including the red star on top of it.

But the practical, quantifiable objectives were not the whole story. The finished building, in the words of Horia Maicu, who headed the architects' collective, would reflect "Man's triumph over nature and over the social forces that have fettered him, his belief in the future, his firm course ahead under the guidance of the party of the working class." The building would also express "the overcoming of the antithesis between theory and practice" and the "concern for mankind," which during these years was always associated with the name of Stalin. And, not least, it would illustrate Socialist Realism: "national in form, socialist in content."

140 Casa Scînteii from the south. Architects: Horia Maicu, Nicolae Bădescu, Marcel Locar, and Mircea Alifanti; built 1950–56. Photograph taken in 1979.

141 Three rejected designs for Casa Scînteii from 1948 and 1949. Bottom: A fourth scheme that provided the point of departure for the final project.

These quotations come from an essay by Maicu in 1951, in which he describes at length the evolution of the project. The assignment was formulated in April 1948 and grew larger as work progressed. Many sites were considered, and many different approaches to the task (Fig. 141). In August 1949 the architects were confronted by representatives of the Party, who firmly rejected the Formalist, Functionalist, and Cosmopolitan tendencies. Three of the entries discarded on such grounds are reproduced in Maicu's essay. All of them are criticized for asymmetry. The first, moreover, is condemned for "a dry, schematic, and machine-like idiom," the second for "heaviness and lack of flight toward the future," and the third for "coldness," "brutal force," and "lack of warmth."

A fourth project, on the other hand, was commended for "the harmony of the stepped composition of its volumes," and this provided the starting point for the work that followed. The architects took this scheme with them to Moscow for consultations with the Soviet experts on printing works and structural engineering. There they also met the architects Simonov and Mordvinov, both from the Soviet Academy of Architecture, of which Mordvinov was president.

The experts' advice, according to Maicu, could be summarized as follows. The building planned would have to be monumental and must be located accordingly, preferably as the end point of one of the main streets of Bucharest (Figs. 142, 143; see Figs. 106, 150). It simply had to be symmetrical and, for all its complexity, must appear as one unit ("no antithesis between intellectual work and manual labor"). For the exterior, "hard, sharp, technical lines" must be avoided, as

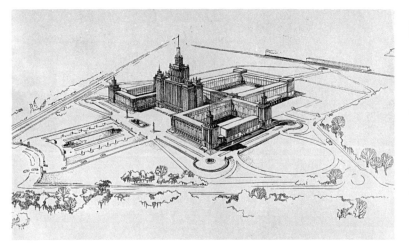
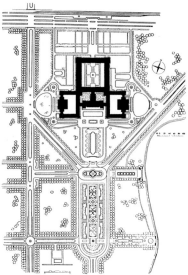

142, 143 Bucharest, Casa Scînteii,
perspective and site plan.

belonging to decadent, bourgeois art. It was wrong to let the material
determine the form. Instead there must be a unity of architecture and
sculpture, an interplay of profiles, an expression of beauty and
enthusiasm. This was to be achieved by studying traditional and
national architecture, but the practical example seen during this visit
to Moscow was the new high-rise buildings that were then under
construction or still on the drawing board. What the Romanians har-
vested here, above all, was technical experience.

Back in Bucharest they had to convert their newfound knowledge into practice, and quickly. The decision on the building project
had already been announced and a big campaign was in progress to
generate ideological enthusiasm and raise money. Construction
began during the spring of 1950 and in the May Day procession the
"builders of Casa Scînteii" carried a large colored perspective showing what the finished building would look like. We have already seen
how national tradition was introduced into the project, and the other
advice from Moscow was followed with equal consistency. The
result—from ground plan and location in the townscape to ornamentation and architectural detailing—came closer to the academic
tradition than was otherwise usual in the people's democracies. Or,
to use another, closely related concept: It came closer to the Beaux-
Arts tradition.

Casa Scînteii was designed to be seen from the south. This
being so, what was it meant to look like from the north, from the
rear? A perspective from 1951 shows the printing workers' entrance,
which, in keeping with the ideals of Socialist Realism, is of monu-

mental proportions (Figs. 144, 145). Here we have the unity of architecture and sculpture, the abundance of detailing, and a bid to upgrade manual labor. That bid, indeed, has been taken to such lengths that the perspective puts one more in mind of a university library than a printing works. The gap between drawing and reality turned out to be all the greater. The back remained just a back, although the perspective was realized, with the sole exception of the surmounting sculptures.

Casa Scînteii ranked with the Danube–Black Sea Canal as the most important construction project in Romania during the 1950s. The canal project failed, but Casa Scînteii was completed. By then, however, in 1956, it was already about to be left behind by political developments, and its original cognomen of "J. V. Stalin" was deleted.

In the 1980s the building was presented to visiting foreigners as "a shame for Romania's architects," in the words of an official repre-

144–147 Casa Scînteii. Top left: Perspective, 1951, showing the printing workers' entrance at the back of the large complex. Top right: The same side in 1979. Above left: Middle section of the main facade. Above right: Arcade of the facade at ground level.

148, 149 Casa Scînteii, main facade, details from the wings, 1979.

sentative of the Romanian Architects' Association. It was intended as the great monument to a new policy and the crowning glory of the first five-year plan, but three decades later it ranked as an architect's blunder. New rhetoric was substituted for old.

The excuses could already be heard before the building was quite finished. Horia Maicu did not only write the essay in 1951 we have just referred to. He returned to the subject in 1956, this time in a different, less enthusiastic vein. Concerning the building that, in every detail, embodied the principles to which he paid tribute in 1950, he now wrote, on behalf of himself and his associates, "We realize that we did not create a consummate architecture."

The political background to these dismissals and excuses can easily be understood. Casa Scînteii belongs to the Stalin era and to the extreme Soviet tutelage characterizing the 1950s in Romania. But insofar as the building can be detached from this context, a different verdict should be possible.

Even then there are reservations. One East German architect whose career began in the 1950s declared, quite bluntly, that Casa Scînteii was not really architecture at all. It was *kitsch.* This verdict is unfair, but there is a grain of truth in it. For, from the viewpoint of the Modernist aesthetic, Casa Scînteii is an even more serious case than Stalinallee and the Palace of Culture in Warsaw. In those buildings, in the midst of all the splendor, there is a touch of discipline, gravity, and dignity. Casa Scînteii, on the other hand, is architecture of a more unsophisticated kind. The architects have tried to achieve the beautiful in a popular sense, on the ideological grounds that the

150 Casa Scînteii, perspective showing south elevation, 1950.

building must convey a readily intelligible picture of the bright communist future. The result, the finished building with its picturesque silhouette, resembles a mirage when viewed from a distance. Or, with its corner towers and its pale cladding materials, a Taj Mahal of "really existing socialism." At close quarters the building is more real. One sees both the carefully worked out national detailing and the neglected maintenance (Figs. 146–150).

The New Center of Sofia

Sofia had been damaged in Anglo-American air raids at about New Year 1943–44, and partly for this reason the new regime announced, very soon after 9 September 1944, a competition for a new city plan.

To assist the jury, the government called in two Soviet specialists, A. V. Shchusev, a member of the Academy, and N. V. Baranov, Leningrad's chief architect. On their advice the jury settled on a design prepared by a team under Liuben Tonev, an influential name among Bulgarian architects during the period that now began. During the processing of this scheme, other Soviet specialists were consulted, including two more members of the Academy, A. G. Mordvinov and K. S. Alabian. This consultation resulted in the idea, current in 1945 and for a few years thereafter, of a high-rise building on the site of the former royal palace, overlooking the newly constructed Ploshtad 9 septemvri. "The experience of the Soviet Union" came sooner to Bulgaria than to the other countries of Eastern Europe.

No high-rise building materialized, but a few years later, on the opposite side of the square, a building was erected that did even more to affirm the new political situation.

The leader of the Bulgarian Communist Party and former secretary of the Comintern Executive Committee, Georgi Dimitrov, died in Moscow on 2 July 1949. He had been a big name in the international communist movement, almost a myth, ever since 1933, when he had successfully defended himself in Leipzig against charges of implication in the Reichstag fire in Berlin (*For a Lasting Peace*, 1949:14). It is this position, not his status as Bulgarian Party leader and head of government, that accounts for the decision now made and immediately put into effect, namely, to install his embalmed body just like Lenin's, in a mausoleum.

The only trouble was that the mausoleum had to be completed in time for Dimitrov's funeral on 10 July. The architects, Georgi Ovcharov and Racho Ribarov of the state planning bureau, were given less than twenty-four hours in which to come up with a design. The result was approved by the Central Committee and Council of Ministers at about noon on 4 July, leaving rather less than six days—138 hours, to be exact—in which to build the mausoleum.

Work was finished on time, however, and at 3.15 P.M. on 10 July Dimitrov's coffin was carried into the mausoleum by members of the Central Committee and Politbureau. Truth to tell, however, another five months were to pass before the mausoleum was quite finished and ready to be opened to the public (Figs. 151, 152).

This is the same dramatic genesis as that of the first version of Lenin's Mausoleum in Moscow's Red Square (1924), and the building has the same practical function as the definitive version of Lenin's

151, 152 Sofia, Dimitrov's mausoleum, exterior and ground plan. Architects: Georgi Ovcharov and Racho Ribarov; built 1949.

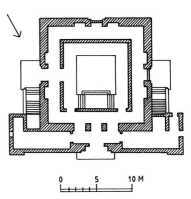

0   5   10 M

Mausoleum (1929–30): inside, a room where the embalmed body of the leader, illuminated by spotlights, can be viewed by a throng of reverent citizens slowly filing past; outside, a building with a ceremonial tribune from which the political leaders can look down on parades and demonstration marches. And the same Boris Zbarsky who embalmed Lenin (and, later on, Stalin) embalmed Dimitrov as well.

But the architecture is different. In both cases, it is true, one finds simplicity, monumentality, and geometrical form, but the cool Classicism of Dimitrov's mausoleum has little in common with the Lenin Mausoleum's expressive Cubism. It has equally little to do with Socialist Realism. On the other hand, it does belong to the native architectural tradition from the 1920s and 1930s, its nearest contemporary in this respect being Georgi Ovcharov's City Hall in Burgas, built in 1946 (see Fig. 14). Close to it in the most literal sense is Tsolov's National Bank, built in 1939 (see Fig. 117).

In November 1951 the government declared that the center of Sofia was to be built up as "an integrated architectural unit reflecting the greatness of our epoch." What this actually meant we can study with the aid of an ideological commentary from 1953 (*Arkhitektura i stroitelstvo*, 7-8), a plan from 1954, and the buildings that actually materialized (Figs. 153, 154, see Fig. 57).

First the changes in the street plan. Bulevard Ruski has been extended westward, past the new Ploshtad 9 septemvri, where it forms a sharp angle toward the abbreviated Bulevard Kniaz Dondukov. This point marks the beginning of a newly constructed T-shaped square, Ploshtad Lenin, the stem of which is sometimes looked on as a square in its own right (called "Largo"), while the crossline is an enlargement of a main thoroughfare from north to south.

Now for the buildings. At the heart of this center we have the Communist Party building, which faces both the newly constructed squares but whose main facade overlooks Ploshtad Lenin (Figs. 155, 156). This is a narrow facade but its importance is underlined by the position and by the dramatically juxtaposed architectural motifs: a colonnade (extending through four stories), the lintel of which is surmounted by the Party emblem (hammer and sickle), above which there is a lantern narrowing into a spire with a five-pointed star on top. In the daytime one's attention is caught mostly by the great assembly of columns, while in the evening and at night the eye-catcher is—or was—the brightly shining red star.

On each side of Ploshtad Lenin ("Largo") are two large rectangular blocks, work on which had only begun in 1954. When finished

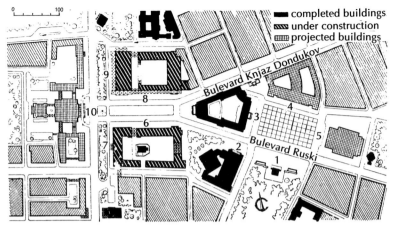

153, 154 Air photograph of the center of Sofia, and site plan from 1954.

1 Dimitrov's mausoleum, 1949
2 National Bank, 1930s
3 Communist Party building, 1950–53
4 Council of Ministers (not built, and former Royal Palace never demolished)
5 Opera (not built)
6 Ministry for Electrification, 1954–56
7 Grand Hotel Balkan, 1954–57
8 Ministry for Heavy Industry, 1954–56
9 TsUM department store, 1954–57
10 House of the City Soviet (not built)

they were to house the Ministries of Heavy Industry and National Electrification, the most important government departments during the period of the first five-year plan. This is where we find the majestic, Byzantine-style vestibule already presented in Chapter Six (see Fig. 119). The facades are heavy and dignified, but aesthetically speaking they are merely sidepieces of the perspective leading to the Party building. This composition prompted comparisons with both the Piazza Campidoglio in Rome and Rossi Street in Leningrad.

The ends of these blocks face the outer part of Ploshtad Lenin and contain, respectively, a department store (TsUM) and a hotel (Grand Hotel Balkan, now Sheraton Sofia), also presented as *national form*. The architectural journals refer to the hotel as a representational hotel intended primarily for big receptions and official guests (see Fig. 118).

The architecture around Lenin Square comes closer to the Soviet prototypes than most of what was built in Eastern Europe during the 1950s. Here we find a heavy, representational idiom that is lacking in native Classicism. But we also find—true to the principles of Socialist Realism—Bulgarian motifs. There are at least three of them in the hotel facade: ox-yoked shapes, the crowning gallery, and the massive, projecting eaves.

The fourth side of Lenin Square remains undeveloped to this day, but for a long time it was earmarked for the city administration building, Dom na suvetite (the House of the City Soviet). This was to have been the tallest building of the new center. A whole succession of schemes are known (Fig. 157). To begin with, they were grandiose and clearly inspired by the high-rise buildings in Moscow (*Arkhitektura i stroitelstvo*, 1953:7–8), but as time went on they grew simpler.

Not even Ploshtad 9 septemvri was completed according to plan. Both the House of the Council of Ministers and the Opera remained on paper, and nothing came of the intended monumental sculptures, Dimitrov outside Dom na suvetite, Lenin in front of the main facade of the Party building, or Stalin in Ploshtad 9 septemvri.

So grandiloquent was the program, however, that the new center was able to serve its purpose although uncompleted. It included a capitolium, in which political power was concentrated (Ploshtad Lenin), and a forum for public political manifestation, for parades, and for the cult of the leader (Ploshtad 9 septemvri). Changing vocabularies, we might say it contained a Kremlin and a Red Square.

The new regime was no transitory phase in Bulgaria's political history. It had come to stay. The historical process inaugurated on 9 September 1944 was irreversible. That was the message proclaimed by the new center. The Dimitrovian epoch was superior to all epochs preceding it. How insignificant was the former royal palace compared with the center! And so, ultimately, it could do no harm where it stood.

Historical necessity was the legitimacy of the new regime. Not only the palace but also Subranieto (the parliament), the monument

155, 156 Ploshtad Lenin with the two ministries on either side and, in the background, the Party building designed by Petur Zlatev and his collective and built 1950–53. The pedestrian tunnel is of more recent date. Above: The top of the Party building.

157 One of several schemes for the unrealized House of the City Soviet, designed in 1953 by Kalin Boiadzhiev.

to the Russian tsar Alexander II, "Tsar osvoboditel" (Tsar and Liberator), the enormous Neo-Byzantine Alexander Nevsky Cathedral (one of the last great works of nineteenth-century European architecture), the Bania Bashi Mosque, the old Byzantine churches, and the remains of the Roman town of Serdica uncovered in the course of construction—all these things could be integrated with the new center as past, inferior staging posts on the highway of historical necessity. Even the government offices from the period immediately preceding 1944 could be integrated quite effortlessly with the new composition. True, they belonged to "the monarchical-fascist period," but what was more important, as architecture they were innocent of "Formalism."

The new regime marked a new beginning in the history of the nation. But there was continuity in its architecture.

The First Socialist Cities

Each of the people's democracies included, or was supposed to include, a *new city*, built up around a steelworks or some other industrial facility occupying a key position in the first five- or six-year plan. On official occasions the city was always referred to as its country's "first socialist city" or "the biggest project of the five-year plan." Often it was also termed "the city of youth." These names indicated the important role of the new cities in political propaganda, hence the overwhelming predominance of ideological content in contemporary presentations of them. The economic, demographic, and technical planning aspects are more elusive.

References to the support and example of the Soviet Union are constantly recurring. And there were precursors: Norilsk, Sumgait, Rustavi, Angarsk—remote precursors, the remotest of all being Komsomolsk on the Amur River. Soviet cities constructed in the Functionalist spirit—Magnitogorsk and Karaganda—could also serve as examples, showing that "deurbanizing tendencies" were not invincible.

In the DDR the new city was called *Stalinstadt* (Eisenhüttenstadt from 1961), in Poland it was *Nowa Huta*, in Hungary *Sztálinváros* (Dunaújváros from 1961), in Bulgaria *Dimitrovgrad*. In Czechoslovakia it was *Nová Ostrava*, an enlargement of the old industrial city of Ostrava (the Poruba district), which came to be dubbed the country's first socialist city. Then there were new towns on a smaller scale: Nová Dubnica and Šaca, both in Slovakia, and Komló in the south of Hungary, its country's "first socialist town of mine workers."

Romania alone was something of an exception. True, it had the city of Gheorghe Gheorghiu-Dej, founded in 1952, but the expansion of that city belonged to a later period and it never became quite the same sort of star turn in political propaganda as the other cities. In Romania that role was reserved for the Danube–Black Sea Canal.

VIII

Stalinstadt

The old German steelworks were located either in the Ruhr, in West Germany, or in Silesia (Śląsk), which in 1945 became Polish. Hence the emphasis of the five-year plan on a big new steelworks, first called "Eisenhüttenkombinat Ost" and then "Eisenhüttenkombinat J. W. Stalin." Conditions, however, were not exactly ideal. Neither iron ore nor coal was available within the boundaries of the new republic, and both had to be imported from the Soviet Union and Poland. This shortcoming, however, could be worded positively, as in a poster from 1952: "Soviet ore and Polish coal become German steel for peace."

In 1950 a site was chosen near Fürstenberg on the Oder–Spree Canal, and construction work began soon afterward. At that stage the city still went by the unwieldy name of "Die sozialistische Stadt des Eisenhüttenkombinates Ost." The name of Stalinstadt was substituted in 1952. The new city was planned for a population of 30,000.

A turning point in the genesis of Stalinstadt occurred when planning had already come a long way and the first apartment blocks had been completed (Fig. 158). It was probably some time in the second half of 1951, fairly soon, one imagines, after *Neues Deutschland*'s attack on Hermann Henselmann. According to *Deutsche Architektur* (1952:3), the first apartment blocks had come in for serious criticism both from Walter Ulbricht and from workers at the steelworks. The magazine quoted furnace worker Günter Kempski: "The time is past when workers only went home to eat and sleep. A good deal of our lives take place in the apartment or its immediate surroundings. But these monotonous buildings make a fatiguing impression. The architects must try and hit on something better."

The buildings thus criticized, with their smooth, plain facades, belonged to the Bauhaus tradition. But the alternative had already been formulated: apartment buildings with Classical facades, a simplified, reduced version of the facades on Stalinallee (Fig. 159, see Figs. 124–126). Here there were bases with banded rustication, window surrounds, bay windows, cornices, and a differentiation of the volume of the building, both horizontally and vertically.

But, of course, what on the face of things was a dispute about facades was really concerned with much more. Its repercussions influenced the whole field of architecture, from detailing to town planning.

The collective that worked out the detailed development plan was headed by Kurt W. Leucht. He was a member of the architectur-

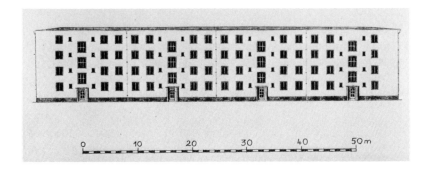

158, 159 Housing development in Stalinstadt: (above) Modernist version rejected in 1951; (below) new version adopted at the same time, complying with the principles of Socialist Realism.

al establishment: director of the School of Town Planning at the Bauakademie in Berlin, and one of the architects of Stalinallee. The first detailed development plan to be published dates from 1951, but it had to go through several revisions before the stipulations of precinct formation, axiality, and monumentality were reasonably satisfied (Fig. 160).

From the steelworks, which were planned to include an architecturally magnificent entrance (cf. Fig. 60), the main street led in toward the city square, with a house of culture on the central axis and with a city hall, Party building, hotel, department store, and post office round about. Perspective drawings show a city of large, verdant precincts, wide, tree-lined main streets curving gently, and monumental public buildings distinctly punctuating the skyline.

For a few years, Stalinstadt really seemed on the way to becoming an ideal city in the spirit of Socialist Realism, hard to believe in view of today's oblivion and decay. Eight architects' collectives competed in 1953 for the monumental axis ("the Magistral") from the steelworks to Zentraler Platz (*Deutsche Architektur*, 1953:5). The competition brief also included proposing a site for a statue of Stalin.

Not many of the public buildings were completed before Socialist Realism was thrust aside, but apartment blocks were built on a large scale: four-story brick buildings with yellow and gray ren-

160 Stalinstadt, urban plan from 1953 with enclosed precincts. House of Culture, City Hall, and Party building overlook the central square.

161 Strasse der Republik, Stalinstadt, later Eisenhüttenstadt. Apartment blocks from 1954 with shops inside the street-level arcades.

dering, massive roof cornices, bay windows and balconies gathered into vertical accents, and arcades in front of the ground-floor shops (Fig. 161). The detailing was simple, the decor sparing.

What seemed rather meager in the early 1950s, however, was later to be extolled as a virtue. "Stalinstadt," Leucht was justifiably able to write in his book about the city, published in 1957, "has none of the exaggerated facade decorations to be found elsewhere in the DDR." The very design of Leucht's book—its asymmetry and Grotesque typefaces—betokens a new message: an explicit continuation of German Functionalism.

Nowa Huta

Nowa Huta was "the biggest project of the six-year plan." When completed, the V. I. Lenin Steelworks would produce as much steel as all the prewar Polish steel mills put together.

The position chosen was a practical one, having transport links with the Vistula and with the mines of Śląsk (Silesia) not far away. But it was also symbolic. Nowa Huta was to be modern, socialist Poland's antithesis of traditional, Catholic Cracow.

Of all the new cities of Eastern Europe, Nowa Huta was the biggest venture and it occupied a prominent role, not only in political propaganda as such but also as a subject of literature, films, and music, for an author like Marian Brandys in *Początek opowieści* (The beginning of a story), for a director like Andrzej Munk in *Kierunek Nowa Huta* (Direction: Nowa Huta), for a composer like Witold Lutosławski in his *Pieśni o Nowej Hucie* (Songs of Nowa Huta).

Nowa Huta was "the pride of the nation," "the forge of our prosperity," and "a work of Polish-Soviet friendship." The name became so pregnant with meaning as to require no expositions. The eight letters of its name, carried in monumental format on demonstration marches through Warsaw, were sufficient in themselves (Fig. 162).

Nowa Huta, though, was not an ideal example in the campaign for new architecture. Many changes were made because, here again, the planners had started on the wrong premise: small tenement buildings of two and three stories, with quite a lot of space in between. For a long time the plans were only partially published. The collective under Tadeusz Ptaszycki responsible for planning had a difficult task. But Nowa Huta as presented in Garliński's *Architektura Polska 1950–1951* still made a telling example of urban development in the spirit of Socialist Realism, interesting above all on account of its link with tradition, which was far more powerful here than in Stalinstadt.

162 NOWA HUTA—the name of Poland's first socialist city—displayed on a demonstration march along Marszałkowska Street, Warsaw, 1952.

163, 164 Nowa Huta. Left: Plan of the city. Right: Model of the center, showing central axis from theater to City Hall with Plac Lenina in between.

The center unmistakably echoes the ideal city of the Renaissance, and in both models and detailed development plans it forms a regular semioctagon (Figs. 163, 164). The central axis was marked by two monumental buildings: a Classical-style theater and a city hall, emulating one of the most famous buildings of the Polish Renaissance, the Town Hall of Zamość (1591–1600). The outdoor staircase, the portal, and the Polish parapet were outright quotations. The massive tower, on the other hand, was more freely interpreted. Its task, according to the prevailing aesthetic, was to give the city an expressive skyline. Both theater and city hall, however, were to remain on paper.

The buildings that materialized in the center include other historical and national associations (Figs. 165–168). Balustrades, window lintels, and portal surrounds are reminiscent of Wawel, the palace of the kings of Poland in nearby Cracow. Streets radiating at an angle of 45 degrees from the center, on the other hand, are not a Polish theme. They were a common feature of contemporary urban design in the Soviet Union, their ultimate precursor being the district south of the Admiralty in St. Petersburg. Also modeled on Soviet lines are the large precincts, shut off from the main streets but both spatially and functionally differentiated within themselves.

The dominant impression conveyed by Nowa Huta today is the contrast between the *city* created by the 1950s and the suburban sprawl of the ensuing decades. And then in the distance, at the end of Aleje Lenina, is the tremendous steelworks with its entrance pavilions (see Figs. 90, 91), surmounted by a Polish parapet.

165 Nowa Huta, facade, Plac Lenina.

166, 167 Nowa Huta, detail of facade viewed from Plac Lenina, and perspective of the City Hall designed by Tadeusz Janowski.

168 Nowa Huta, street facade of Osiedle C. precinct.

Sztálinváros

Construction of this city, on the right bank of the Danube 70 km south of Budapest, began in May 1950; at that time it was still called Dunapentele, after a village on the site (Figs. 169–171). The city and steelworks were "the greatest project of the five-year plan," but Hungary, like the DDR, had neither the iron nor the coal that were needed.

The new plant immediately came to the forefront of political propaganda. An artists' collective, led by Zoltán Szemerei, executed an enormous oil painting (325 x 240 cm) that was displayed at the World Youth Festival in East Berlin during the summer of 1951. It had a long title: *The building of the Dunapentele Steelworks. Young workers receive advice from the Soviet Stakhanovite Amozov.* This theme was an almost exemplary digest of the political message. It packed in everything: planned economy, heavy industry, mobilization of youth, help from the Soviet Union, new working methods, socialist competition. In form, however, this was not yet Socialist Realism in the Soviet sense. There is no unity of action. The precursors, if any, are more to be found in the social tendency painting of the Italian Renato Guttuso. One year previously, in Warsaw, Guttuso had received the prize awarded by the World Council for Peace.

Then, in the autumn of 1951, came the attack by József Révai, the Minister of Culture, on Máté Major and on Cosmopolitanism in architecture, with specific reference to "the ugly buildings in Dunapentele." Later that year the city acquired its new name, Sztálinváros (altered in 1961 to Dunaújváros).

The main architect of the new city was Tibor Weiner, a former Bauhaus pupil who went to the Soviet Union in the 1930s (as a member of a group of German architects led by Hannes Meyer), where he joined in the campaign against Formalism. There are at least two versions of the central parts of Sztálinváros, both of them produced under Weiner's direction. The first belongs to the period preceding Révai's attack and shows a freely interpreted Classicism in the spirit of the interwar years (Fig. 172). There are points of similarity here, for example, with the vocabulary of Gunnar Asplund. The six towers on the long facade facing the main street suggest that the architect also allowed himself to be inspired by the Roman antecedents of the place (the frontier fortress of Intercisa).

The second version is more symmetrical, a modification in favor of greater weight and monumentality (Fig. 173). The main street is now wider. The lateral axis is more pronounced, opening out toward the Danube (Duna) and accentuated by a statue of Stalin.

169 *The building of the Dunapentele Steelworks,* oil painting by Zoltán Szemerei et al.

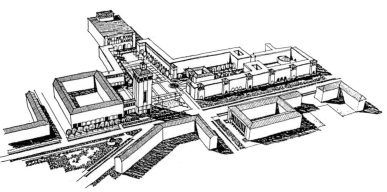

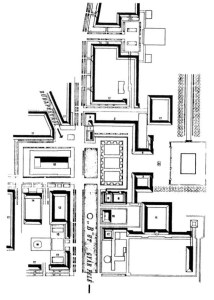

170–173 Sztálinváros, now
Dunaújváros. Top left: Hotel interior.
Top right: West side of the main street,
including a tower block (see also Fig.
77) and a hotel. Middle: Perspective of
the city center, with the north-south
main street running from left to right
and the cross axis toward the Danube
pointing upward. Bottom: Plan of the
city center in the revised, more
monumental version, with the cross
axis toward the Danube now facing
right (east). The steelworks comes
outside the plan, to the southwest.

This is the same in-process modification as we have already seen in the cases of Stalinstadt and Nowa Huta.

The other point of emphasis in Sztálinváros is the main entrance to the steelworks, in the style of a Classical propylaeum (Figs. 174, 175). Monumental factory gates were a staple item in the architectural iconography of the people's democracies. The Classical vocabulary on the other hand, was indigenous, rooted in the inter-war years.

Inside the colonnade, above the three doorways, a monumental mural (3 x 17 m) was installed in 1955, depicting nine steelworkers, with pokers and leather aprons, and nine women bringing them bread. The artist, Endre Domanovszky, emulated, both in color and in figure drawing, the famous nineteenth-century Hungarian painter Mihály Munkácsy, frequently referred to as an example in the heyday of Socialist Realism.

174, 175 Sztálinváros (Dunaújváros). Entrance to the steelworks, at that time called Sztálin Vasmű, by László Lauber and Jenő Szendrői, 1954. Mural by Endre Domanovszky was added the following year.

Dimitrovgrad

Dimitrovgrad, construction of which began in 1947, was the first of the new cities of Eastern Europe. It is located on the River Maritsa, in the south of Bulgaria, near the great lignite field of Marbas. The starting point was a number of newly established factories, the most important of them being the big J. V. Stalin Chemicals Combine, which mainly produced nitrogen fertilizer, both for export and for the country's own recently collectivized agricultural sector (see Fig. 39).

The city was named after Georgi Dimitrov, the legendary leader of the Bulgarian Communist Party. It was also called "the city of youth," an epithet of which it was perhaps more deserving than the other new cities. Vast numbers of young Bulgarians took part in the work of construction during the early years.

The original plan was for Dimitrovgrad to be a garden city, and building work began with this end in view. Those plans were soon put aside, however. The critics found that fatal errors had been committed here. The housing areas were poorly planned, single- and two-story buildings were scattered about at random, the architecture was meager and not properly thought out, and no expression had been given to the grandeur of the Dimitrovian epoch.

The Ministry of Building (MKSB) ordered a new plan. This was drawn up at Glavproekt, the state planning bureau, under the direction of Petur Tashev, and it was completed in 1950. The new version made Dimitrovgrad monumental, instead of "petit bourgeois" and "idyllic." It was now a city, and no longer a village. Accordingly, the land was more heavily developed and the buildings were closer together, designed to accommodate 250 residents per hectare instead of just 93 as before. Consequently the new plan was also more economical. Construction costs were estimated at 3,000 leva per m^3 housing, as against 4,000 previously (*Arkhitektura i stroitelstvo,* 1951:2–3).

Bulevard Georgi Dimitrov, the wide main street, is lined with five-story buildings with shops inside their ground-floor arcades (Figs. 176–178). This is a prosperous-looking environment for the inhabitants of "Bulgaria's first socialist city," and the buildings are grouped and designed in deference to the buzz words of Socialist Realism: the ensemble, the block, the street, the facade, detailing. The National Bank building, which to an outsider may seem reminiscent of both Italy and Scandinavia during the interwar years, is a direct continuation of Bulgarian architecture of the 1920s and 1930s. The House of the City Soviet (Dom na suvetite), on the other hand, which

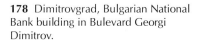

176, 177 Dimitrovgrad, Bulevard Georgi Dimitrov. Arcade interior from the 1950s, and apartment block with shops and arcades.

178 Dimitrovgrad, Bulgarian National Bank building in Bulevard Georgi Dimitrov.

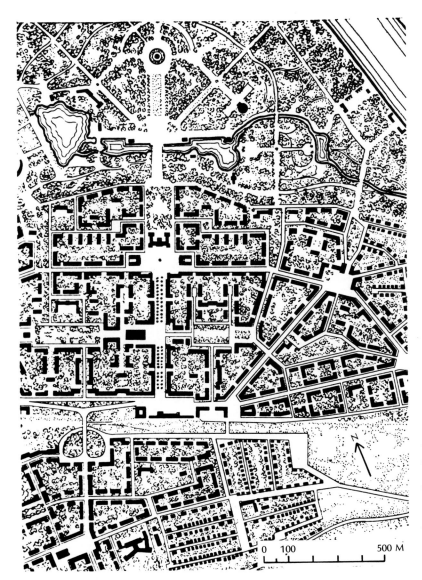

179 Dimitrovgrad, plan of the central districts of the city. The tree-lined Bulevard Georgi Dimitrov extends from the railway station in the south to a monumental square dominated by the House of the City Soviet. Farther along the same axis, a large cultural park. South of the railway, in the bottom left corner, the square of the Tolbukhin district.

should have been the end point of the main street, was designed in keeping with Soviet precedent (Fig. 179). Its central section was a high-rise building that was to have dominated the skyline (*Arkhitektura i stroitelstvo*, 1953:1).

A perspective from the early 1950s shows us the intended Tolbukhin district, viewed from north to south (Fig. 180). The square in the middle is included in the general plan, bottom left (Fig. 181). The street from the center (Bulevard 9 septemvri) leads obliquely into the square, in the center of which is a statue of Marshal

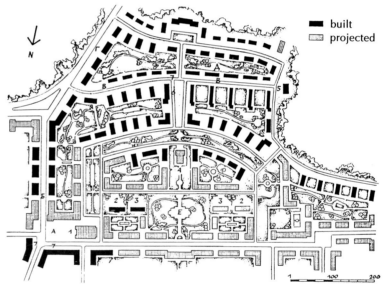

Tolbukhin, who led the invasion of Bulgaria by the Red Army in 1944. At one end of the square is the district house of culture, resembling a Classical temple. Along one side is an administrative building with a restaurant inside the ground-floor arcade and with an emphatic corner tower, alluding to the clock towers that were a typical feature of Bulgarian towns and cities in the eighteenth century. On the right, in the foreground, is a large housing block with plantings and with a fountain set in a spacious courtyard (see Fig. 180).

The mode of presentation, vigorous and detailed, is part of a long tradition of Academic architecture which, at the beginning of the

1950s, was hardly being practiced anywhere outside the Soviet Union. Petur Tashev, it is true, was trained in Yugoslavia, but after the war he had continued his studies in the Soviet Union.

In content, too, this is one of the most exemplary perspectives of Socialist Realism, with never a trace of Formalist tendencies. In the plan of the same district, though, one can easily identify the irregularly shaped southern precincts, the first to be built in the Tolbukhin district. Tashev and his collective were afterward given the task of integrating—or perhaps rather concealing—this development in a more regular, monumental scheme of town planning.

The Tolbukhin district, however, had one incurable defect. Both practically and aesthetically it was isolated from the center of Dimitrovgrad on the other side of the railway line. This was a legacy from the "deurbanizing" period in which it had been founded.

The New Cities: a Glimpse of the Future

The new cities have many points in common. Their origins were closely bound up with the introduction of the planned economy and they were planned in close conjunction with Soviet precursors (Figs. 182, 183). They were rather like flagships of the five-year plans, their mission being both practical and symbolic. Work on building them, however, had already begun before the launching of Socialist Realism, or at all events before its elevation to normative status.

Consequently there are two dramatic turning points in their evolution. First there is the rejection of Formalism and the affirmation of Socialist Realism. Then comes the backlash. Only a short period separates these turning points, but it was long enough to leave a definite mark on the centers of the new cities, which to the present-day visitor have the appearance of a historic nucleus surrounded by suburbs from the sixties and seventies.

There are enclosed precincts here, just as in the old European city, but since the precincts are large and not divided among different owners, there are no dark, congested backyards. Streets are few in number, but broad. The main street is a tree-lined boulevard, flanked by large apartment blocks with shops at street level, sometimes with arcades as well.

The main street leads to a square, spacious enough to accommodate large political manifestations. The town hall, or House of the City Soviet, would have stood here. The high towers would have given these cities the vigorous skyline usually prescribed in articles on Socialist urban development. But time ran out and they stayed on paper. The monumentality and national form of the centers of the new cities became only a pale reflection of what they should have been.

182, 183 Socialist urban ideals were realized on a large scale in the Poruba district of Ostrava, often presented as "the first socialist city of Czechoslovakia." Designed at Stavoprojekt Ostrava by Miloslav Čtverniček, Rudolf Spáčil et al. The main street running diagonally across the photograph corresponds to the west-east central axis in the plan, right. In the southeast corner of the plan is a district of parallel apartment blocks from the earliest postwar years; its impact on the townscape has been softened by means of a large, semicircular apartment block.

The other point of architectural emphasis is the entrance to the factory, a couple of kilometers from the center, which is the economic base of the city. In Nowa Huta it is flanked by the "Polish" administration buildings. In Sztálinváros it takes the form of a propylaeum, while in Dimitrovgrad it is a city gate or triumphal arch.

There was a sharp line of demarcation between town and country. In Dimitrovgrad it had actually been proposed to build city gates. Town was town and country was country.

One perpetual ingredient of the urban-development theory of Socialist Realism was polemic against the "deurbanizing" ideals of the West. After hesitant beginnings, Stalinstadt, Nowa Huta, Sztálinváros, and Dimitrovgrad were planned in deliberate contradistinction to the British new towns (Stevenage, Basildon) and the Scandinavian satellite towns (Tapiola, Vällingby). The polemic still included assertions of the artistic aspect of urban development. "The city must be viewed as one great work of art, saturated with the abundant ideological content of our epoch," to quote Petur Tashev, writing about Dimitrovgrad (*Arkhitektura i stroitelstvo*, 1953:1).

The ideological pretensions were enormous. The political rhetoric charged the new cities with an ideological content, and city plans and buildings had to make reference to this political context. The content was conveyed by news material and articles on the progress of building operations, by films and novels, poems and paintings, cantatas and popular music. As political symbols, the new cities became almost as important as the red flag.

Why did they acquire such a prominent role in political propaganda? The reason has to be looked for in political ideology, in the notion of the physical environment as a *mirror* of the political order.

The new social system had been introduced. Private ownership of the means of production was abolished or restricted to a minimum. But the built environment from the old social order lived on. Cities, towns, and villages looked roughly the same as they had a few years earlier (Fig. 184). In some cases, it is true, a positive value could be put on the old environment—as part of the progressive national tradition—but mostly it bore the mark of capitalism and of "man's exploitation of man."

Things were different in the new socialist cities. In their case, the new conditions had prevailed from the very beginning. Here there were no links with the old society. Here "concern for mankind" had already been transmitted into buildings, housing, day nurseries, parks, and houses of culture. Here the workers could develop in liberty, for the first time in the history of their country. Here were all the prerequisites of *the new man* (Fig. 185).

The new cities were *typical* in the special sense that the word had acquired in the Soviet Union—not typical in the sense of being ordinary or occurring frequently, but typical of the direction of the ongoing historical and social process. In a word, the new cities were a

184 Presentations of the new cities would include contrasting pictures of the past. Here the village of Mogiła near Nowa Huta.

185 It was in the new cities that "the new man" was in the making. Pictured here are worker Józef Zych and his family in Nowa Huta in the early 1950s.

glimpse of tomorrow's reality. This is the sense in which they were typical, and this is why they were always referred to as their country's "first socialist city." The other cities would follow suit.

Long before the events of the late 1980s the new cities more or less faded into oblivion. They played no part in political propaganda and they occupied but a modest position in the literature on urban development. The stranger wanting to travel there was met with astonishment. Thus a travel agency clerk in Hungary:

"Dunaújváros? It's the ugliest town in the whole country!"

Or an elderly Bulgarian architect:

"Dimitrovgrad? No, I haven't been there for twenty-five years. What on earth do you want to go there for?"

The Logic of the Situation:
Eight Biographical Sketches

The initiatives leading to the big changes in Eastern European architecture at the end of the 1940s did not come from the architects. On the contrary, the architects felt themselves drawn into a compulsive sequence of events, like actors putting on a play. They had little scope for independent action.

This is not to say that all of them were in the same position, still less that they all reacted in the same way. Their values and loyalties were also part of the situation. And even in compulsive situations one still has a choice. The actions of the individual are made neither less interesting nor less important by a diminishing scope for maneuver. The eight brief biographical sketches that now follow have been arranged in pairs, by nationality: two Czechs, two Hungarians, two Poles, and two Germans. Every such pair of examples contains an antithesis between the one who put up more and the one who put up less resistance or none at all to the new policy and the new architecture. Seven of the eight were architects, while one (Teige) was a critic closely allied with the architectural profession.

The examples have been chosen to illustrate the individual variations and the way in which individual action in the constrained situation that prevailed around 1950 was determined not only by political and social pressure but also by personal background, individual psychology and morality, aesthetic values, and ideological commitments.

Karel Teige and Jiří Kroha

In 1947 there was published in Prague a book on modern Czech architecture. It appeared in Czech, French, and English editions, the last titled *Modern Architecture in Czechoslovakia*. The author, Karel Teige (1900–51; Fig. 186), had long been an important figure in Czech

186 Karel Teige, in the 1930s.

Modernism. He was a critic with wide-ranging intellectual and aesthetic interests, from poetry to architecture. Between 1923 and 1931 he had edited the journal *Stavba,* one of the first European magazines to specialize in modern architecture. In 1930 he had served on the staff of the Bauhaus in Dessau as a visiting lecturer in the sociology of architecture. Politically he belonged to the left, but in 1937 he had left the KPČ, which under Gottwald's leadership had developed into one of the most pro-Moscow Communist parties in Europe.

Teige had designed the book himself, and the cover illustration showed what was internationally the most famous building to have come out of Czech Modernism: the pavilion at the 1937 World Exposition in Paris. The very first sentence would soon be sufficient in itself to put the author right beyond the pale: "Modern architecture is principally international and universal in character." And a few lines farther down he refers to "a cosmopolitan style for the greater part of the world." Teige adheres to the usage of the interwar period: The cosmopolitan is concerned with world citizenship. It makes no difference to him that, in the Soviet Union and among orthodox Communists, the word *cosmopolitanism* has now taken on a different meaning: betrayal of the nation and of socialism.

No less controversial was Teige's view of socialism and modern architecture as parallel phenomena, products of the same historical development. Indirectly this was criticizing the line represented by the Soviet Union and, before long, by the KPČ as well.

Teige's text ends with a caveat: He has tried to be objective, but the opinions expressed are disagreed with by many and are to be thought of as his personal opinion. The reader senses that there have been doubts about publishing this book and that the publishers wanted to clear themselves. And indeed, it was published at the eleventh hour. After February 1948, any plea for a "cosmopolitan" culture was out of the question. In every connection, the example of the Soviet Union was held forth, and in every sector of the community a campaign was prosecuted that, in English, came aptly to be termed *de-Westernization.*

Karel Teige's time was up. True, his views of Czechoslovakia's architecture and art were shared by many, but this did not help him. Night after night he worked on his magnum opus, "The phenomenology of modern art," but with no hope of getting it published. He was isolated and died in October 1951, perhaps, as many believe, by his own hand. This, however, is contradicted by Jaroslav Seifert, who recalls Teige in his memoirs and was one of the few people to attend his funeral.

Before Teige's book on modern Czech architecture was consigned to oblivion, it did serve as a target for attack. In the Communist weekly *The New Central European Observer* (11 and 24 December 1948), the British architect Kenneth John Campbell inveighed against Teige's opinions, fully endorsing the Soviet standpoint: "Modern architecture is in fact the architecture of modern capitalism." There were probably very few architects in Western Europe, even among the convinced communists, who shared Campbell's views. The following year his article was published again in Poland, as part of the campaign against "Formalism" (*Architektura,* 1949:3).

Not until the 1960s did it become possible to mention the name of Teige, and a selection of his writings on art theory was then republished.

At the same time that Karel Teige was ejected from the cultural life of Czechoslovakia, Jiří Kroha was nominated *národní umělec,* National Artist. This was a new title instituted in accordance with Soviet precedence, by the regime that took over in February 1948. But it was more than just an honorary title. A National Artist had to be the foremost in his field and must take the lead in the redirection and politicization of cultural life that the regime was bent on accomplishing.

The name of Jiří Kroha (1893–1974; Fig. 187) carried prestige. As a young architect at the end of World War I he had belonged to the Cubist direction in Czech art and architecture ("Cubo-Expressionism"). In the 1920s he became one of the exponents of Czech Functionalism, which also aroused international attention. In 1930 he was the subject of a monograph, written in Czech and German and published in Geneva, that paid special attention to his expressively Modernist vocational school in Mladá Boleslav and his own house in Brno.

Like so many other members of the young intelligentsia between the wars, Kroha was a Communist, and he wrote enthusiastically about modern architecture in the Soviet Union, about developments down to the beginning of the 1930s. He was above all a theorist and as a teacher at the Czech (not German) Institute of Technology in Brno (Brünn), he was greatly admired by the radical students. He organized seminars on "Marxism and architecture." On occasions like this, however, his growing deafness was a problem, and he did most of the talking himself.

During the war years, according to *Architektura ČSR,* he was "persecuted on account of his socialist opinions." After the war, his life seems first to have continued on the same lines as before. Together with Vilém Kuba and Josef Polášek he designed a housing

187 Jiří Kroha in 1930.

development in Brno-Tábor (built 1946–48), still in the spirit of classical Functionalism.

But then came 1948, and Kroha became National Artist. He was the main architect for the Slovak Agricultural Exposition in Prague. *Architektura ČSR* (whose editorial board included Kroha himself) devoted an entire issue to him (1948:9), and in the years that followed he had published, in the same journal, a spate of ideological articles, renouncing nearly all of his earlier beliefs about architecture: He and his colleagues had not perceived the antipopular content of Cosmopolitan architecture, meaning Modernism.

He also disavowed himself as a practicing architect. The projects he published were abundant in form, almost motley, without any counterpart in the other people's democracies. Take, for example, his design for a building for the Faculty of Medicine in Olomouc, for the University Library in Brno, or for the Institute of Chemistry in Pardubice. Much is derived from Soviet architecture, but there are as well traces of the Cubist Expressionism of his youth.

He was involved in every project of importance. He drew a detailed development plan for the new city of Nová Dubnica in Slovakia, and together with the sculptor Karel Pokorný he took part, in 1949, in the competition for a Stalin monument on the Letná Mountain, Prague (see Fig. 207).

Many people changed their opinions in postwar Czechoslovakia, but Kroha's about-face was *too* fantastic, *too* demonstrative. It was hard to take seriously, and those colleagues of Kroha's who changed their standpoints with a little more discretion were probably more useful to the regime. Even so, a stance like Kroha's was not ineffective. It showed who had the upper hand.

During the 1930s, Teige and Kroha had both belonged to the intellectual left-wing organization *Levá fronta* and both had believed in the inseparability of socialism and Modernism. But that idea had now been put aside. Teige and Kroha went in different directions. Teige kept faith with Modernism and with the strong Western European tradition in Czech culture, Kroha with the Party and the Soviet Union. Nobody needed to ask twice who had won and who had lost, but in the 1960s, when Teige was given something of a posthumous reinstatement, Kroha was made to look tragic, if not ridiculous.

Under the Husák regime in Czechoslovakia it was then Kroha's turn for reinstatement, and shortly before his death he was able to publish a presentation volume on his old speciality, 1920s avant-gardism in the Soviet Union.

József Fischer and Máté Major

On the morning of 21 February 1948, József Fischer, architect and director of town planning in Budapest, was telephoned by a government official who told him that his office would be closed down within twenty-four hours. Not long before that, Fischer had realized that *Tér és forma,* the architectural journal he had been editing for the past six years, would have to cease publication. The February 1948 issue would be its last. He was, however, allowed for the time being to continue drawing his salary as director of town planning.

Fischer's deposition was brought about by his independence and by his activities in the Social Democratic Party. He had belonged to the segment of the party that opposed the enforced amalgamation with the Communist Party. It was his involvement in the wartime resistance that saved him from more serious reprisals. His being a convinced Functionalist, on the other hand, meant nothing. The campaign against Cosmopolitanism had not reached Hungary. His deposition had nothing to do with architecture.

It was, however, as an architect that József Fischer (b. 1901; Fig. 188) was known, and as one of the Hungarian pioneers of Functionalism. The villas he designed were distinguished by austere elegance. He was inspired by Ernst May and the new housing design in Frankfurt am Main. Together with Farkas Molnár and others he

188 József Fischer in 1985.

formed, in 1928, the Hungarian section of the CIAM (*Congrès interna-tionaux d'architecture moderne*). The group's journal was the above-mentioned *Tér és forma* (Space and form).

The CIAM group was dissolved in 1938 and its members scattered. Politics took over. Fischer had belonged to the Social Democratic Party since 1926 and became involved in the resistance movement. The Molotov-Ribbentrop Pact in 1939 spread confusion. Molnár, the most famous architect in the group, transferred his sympathies from the Communists to the Hungarian Nazis (alias the Arrow-Cross Party).

In January 1945, while shooting was still going on in Budapest, the four-party commission that now took over the administration put Fischer in charge of the Town Building Office *(Fővárosi Közmunkák Tanácsa)* and with it the reconstruction of the city. Before long he was also made reconstruction commissar for the entire country.

Practical and organizational problems predominated, especially in the beginning. How extensive was the damage? Which ruins were liable to collapse, causing further harm? How were the labor duties of the citizenry to be organized? How were tiles and flat glass to be procured? Before long, though, planning questions of different kinds also cropped up, not all of them due to the war. The project, already presented, for the renewal of the Erzsébetváros district of Budapest, entirely in the spirit of radical Functionalism, dates from 1946 (see Fig. 15).

But then in 1948 Fischer was sacked. Others were prepared to step into his shoes, including Imre Perényi, who had returned from the Soviet Union. A year later, Fischer was given a junior appointment at an office working on the reconstruction of the Old City of Budapest.

For a few days in the autumn of 1956 he returned to the limelight as one of three Social Democratic ministers in Imre Nagy's coalition government. All that was ended, however, by the entry of Soviet troops on 4 November. Many of the ministers were taken prisoner, and two eventually were executed. Fischer was soon released but never recovered his job. Another of Imre Nagy's ministers, János Kádár, took over as head of government with Soviet support.

Fischer moved to the USA in 1965 but returned to Budapest in 1979.

In the autumn of 1951, at an architecture congress arranged by the Party, the Hungarian Minister of Culture, József Revai, gave a long speech entitled: "Questions in the new Hungarian architecture" (*Építés-Építészet*, 1951:9–10). The title contained a message. "Questions" was the Soviet way of presenting the Party line. The speech was widely publicized and published in at least three of the other people's democracies. It was one long castigation of Functionalism and of the architect Máté Major, who ranked as its foremost advocate now that Fischer and others were out of the running. Major had claimed that modern architecture was not tied to capitalism and that it was based on principles that were also valid for Hungary. He had actually said—though Révai did not mention this—that Functionalism was "Stalin's concern for mankind" applied to architecture (*Építés-Építészet*, 1949:6–7).

Révai was Hungary's counterpart to the Soviet Union's Zhdanov, the man who was to exterminate Cosmopolitanism in cultural life. He no longer had any bourgeois opponents to bother about, and the thing now was to deal with deviants in the ranks: the literary historian György Lukács, the author Tibor Déry, and—Máté Major. His criticism was fierce and dangerous. What would the next step be? But Major's political credibility was not called into question. The intention was to warn him and call him to order.

Máté Major (1904–87; Fig. 189) had belonged to the same circle of young architects as Fischer, but as an architect he had not enjoyed the same success. He had belonged to the Hungarian Communist Party since the 1930s, but one kept quiet about things like that under the Horthy regime and during the German occupation of Hungary. At the end of the war, in 1945, he was sent into Soviet captivity on

189 Máté Major in the 1980s.

purely arbitrary grounds. He was released after a while, apparently after the Soviet architect Boris Iofan, visiting Budapest, had been told before returning home that Major's assistance was essential to the work of reconstruction.

Returning to Hungary, he worked for a while under Fischer in Budapest and designed a number of apartment blocks in the mining town of Tatabánya. But otherwise he devoted himself full time to writing about architecture. That, however, was a complicated activity. The battle in Hungary concerned not the buildings but the periodicals and the written word. Journals were closed down and new ones founded in their place, and always the reason was an ideological and political complication.

When *Magyar Építőművészet* began to appear in 1952, it was the third Hungarian architectural journal to have been started up since the war; an equal number had been closed down. Major contributed to all of them but only sporadically between 1950 and 1953. He demonstrated his loyalty to the Party, but—unlike Kroha—without self-denunciation. And the task of pleading for a new Hungarian architecture based on Neo-Classicism was left to others. In Eastern Europe during the early 1950s, few of those who were publicly denounced for lack of orthodoxy got off as lightly as he did.

The turning point for Major came in the spring of 1956, less than five years after Révai's attack. The Hungarian Rising, eventually put down in November, was already in the making. The opposition burst forth in all sectors of society. Following a secret ballot among the members of the Hungarian Architects' Association, all the Communist architects making up its executive committee were forced to resign—all, that is, except Máté Major.

The sequel was less dramatic. As a member of the Hungarian Academy of Sciences, Major ranked higher than any other architect in the country. As a theorist and writer on architectural history he played an important part, but the respect he enjoyed among his colleagues was founded on his resistance to Socialist Realism at the beginning of the 1950s.

Major and Fischer had both belonged to the circle of pioneers in Hungarian Functionalism. For a short time they had both worked on the reconstruction of Budapest, but in 1948 their fates diverged. Fischer's career came to a sudden end. Major too got into difficulties, but they were transitory and led on to success.

I met both men in Budapest in the autumn of 1982, more than thirty years after the events described here. Fischer was eager and committed, a loser but unbroken. Major was more prudent, diplomatic in his view of the past.

Szymon Syrkus and Bohdan Pniewski

In issue no. 5, 1949, of the Polish journal *Architektura,* there was an article by Szymon Syrkus entitled "On the question of developing architectural creativity." It was a short, one-page article that would have passed almost unnoticed if written by a less famous author.

The article takes the form of a synopsis. It contrasts the modest condition of architecture under the interwar capitalist regime with the tremendous opportunities of the socialist build-up phase. Cosmopolitanism is contrasted with Socialist Realism, Western influence with experience from the Soviet Union. But for all these and other ideologically orthodox touches, such as the reference to Michurin and Lysenko, readers must still have found the article a trifle unclear. Had Syrkus performed a complete *volte-face?* Was he rejecting Functionalism, or was he making ideological concessions in the hope of practical compromises? It was hard to say, but one message was clear enough: No resistance was to be expected from Syrkus.

Szymon Syrkus (1893–1964; Fig. 190) was the great pioneer of modern Polish architecture, and perhaps the foremost exponent of Functionalism anywhere in Eastern Europe. He had studied in Vienna, Graz, Riga, Moscow, and Warsaw, spending the next few years (1922–24) in Berlin, Weimar, and Paris. He was a founding member of the CIAM in 1928 and one of the authors of *La Charte d'Athènes* in 1935. He founded the journal *Presens* in 1928 and, together with Jan Chmielewski, presented in 1934 a plan for the Warsaw region entitled *Warszawa funkcjonalna.* Otherwise, as a planning architect, he always collaborated with his wife, Helena Syrkus (1900–82).

Szymon Syrkus came of a Jewish family and was interned in 1942 in Auschwitz. When liberated in 1945 he was badly marked by his ordeal, and people close to him said that he never recovered. Yet during the earliest postwar years he came to be intensely active.

Syrkus's name carried prestige, and Modernism was now to accomplish what had previously been denied it. In addition to a large number of competition entries, Szymon and Helena Syrkus designed two large housing areas in Warsaw: Praga I and Koło. The latter especially is a fine example of the gentle Modernism of the 1940s.

In 1949, the year when Socialist Realism was launched in Poland, Syrkus became a professor at the Warsaw Institute of Technology, a position in which he could not easily keep out of polemics. Instead he pleaded the cause of Socialist Realism so vigorously that his closest friends and acquaintances at least took it for irony. Whereas formerly he had been so prolific, he now gave up

190 Szymon Syrkus in the 1930s.

drawing and wrote hardly anything. Koło was completed, but phase by phase it grew less and less modern. The final blocks were cast in the mold of Socialist Realism.

Teige, Kroha, and Syrkus had all believed in the combination of socialism and Functionalism. Whereas Teige stuck to his ideals and Kroha changed course altogether, Syrkus evidently hoped for some kind of compromise. That compromise, however, was a chimera, at least for a Functionalist as convinced and theoretically oriented as Syrkus. He lost, if not his social position, then at least his leading professional status and his self-confidence.

Private architects' practices in Poland were abolished during 1949 and here, as in the other people's democracies, the architects became employees of large state planning bureaus.

One of them, however, was able to continue as before. Bohdan Pniewski kept up his private office, in his big villa in a park in the center of Warsaw. He had never shown any interest in communist ideology, nor did he do so now. But from his fortresslike villa he masterminded some of the really big architectural briefs in the newly founded people's republic: the new National Bank (*Narodowy Bank Polski*), the rebuilding of the Parliament building (*Sejm*), and the rebuilding of the Opera (*Teatr Wielki*).

Bohdan Pniewski (1897–1965; Fig. 191) had always been successful. He belonged to the first generation of architects trained in Poland (no program of architectural studies existed there until 1915). From 1925, when he opened his own practice, and until the outbreak of World War II he took first prize in no less than nine competitions. From 1931 onward he was a professor at the Warsaw Institute of Technology. His style was a modern, personal Classicism. Mostly he designed for the state, but he also had assignments from the Catholic Church and for wealthy private individuals. He understood his clients and, without relinquishing his artistic demands, gave everybody what they wanted. His architecture was modern without being provocative, traditional without seeming old-fashioned. To Zygmunt Stępiński, who at one time was employed in his office, he said that a good architect must be able to draw *everything* (*Architektura*, 1978:1–2).

The seal of his success was his own villa, which he moved into in 1935 and where he also had his office. But it was no ordinary architect's villa. It would have made a good embassy building, such was its splendid self-containment. Today it is a museum of geology. The courtyard facade incorporates parts of a garden pavilion in the Doric style, built in 1781 for a member of the Poniatowski family.

191 Bohdan Pniewski in the 1950s.

The war years made a gap in Pniewski's career, but in 1945 he picked up where he had left off in 1939. Once again it was he who received the big status assignments and he got through 1949, such a fateful year for others, with both his assignments and his office intact. A certain adjustment to the principles of Socialist Realism was all that was needed. On the whole, Bohdan Pniewski could remain as he was.

Architecture was politicized, but the implications of this for the individual architect were not predetermined. Syrkus, who belonged to the left and the avant-garde, was thrust aside. Pniewski who belonged to the bourgeoisie and tradition, prospered all the more. To Syrkus, ideas were the breath of life, while for Pniewski what counted was practical reality. Syrkus was a man of strong convictions, Pniewski was not, at least not outside his architect's practice. And as an architect, it was Pniewski who was useful. Whereas Syrkus lost his footing, Pniewski the pragmatist had his feet well and truly on the ground all the time.

Hermann Henselmann and Kurt Liebknecht

On 29 June 1951, the Party journal *Neues Deutschland* carried an article by its editor-in-chief, Rudolf Herrnstadt, entitled "On the style of building, political style and Comrade Henselmann."

The article was, first, a general assault on Functionalism, which was portrayed as a tool of imperialism and a product of "the profit hunger and misanthropy of dying capitalism." Second, it described a meeting of some members of the Central Committee and a number of leading architects. That meeting had ended with the architects being given eight days in which to present new schemes for the development of Weberwiese, near Stalinallee. Finally, the article was a personal attack on Henselmann, who had expressed himself in dubious terms concerning the new Soviet Embassy in Unter den Linden and clung doggedly to his Functionalist values. He was called upon to mend his ways, "politically and professionally."

Only a few days later, Henselmann put forward a new scheme for Weberwiese in which the detailing especially marked a renunciation of Functionalism (see Figs. 84, 122). *Neues Deutschland* responded immediately (3/8 1951), congratulating Henselmann on his susceptibility to criticism. The scheme was accepted and soon afterward came proposals by Henselmann and his colleagues—once again, a result of the earlier criticism—for Stalinallee. There were no more galleried apartment buildings—or "sanatoria" as Walter Ulbricht had branded the first new buildings in Stalinallee (see Fig. 120). Instead there was monumental big-city architecture true to Moscow precedent, although some of the detailing put one in mind of Berlin Classicism in about 1800. Presumably the consequences must also be taken to include an article by Henselmann in *Neues Deutschland* (4/12 1951) on "the reactionary character of Constructivism."

The impact and relevance of the Henselmann episode extended far beyond Henselmann personally. In architecture as in other fields, the DDR was now conclusively shepherded into the same camp as the other people's democracies. Another result of the episode, however, was to put Henselmann personally into the limelight for a long time to come.

Hermann Henselmann (b. 1905; Fig. 192) was an unknown quantity when, in the summer of 1945, he was commissioned by the newly appointed administration in Thuringia, in the Soviet zone of occupation, to reorganize and resume classes at the Weimar School of Arts and Crafts. He was a young architect sympathetic to Functionalism and communism, no more. On arriving in Weimar he declared to the remaining staff, at all events if we are to believe his memoirs, published in 1981: "I have come to restore the continuity broken by the Nazi government in the development of this school and to remove the reactionary body of ideas fabricated here for the past fifteen years."

This was the same school that Henry van de Velde had headed before World War I, which was taken over by Walter Gropius after the war and turned into the Bauhaus, and which from 1930 onward was headed by Paul Schultze-Naumburg, appointed by a National Socialist minister with the express task of reestablishing a *German* architecture. But now it was once again time for Modernism, the return of which was a natural consequence of the Nazi defeat.

In his address at the reopening of the school in August of the following year, Henselmann turned to consider the question of architecture and politics as it was being asked by many people in the Soviet-administered part of Germany:

> I know very well that the German artist is afraid of the term "realism," and that he is particularly afraid of having a new, extra-artistic program dictated for him. And, let us be quite frank about this, there are a large number of artists who are waiting for a dictate of this kind from the Soviet administration.

But Henselmann saw no cause for any such fears:

> The Soviet administration is generally run by Marxists. Marxists know that art grows out of the social situation of an

192 Hermann Henselmann in 1952.

entire age. It would be un-Marxist to try and force a particular kind of art upon people by means of devices and dictates. Realism is an attitude, not a style.

And to begin with, indeed, it looked as if Henselmann was right. During the early years it was only in the monuments to the Soviet Army that "realism" became visible, and the German artists and architects had nothing to do with them.

At the beginning of 1951, without being called upon to recant, Henselmann—like Paulick and Hopp—was put in charge of an outstandingly qualified architects' practice, known as a *Meisterwerkstatt*. But when the dictate came a few months later it was, ironically enough, directed at him personally.

The biography of Hermann Henselmann contains—leaving all other comparisons aside—the same contradictions as in the life of Dmitrii Shostakovich. They were at one and the same time recalcitrant and loyal. They incurred both praise and reproof. But perhaps there is one more similarity: The work they did reluctantly and under coercion was not necessarily inferior to the work that coincided with their own values.

The newly founded Deutsche Bauakademie in East Berlin was opened in December 1951. One of its main tasks was to promote the new cultural policy in the fields of architecture and urban development. Its president was Kurt Liebknecht.

Liebknecht was a resounding name in the newly established German Democratic Republic. His grandfather, Wilhelm Liebknecht, had been a close friend of Karl Marx and one of the pioneers of German social democracy. His uncle, the revolutionary Karl Liebknecht, had been murdered for leading the Spartacist Rebellion in 1919. Kurt Liebknecht, however, was fairly unknown and—unlike Hermann Henselmann and in spite of his official status—was never to become a public personality. Even so, he occupied a stronger position than any other architect in the DDR during the years of Socialist Realism.

Kurt Liebknecht (b. 1905; Fig. 193) had studied architecture at the Berlin Institute of Technology. Like other Communist students he had chosen Hans Poelzig as a teacher. After only a brief period of practice as a qualified architect he had moved to the Soviet Union in 1931, joining up with a group of German architects led by Ernst May, which had arrived there the previous year. Like the other members of that group, he represented modern, German architecture. He designed a hospital for Magnitogorsk and took part in the 1932 com-

193 Kurt Liebknecht as president of the Deutsche Bauakademie, photographed in the 1960s.

petition for the Palace of the Soviets in Moscow. Most of the foreign specialists left the Soviet Union again after a few years, but Liebknecht stayed on as a member of the staff of the Moscow Academy of Architecture. By the time he returned to Germany in 1948, after seventeen years in the Soviet Union, he was an initiated exponent of Socialist Realism and of the Soviet view of architecture. Hence his authority.

In the early years he headed the Urban Planning Division of the *Ministerium für Aufbau* (Ministry for Reconstruction), which under his leadership drafted the "Grundsätze des Städtebaues," adopted by the government in July 1950, which was to have such a momentous effect on building in the DDR. In 1951, as we have already seen, he became president of the Bauakademie, a position from which he was to lead the campaign against Formalism and Cosmopolitanism. Liebknecht became the ideologist of DDR architecture. "The profound difference in architectural development corresponds to the fundamental difference between progressive politics in the German Democratic Republic and reactionary politics in the western part of our fatherland," he wrote in the first issue of the journal *Deutsche Architektur* (1952:1), published by the Bauakademie.

The common denominator of Liebknecht's authorship and the Bauakademie's activity under his direction—its prolific publication of books and brochures, for example—was fidelity to "das grosse Vorbild" (the great model), that is, the Soviet Union.

Liebknecht was close to the power in the land. His 1953 article about Walter Ulbricht and architecture is as well-informed as it is submissive (*Deutsche Architektur*, 1953:4).

Both Henselmann and Liebknecht still retained their positions after the 1950s: Henselmann as extrovert, successful architect, Liebknecht as a senior bureaucrat.

The Architects: Aesthetic and Ideology

Any notions that may exist, outside Eastern Europe itself, concerning the situation for Eastern European architects in the 1940s and 1950s are bound up with Hermann Henselmann. He was the competent professional who tried to accommodate both the political demands and his own architectural ideals, and who, when forced to choose, put his ideals aside and, thanks to his professional skill, invariably landed on his feet. Henselmann, however, is no more typical than the others who have now been presented. There was a wide spectrum of standpoints, and it is tempting to try and place our eight examples on a continuous scale of standpoints, from orthodoxy to heresy (8):

Liebknecht, Kroha, Henselmann, Pniewski, Syrkus, Major, Fischer, Teige.

This constellation, however, conveys the misleading impression of there being just one standpoint, when in fact the key to understanding these things is a combination of *two* standpoints. It is only toward the beginning and end of the series of names that the ranking order between them is perfectly straightforward.

The fact that there were two standpoints involved—one political, one aesthetic—gives us cause to return to the figure already presented in the introduction to this book in order to show how, in the architects' opinion, the standpoints were interconnected (Diagram A). The great majority of architects are located along the dashed diagonal: The Modernists belonged to the left, the Traditionalists to the right.

But the official interpretation of the relationship between politics and architecture was different; schematically, it is represented by the lower of our two figures (Diagram C). Here the dashed diagonal shows what the relationship between politics and aesthetics *ought* to look like, with the Modernists to the right and the Traditionalists to the left. Where the great majority of architects were concerned, it was as if a map had been published with the points of the compass reversed. But it was no easy situation for the regime either. The architectural profession did not look the way it ought to. Schematically it could be divided into four groups:

1. Architects with *the right ideology and the right aesthetic.* The official aim, of course, was for everybody to come within this category, but to begin with the category only included a very small group of architects who had spent the war years in the Soviet Union and been trained there. Kurt Liebknecht in the DDR, Edmund Goldzamt in Poland, and Imre Perényi in Hungary came to be very important as interpreters of Socialist Realism and "the example of the Soviet Union," but not as practicing architects. This category also included the Hungarian Tibor Weiner, the architect of Sztálinváros.

2. Architects with *the right ideology but the wrong aesthetic.* This category included the large group of Modernists with left-wing sympathies, which for a long time meant the same thing as communist sympathies. The group, however, was by no means homogeneous and it varied a great deal in its willingness and ability to rectify its aesthetic. Kroha seems to have changed quickly and easily, Henselmann only after heavy pressure had been put on him. Syrkus and Major too were good Communists, but both of them appear to have hoped for some kind of compromise where architecture was

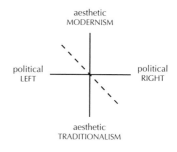

Diagram A

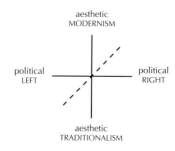

Diagram C

concerned. Others looked for duties where they could avoid confrontation with Socialist Realism, for example, jobs in planning bureaus for industrial buildings or positions in the bureaucracy.

3. Architects with *the wrong ideology but the right aesthetic*. This again was a large group if taken to include all the elderly and middle-aged architects working on the basis of tradition. And they were indispensable. They were in demand, but for the most part they remained in subordinate positions. In Poland especially, however, they could go far, as in the cases of Pniewski and Stępiński. This category also included most of the better-known Bulgarian architects. "Wrong ideology" was, from a practical point of view, much less of a problem than "wrong aesthetic."

4. Architects with *the wrong ideology and the wrong aesthetic*. These included not only the Modernists who were liberals or "bourgeois nationalists" but also Social Democrats like József Fischer, even though he was purged at such an early stage that there was never time for his architectural views to be used against him. This category also included Karel Teige. On paper this was a small group, but in reality it was a good deal larger. It has grown subsequently, and most of the people surviving from the 1950s apparently want to be included in it.

Whatever group they belonged to, however, the architects as a collective were highly regarded as a professional group. In the course of conversation they frequently point out that, despite all difficulties (even night work without pay was if anything routine), they felt more significant then than at any other time before or since. There are no statistics to show the occupations of people who defected to the West during the period we are dealing with—not even for those who crossed the border between the DDR and the Federal Republic do we have sufficiently detailed figures—but all the indications are that there were few architects among them. The majority adjusted successfully to the dramatic change in their professional conditions. The architect's position was respected and, in spite of all complications, was less hazardous than most other intellectual and aesthetic activities.

Four Political Works of Art

Pass Me a Brick—Building as a Symbol

X

One of the best-known paintings from the 1950s in Poland is called *Pass Me a Brick! (Podaj cegłę!)* (Fig. 194). Painted in 1950 by Aleksander Kobzdej (1920–72), it was exhibited the same year in Warsaw at the First All-Polish Exhibition of Art, where it took third prize. Through reproduction it quickly became known everywhere in the country. The original is now to be seen at Muzeum Narodowe in Wrocław. It measures 133 by 162 cm.

We see three men working on a building site, three bricklayers. We see them from below, so that they stand out monumentally against the background sky. The man on the far right is shaping bricks with his hammer. The others, trowel in hand, are laying bricks. One of them has straightened up, and the words giving the painting its title must be his.

This is a realistic painting, but without the detailed, photographic realism of contemporary painting in the Soviet Union. Kobzdej's painting belongs to the Polish variant of Socialist Realism, referred to as the Sopot School (in which the colors are more important than the line). The forms are quite cursory and the faces are merely hinted at. The colors are few in number, but they are applied with vigorous strokes of the brush: Contrasting with the red brick wall we have the bright blue sky.

Looking at the painting without prior knowledge of its context, one cannot readily understand that this is a piece of political art with a very exact message. But there are two reasons for suspicion: the rhetorical title and the monumental gesture of the bricklayer who is standing up.

In Poland in 1950, it was obvious that a picture of three bricklayers was about the reconstruction of the war-torn country and, in

194 *Pass Me a Brick!* oil painting by Aleksander Kobzdej, 1950.

particular, about Warsaw, the most ruined of all the ruined cities of Europe. Reconstruction demanded tremendous material resources in a country where practically everything was in short supply. Even modest demands for increased private consumption had to be put off, added to which the Poles expected the regularly recurring money-raising campaigns to yield voluntary funds for the reconstruction of Warsaw. These appeals were organized by 50,000 local committees. One out of every six people living in Warsaw was employed on reconstruction. In 1945 practically everybody had been thus occupied. "Pass me a brick!" meant: "Play your part in the reconstruction of Poland. Your country needs you!" (Fig. 195).

But the painting had another content, which was almost as self-evident in 1950, though not borne up in the same way by a united population. The painting was also about the Party.

Reconstruction paralleled the building-up of a new political system, and in both cases work was headed by the Polish Communist Party or, as it had been called following the enforced annexation of the Social Democrats at the end of 1948, the United Polish Workers' Party (PZPR).

At first the Party had toned down its ideological ambitions in order, if possible, to overcome the profound national disunity, which was a continuation of the antithesis, during the war years, between two different resistance movements, the AL (Armia Ludowa), supported by the Soviet Union, and the much larger AK (Armia Krajowa), supported by the Polish exile government in London. From 1949 onward, however, it was instead the specifically Communist targets that were emphasized.

The popular-front spirit was gone and the single-party state took over. The objectives were to build up Poland again, and to build up—on Soviet lines—a new political system, and the first objective became part of the second. This may seem farfetched to a Western reader, decades after the event, but it was not farfetched in Poland in 1950: The bricklayer with the commanding gesture is Poland's United Workers' Party. "Pass me a brick! Let us join in building socialism, the new, good society. Beyond the rigors of everyday life, the bright blue sky of the future is already visible."

There is ample support for this kind of interpretation. In Adam Ważyk's once famous poem "The People Move to the Center" (*Lud wejdzie do śródmieścia),* the first lines read: "See how the Party stands there/perseveringly on the scaffolding." And in a painting from 1949 by Włodzimierz Zakrzewski, *Comrade Bierut among the Workers,* we see the leader of People's Poland amid the workers on a building site, a building site that is of course a picture of the new Poland. Here we meet another main theme in the iconography of Socialist Realism: the close relationship between leader and people.

But, at the time Kobzdej's painting was put on exhibition, building also had a third meaning in political language. The ruins were a product of the war. Building, to a corresponding extent, belonged to *peace.* To build was to have faith in the future, to defy the opponent in the Cold War, and to assert the cause of peace.

The peace movement was everywhere in evidence, and strikingly often its message was conveyed with the assistance of buildings and bricks. The walls of buildings were hung with banners

CAŁY NARÓD BUDUJE SWOJĄ STOLICĘ
The whole nation is building its capital.

NIECH ŻYJE I ROZKWITA STOLICA NASZEGO KRAJU, MIASTO REWOLUCYJNYCH TRADYCJI NARODU POLSKIEGO—WARSZAWA
May our country's capital live and flourish, the city of the revolutionary traditions of the Polish people—Warsaw.

PRACA DLA WARSZAWY JEST SPRAWĄ HONORU I OBOWIĄZKIEM KAŻDEGO POLAKA
Working for Warsaw is a point of honor and the duty of every Pole.

SOCJALISTYCZNA STOLICA—MIASTEM KAŻDEGO OBYWATELA—ROBOTNIKA, CHŁOPA I PRACUJĄCEGO INTELIGENTA
The socialist capital is every citizen's city—the worker's, the peasant's, and the intellectual's.

CHWAŁA BUDOWNICZYM SOCJALISTYCZNEJ WARSZAWY!
Honor to the builders of socialist Warsaw!

CHWAŁA BRACIOM RADZIECKIM POMAGAJĄCYM W BUDOWIE WARSZAWY!
Honor to the Soviet brothers assisting in the building of Warsaw!

NIECH ŻYJE PIERWSZY BUDOWNICZY WARSZAWY, BOLESŁAW BIERUT!
Long live Bołeslaw Bierut, the foremost builder of Warsaw!

NIECH ŻYJE PRZODUJĄCA W OFIARNOŚCI NA SFOS KLASA ROBOTNICZA!
Long live the working class, leaders of self-sacrifice for SFOS!

SFOS ŁĄCZY ROBOTNIKA, CHŁOPA I INTELIGENTA WE WSPÓLNYM WYSIŁKU PRZY SOCJALISTYCZNEJ WARSZAWIE
SFOS unites the worker, the peasant, and the intellectual in a common endeavor for socialist Warsaw.

BUDOWA WARSZAWY TO SYMBOL TWÓRCZYCH I POKOJOWYCH DĄŻEŃ NARODU POLSKIEGO
The building of Warsaw is a symbol of creativity and peaceful endeavor of the Polish nation.

BUDUJEMY SOCJALISTYCZNĄ WARSZAWĘ DLA POKOJU I SZCZĘŚCIA NARODU
We are building socialist Warsaw for peace and for the felicity of the people.

BUDOWA NOWEJ SOCJALISTYCZNEJ WARSZAWY TO WALKA O POKÓJ I SILNĄ POLSKĘ TO CIOS W ZBRODNIARZY WOJENNYCH
The building of the new socialist Warsaw is a struggle for peace and for a strong Poland, a blow against the war criminals.

ZESPALAJMY WYSIŁKI WSZYSTKICH PATRIOTÓW WOKÓŁ NARO-DOWEGO DZIEŁA BUDOWY SOCJALISTYCZNEJ WARSZAWY
Let us unite the endeavors of all patriots round the national task of building socialist Warsaw.

195 Every September in postwar Poland was devoted to a nationwide campaign for the rebuilding of Warsaw. These slogans, for 1952, are taken from the September issue of *Architektura*. SFOS is short for Społeczny Fundusz Odbudowy Stolicy (the Social Fund for Reconstruction of the Capital).

reading, "Every additional brick is a blow to the American imperialists." And on May Day the school children chanted, "In reply to the atom bombs, we are building new houses." Or to quote Marian Brandys's novel about Nowa Huta: "Every building in Nowa Huta is a brick in the wall shielding mankind against war." The 1949 Congress, which introduced a decisive phase in the rebuilding of Warsaw, assembled under the motto: "The Rebuilding of Warsaw is our reply to the warmongers." In this latter instance the Americans and their allies were not the only targets. The Congress opened on 1 September, the tenth anniversary of the invasion of Poland by Nazi Germany. It was typical of the Cold War that both sides did everything in their power to implicate each other with fascism.

Phraseology like this was the same everywhere in the Communist bloc. In January 1953 the Cominform weekly wrote: "Stalinallee has become a battlefield for peace." And concerning the political significance of building, Hermann Henselmann declared, "We are building, not because we need dwellings but because we feel young and strong and because we desire peace" (*Der Spiegel,* 14/5 1952).

On Warsaw's biggest construction site, MDM in Marszałkowska Street, a pennant proclaimed WARTA POKOJU (On guard for peace). No such pennant was needed in Aleksander Kobzdej's painting, and it would not have improved the picture. The point was made all the same.

Of course, building has been used before as an image of society, but this idea gathered new impetus in the Soviet Union during the 1920s, and during "the construction of socialism" it was powerfully supported by the political language. Building, however, had not only a practical purpose and a symbolic significance, it had an immediate impact on people's senses. Or perhaps more accurately, it was expected and required to have that kind of impact.

For the simplest way of putting this, we can turn to a commentary on the new Marszałkowska Street in 1952: "It is not only the street that has changed, but also we ourselves" (*Det nya Polen,* 1952:8–9). Or, at somewhat greater length in the above-mentioned novel by Marian Brandys: "It was people who raised the walls. But the walls in their turn uplifted people. This was Nowa Huta."

All major construction projects were accompanied by similar remarks. The urban scene was transformed and with it—according to this popularized Marxist argument—an important part of the great material context that makes up people's awareness. Building as a direct impulse in the fashioning of *a new man*—one can hardly go any farther than that in thinking of architecture as an ideological force.

Political declarations without some form of rhetoric are barely

196 Mateusz Birkut and his fellow workers in *The Man of Marble,* 1976. Andrzej Wajda's film was, among other things, a sequel to Kobzdej's painting.

conceivable, but all the same, rhetoric is the perpetual threat to political credibility. When the gap between words and reality grows too wide, rhetoric backfires.

This is exactly what eventually happened in Poland, and perhaps it did so there with greater emphasis than in any of the other people's democracies. In Poland, of all countries, state-managed collective enthusiasm was outstandingly alien to cultural tradition. In the end, the command "pass me a brick" took on an ironic sound, the height of the irony coming in *The Man of Marble (Człowiek z marmuru),* the great film about the Stalin era by Aleksander Ścibor-Rylski and Andrzej Wajda, made in 1976 (Fig. 196). This, of course, is a film about a bricklayer.

What happens when Mateusz Birkut's luck deserts him? Once a shy country lad, he is now a famous elite worker, self-assured but as pure-hearted as ever. He travels all over the country to inspire socialist competition among his fellow countrymen. His appearances are a kind of festive, public theatrical performance, a far cry from the gray drudgery of everyday work. Together with his fellow worker Witek he is now to demonstrate once more the new methods of bricklaying (Fig. 197). They are met with great expectation, but they have hardly got started when Birkut screams with pain. He has burned his hands badly on a hot brick.

This happens at a time when the Party, aided by the security service, is looking for opponents and saboteurs—real or imaginary—even among its own ranks. There are no holds barred in demonstrating how the enemy ("the Anglo-American imperialists," "the fascist Tito clique," etc.) can infiltrate in the most unexpected connections. Witek is sacrificed and Birkut quickly goes from bad to worse.

Disappointed and pretty drunk, he is spending his last night of liberty at a tavern in Floriańska Street in Cracow. He has, wrapped in a newspaper, the brick he was holding in his hand when, as leader of his team, he set his great record of 30,509 bricks in one shift. To the strains of "The Bricklayer's Waltz" he leaves the tavern and takes a horse-drawn droshky to the security service building. He throws his brick through the doors with tremendous strength and is immediately arrested.

Birkut's brick, of course, is not just a personal souvenir of which he divests himself in his disappointment. It is also the brick of Aleksander Kobzdej's painting (which, incidentally, puts in a fleeting appearance in the film, in a few frames from a 1950s newsreel). The Party has appealed for solidarity, it has responded with manipulations and broken promises, and it now gets the brick thrown at it.

Ścibor-Rylski and Wajda, however, are not alone in referring back to the construction symbolism of the 1950s. Of the many posters appearing in 1980 and 1981, one in particular had an outstanding impact (Fig. 198). Like most of the others, it is in small format, plainly executed, and printed in either red or black.

The subject is as follows. Behind the scaffolding one can make out a house in the shape of a stylized map of Poland. In front there is a sign reading: WARNING! REPAIRS IN PROGRESS. NO UNAUTHORIZED ACCESS. This was a discreet but telling way of declining outside interference. It was also the opposition's way of using the dog-eared symbolism of reconstruction. The social system presented to the people for the last thirty years as an edifice of increasing perfection won't do! It needs to be repaired and rebuilt.

There were three themes in Aleksander Kobzdej's painting: reconstruction, the Party, and peace.

How did *reconstruction* fare? Many grandiose projects remained on paper, but the amount that did materialize was impressive enough. Much comment was aroused by reconstructed historic city centers, not only in Warsaw but also in Gdańsk, Poznań, and Wrocław. This reconstruction gave Poland a tremendous, and abiding, international prestige.

How did *the Party* fare? Much worse. But in 1956, under Gomułka's leadership, it was given a second chance. Hopes ran high, but again they were dashed. Then came the third attempt under

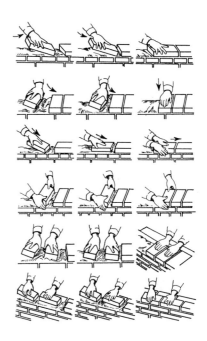

197 The technique of fast bricklaying as illustrated in a Polish book of instruction. The fast tempo was made possible by dispensing with the trowel and by smoothing the mortar and laying the brick in a single operation.

198 The symbolism of construction backfires. Poster from the Solidarity period, 1980–81.

Gierek in 1970. Ten years later the Party's good will was definitely exhausted, and the people's patience with it.

What about *peace?* The Cold War gave way to peaceful coexistence, but the military continued to enjoy an exceptionally favored position, which, if anything, was reinforced toward the end of the 1970s. This did not alter the Polish people's view of peace, but it augmented their distrust of the official rhetoric. Martial law was proclaimed on 13 December 1981, and the peacekeeping forces (as the army was often and officially called) were sent in against their own people.

Young Bricklayer of Stalinallee—"the Typical" in Art

Young Bricklayer of Stalinallee (Junger Maurer von der Stalinallee) is an oil painting on canvas done in 1953 by Otto Nagel and exhibited in Dresden in March that year at the III. Deutsche Kunstaustellung (Fig. 199). It measures 115 by 80 cm and belonged to the city authorities of Gross-Berlin (DDR), later to the Otto Nagel Haus (East) Berlin.

In old-fashioned terminology, this painting is a knee-length portrait, but at the same time it is really no portrait at all, as we can sense immediately. We see a young man in the white overalls of a bricklayer. He is facing the beholder, left hand at his waist. In the background we see scaffolding receding at an angle from right to left. Farther away we see some flags and a few small figures—building workers. Otherwise the background tells us nothing, except that something big is under construction. But we understand from the title that this is Stalinallee.

On the strength of the previous section, we could say that, once again, we are confronted by "building as a symbol," and once again we are dealing with *reconstruction, the Party,* and *peace.* There may be something in this, but it is still rather wide of the mark, because here it is clearly the bricklayer who is important—the *worker,* not the work.

Otto Nagel was born in 1894, and by the time he came to paint this bricklayer he had a long artistic career behind him. He had been a Communist for a long time and had devoted most of his creativity to the proletariat of Berlin. In Soviet terminology, he was a *critical realist.* He could have the pathos of Käthe Kollwitz and the satirical quality of Otto Dix. As regards choice of themes, he also had a certain amount in common with Heinrich Zille. He had painted gloomy views from the working-class district of Wedding. He had depicted the workers as profoundly marked by their social situation, whether subdued or rebellious. There was always something dismal and suppressed about his characters.

199 *Young Bricklayer of Stalinallee,* oil painting by Otto Nagel, 1953.

Nothing, however, could be farther from the case with this bricklayer in Stalinallee. He gives the impression of being quite unmoved by his work, just as his overalls are neither soiled nor mended. Sustaining the realist fiction, we might say that this is because of the model, because of his youth, but Nagel had never previously given such figures a second glance. He does so only now, when he is required to proceed from critical realism to *Socialist Realism.* But before proceeding any further with Nagel and his bricklayer, let us see what his colleague among the authors, Johannes R. Becher, made of the theme of Stalinallee.

Becher was a contemporary of Nagel's, born in 1891, and known since the 1920s as an Expressionist poet. He too was a long-standing Communist, but unlike Nagel he had spent the Hitler era in exile in the Soviet Union. Like Pieck, Ulbricht, and Kurt Liebknecht, then, he belonged to the "Muscovites" within the Party, who in every field took precedence over the "home Communists." Becher became Minister of Culture in the DDR, but he also became the DDR's National Poet, author among other things of the national hymn "Auferstanden aus Ruinen." He responded sensitively to all the demands the Party made. The following poem dates from 1952.

STALINALLEE

Columns and stone blocks like footsteps
Set firmly on the earth—
And a blooming center:
Glorious today and now!

Glorious today and here!
Banner of shining words.
Flag-festooned is the gate
Through which peace marches—WE!

Swaying, waving course
Like a triumph without end.
See the rejoicing of hands uplifted
In the song of the people!

Name that everyone knows,
More radiant today than ever:
Street—his monument!
Proud Stalinallee!

STALINALLEE

Säulen und Quadern wie Schritte,
Fest auf die Erde gesetzt—
Und eine blühende Mitte:
Herrliches Heute und Jetzt!

Herrliches Heute und Hier!
Spruchband leuchtender Worte.
Fahnenumkränzt ist die Pforte,
Durch die der Friede zieht—WIR!

Schwingender, winkender Gang,
Wie ein Triumph ohne Ende.
Seht der erhobenen Hände
Jubel im Völkergesang!

Name, den jeder kennt,
strahlender heute denn je:
Strasse—sein Monument!
Stolze Stalinallee!

There is not much here of Becher's Modernist past. This is a panegyric poem in the grand style. And in content it represents a very old genre, *tribute to the sovereign.*

Nagel, of course, could have adopted a similar approach. He could have painted Stalinallee on May Day or perhaps, better still, on "Liberation Day" (9 May). He could have included in his picture the statue of Stalin in front of the Deutsche Sporthalle. The previous year he had painted *Street at the Sector Boundary*: on the western side, emptiness and ruins, on the eastern side, flag-bedecked facades, bustling crowds. But instead he chose to paint the construction worker.

The best construction workers from all over the newly founded republic came to Stalinallee. So too did Polish and Soviet bricklayers, to teach new methods. This is where the principle of *socialist competition* was introduced and where honorary titles—"bester Bauarbeiter" and "bester Facharbeiter"—were conferred. The title of "beste Baustelle" was awarded on 1 May 1952 to the building workers from Magdeburg, who also received 10,000 marks and "das rote Banner der Stalinallee," the red banner of Stalinallee.

But Nagel's bricklayer is not a proletariat muscle man, nor does he represent a corps of exalted skilled workers. He is the representative of youth and tomorrow, *the new man* in the making during "the construction of socialism." In Soviet terminology recently authorized by Malenkov at the 1952 Soviet Party Congress, he is a *typical* bricklayer, not typical in the sense of ordinary but typical of the direction of current social development. The young bricklayer as an individual is a *tabula rasa*, but the socialist future is firmly staked out: the construction project in progress in the background.

And yet it was among these very building workers of Stalinallee that rebellion broke out. It was they who had the self-confidence to protest against "norm elevations" (wage cuts). A demonstration march of three hundred workers assembled on the morning of 16 June 1953 at "Baustelle Block 40." Carrying a banner inscribed "We demand a reduction of the norms," they marched past the other construction sites, and before long there were two thousand marchers. They went on to the trade union building in Wallstrasse, which was closed, and by the time they reached the Ministry building at Leipziger Strasse there were ten thousand of them. Venting a discontent that had long been brewing, they demanded the government's resignation.

The following day, 17 June, there were strikes and demonstrations all over the DDR. There were demands for free elections and "down with goatee beard" (Ulbricht). That very same day, though, a state of emergency was declared and the rebellion was quickly put down by Soviet tanks, at the same time as the norm elevations were retracted.

A broadsheet appealed to the population to try and regain the confidence of the government by doubling the work output. Bertolt Brecht replied with the famous lines: "Then wouldn't it be simpler for the government to dissolve the people and elect another one?"

According to the government and Party leaders, however, the rebellion was a fascist provocation, staged by "bandit columns" controlled from the West. Or else it was even an "attempted fascist coup." That was the only acceptable explanation. Workers could never, on their own initiative, rebel in a workers' state. The rebellion was a fact, but it was not *typical* of the building workers of Stalinallee.

Otto Nagel remained a big name in the art of the DDR, and even since his death in 1967 he has continued to be looked on as an important artist and his works have been published at frequent intervals. But the standing selection does not include the *Young Bricklayer of Stalinallee.*

Contemporaries were already doubtful. The painting complied with official ideals, but was it convincing? "More artificial than experienced" was the verdict of *National-Zeitung* (11/3 1953), published in East Berlin. Posterity too has been embarrassed by the title. The renaming of Stalinallee in 1961 operated retroactively. One solution was the abbreviated *Junger Maurer*, as if the subject had been just any bricklayer. In the latest survey of art in the DDR, however, the painting was included under its original title.

The Stalin Monument in Budapest—*damnatio memoriae* I

The Stalin Monument in Budapest was a gift from the Hungarian people to Stalin on his seventieth birthday, 21 December 1949—not the finished monument, that is, but the promise to erect it. The unveiling did not take place until two years later, almost to the day.

On Sunday, 16 December 1951, according to a lengthy account in the party newspaper *Szabad Nép* (28/12 1951), eighty thousand workers had assembled on Dózsa György út in Budapest. On the stroke of ten a fanfare rang out and Mátyás Rákosi, Secretary General of the Party, took up his position on the tribune forming the base of the statue, accompanied by the members of the Politburo, by the Soviet ambassador, and by the ambassador of the People's Republic of China. The speech for the occasion was made by the Minister of Culture, József Révai.

He explained that the statue portrayed Stalin as the Hungarian people saw him, "great in his simplicity, simple in his greatness." He said that Stalin had given the Hungarians the greatest thing that can be given to a people: "freedom, independence, self-confidence, and the opportunity of freely developing their own powers." Stalin was "the Hungarian people's best friend."

Révai dwelt on the material assistance received from Stalin, but the most important assistance of all was teaching—Stalin's writings. Stalin deserved credit for everything. It was he "who released from Horthy's prison and restored to us our beloved Comrade Rákosi." This was one of many turns of phrase eliciting applause. But the speech also included warnings about "the mendacious imperialists." It ended with cheers, with the Soviet national anthem, the Hungarian national anthem, and the *Internationale*.

The newly unveiled monument stood on the edge of Városliget, Budapest's city park, where Dózsa György út had been widened, soon to be renamed Sztálin tér (Stalin Square). This was an excellent setting for parades and demonstrations, but for one defect: Opposite the statue of Stalin was MÉMOSZ, the house of the builders' unions, denounced by Révai as a horrendous example of new Hungarian architecture, replete with Cosmopolitanism and Western influence.

The Stalin Monument was not just a monument to the leader, then, it was also a tribune for the political leaders. This was a frequent combination in the Soviet Union, as for example with the Lenin Monument in Yerevan, the Ordzhonikidze Monument in Ordzhonikidze, and the Stalin Monument in Gori (the only Stalin Monument surviving de-Stalinization).

The Budapest monument was a big one: The tribune was 18 meters wide and, in the middle of it, on a 4-meter-high limestone base, stood the 8-meter-high bronze statue. Stalin was portrayed as a speaker, but a speaker with restrained gestures and a rigid posture.

200 Budapest, 4 April 1956, the Hungarian national day. Military parade in Sztálin tér in front of the Stalin statue and Party leaders assembled on the tribune.

It was a figure with no artistic authority. There was no wind of change blowing any longer, as there had been over the Stalin figures of the 1930s. Everything had already been achieved.

The monument was the work of sculptor Sándor Mikus, and it was already rewarded before the official unveiling with the Kossuth Prize, the finest distinction that a Hungarian artist could possibly receive, for by definition a monument to Stalin—given the loftiness of its subject—must be a masterpiece. But it still remained for Mikus to produce reliefs for the tribune, two long, high reliefs on the subject of "the Hungarian people welcoming their Soviet liberators."

We can see from a photograph taken on the national day in 1956, 4 April—the eleventh anniversary of "the liberation"—what the monument looked like when the reliefs were in position and when it was actually being used (Fig. 200). Just over a month earlier, Khrushchev had torpedoed the cult of Stalin at the 20th Party Congress. The age of Stalinist rhetoric was over, but the monument was still there. Before long the city authorities were to raise the question of its relocation or complete removal. That question, however, was to be settled by a special event.

On Tuesday, 23 October 1956, there took place in Budapest a big demonstration of sympathy for the rebellious Poles, who had just secured acceptance of their demands for changes in their political leadership. It was an unofficial demonstration. The national poet Petőfi's famous "Song of the Native Land" was recited in front of his statue. Written in 1848, on this day it sounded as if it had just been written:

> Hungarians arise! Your land summons You.
> The time is ripe, now or never!
> Shall we be slaves? Shall we be free?
> That is the question—what is Your reply?

The marchers grew in number as they progressed through the city, until finally there were more than 200,000 of them. Some of them went to the radio station and asked for their demands, under sixteen headings, to be broadcast. They were met by troops from the security service (ÁVÓ), but, at dawn the following day, they managed to occupy the radio station. This was the prelude to the uprising.

One of the sixteen demands was the dismantling of the statue of Stalin, and a large number of the demonstrators had gone there. When the chief of police was informed, the number of persons assembled at Stalin Square and Heroes Square was estimated to exceed 100,000. Facing them were twenty-five armed police. The crowd was exhausted and disobedient. Somebody had fastened a

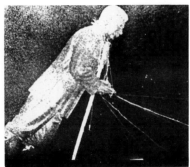

201–204 Budapest, 23 October 1956 and the following day.

placard to the statue, putting into Stalin's mouth the words: RUS-SIANS, WHEN YOU RUN AWAY DON'T LEAVE ME BEHIND!

A lot of people had climbed up onto the monument. Ladders had been put up against it and the boldest besiegers fastened ropes and steel hawsers to Stalin, so as to pull him down (Figs. 201-203). The ropes, ladders, and small figures swarming around the giant—it was like the Lilliputians on Gulliver. One of them was up on Stalin's head, probably the same person as had lashed a rope around the fingers of his right hand. Trucks arrived with oxyacetylene cutters and oxygen tanks. Stalin was cut off at the tops of his boots and at 9.30 P.M. he fell to the ground. Remarkably enough, no one was hurt.

"W.C." and other denigrating remarks were scrawled on the fallen statue. The destruction continued. Stalin was broken up and, in a frequently reproduced photograph, we see his severed head in the middle of the street among the tramlines (Fig. 204). It looks as if somebody has jabbed a road sign into the right side of the head—a primitive, ritual revenge. Degradation and humiliation of the man who, until very recently, was praised as "the Hungarian people's best friend." Without the people being consulted.

Perhaps there was somebody who recalled what Révai had said in his speech at the unveiling, four years earlier: "The bronze in which we have cast the figure of our beloved Stalin, the stone on which we have placed him, symbolize the enduring nature of his work, which defies the passage of time . . ." The brutal treatment of the statue was, on top of everything else, a retort to phrases like this, to Stalinist rhetoric and its claims to perpetuity.

A photograph taken a day or two afterward shows the remains

205 The remains of the monument.

of the monument (Fig. 205). Nothing is left of Stalin but his boots and a few bent reinforcement bars. Inquisitive Hungarians are investigating the boots or strolling about unconcernedly on what had until very recently been a tribune for the top leaders of the state. Someone has rigged up a Hungarian flag next to Stalin's boot, cut down so that the emblem of the People's Republic of Hungary is no longer visible. Gone too is the bronze lettering on the base, spelling in Hungarian the name of the leader and teacher: SZTÁLIN. That had already been removed before the statue was demolished.

Sealing the fall of a regime by removing the image of the leader,

206 Budapest, Dózsa György út. The remodeled base of the Stalin monument, twenty years afterward.

his name, and other symbols is a mode of action so ancient that there is a Latin name for it: *damnatio memoriae*, obliteration of the memory. In Budapest in 1956, it was rebellious citizens who did the obliterating. But this was unusual in post-Stalinist Eastern Europe; the usual thing was—and had been ever since the days of the Roman emperors—for the successor in power to try and legitimize his position by denouncing his predecessor, pulling down the statues and erasing his name. We will return to this theme in our next section.

The tribune survived for a long time, acquiring in 1965 a companion piece in the form of a nearby statue of Lenin. It was not radically reconstructed until 1974–75. The result then was a completely new tribune, Modernist in form, emulating Mies van der Rohe, and with a discreet national coat of arms as its only piece of ideological identification (Fig. 206). And Sztálin tér recovered its old name of Dózsa György út.

Not even this tribune, however, seemed to be the ultimate solution. In the successful Hungary of the early 1980s, a new national theater was proposed for this very site. One with a generously proportioned balcony.

The Stalin Monument in Prague—*damnatio memoriae* II

The big Stalin Monument in Prague also dated back to a promise on the occasion of Stalin's seventieth birthday, on 21 December 1949. But this was an even bigger undertaking than the Budapest monument and was to be the biggest outside the Soviet Union. It also took longer to complete. It was, at one and the same time, the last Stalin Monument to be completed in Eastern Europe and the one that remained longest in position. Its eventual demolition was quite different from what happened in Budapest in 1956.

The brief history of this monument can be presented with reference to five dates: 1949, 1950, 1955, 1960, 1962.

1949. This was the year after the Communists had conclusively taken power in Czechoslovakia. A meeting took place of "the State Commission for Coordinating the Celebration of Generalissimo Stalin's 70th Birthday." The proceedings were chaired by the Minister of Information, Václav Kopecký.

The birthday celebrations were nearly as important a concern in the people's democracies as in the Soviet Union. In Bucharest, Budapest, and Prague alike, it was decided to put up statues of Stalin. But events were soon to prove that it was the Czechs who were going to make a really big thing of their project.

Compared with Berlin, Warsaw, and Budapest, Prague had suffered very little damage during the war and there had not yet been any cause for conspicuous new public buildings as a manifestation of the new regime. But an opportunity had now arisen to make the new political cause visible, and the Stalin Monument in Prague would have to be something out of the ordinary.

Kopecký explained to the committee that a square or riverbank was insufficient for such a tremendous monument as this, a monument to Stalin, "the immortal genius of the working class." Only a mountain could set off the monument in its true grandeur and help to elevate the beauty of Prague. And so the choice had fallen on the Letná Mountain, which was widely visible from the central city. The design of the monument would be settled by means of a competition, and eighty artists and architects had already requested to be apprised of the conditions.

Thus when the foundation stone was laid by the head of government, Antonín Zápotocký, on 21 December, Stalin's birthday, it was still not known what the monument would look like, but site preparations, guided by the terms of the competition brief, had already made some progress.

1950. This year the competition was settled and the results presented at length in *Architektura ČSR* (1950:3–4). There were comments from Oldřich Starý, who together with Jiří Kroha ranked as the leading ideologist and interpreter of Socialist Realism. Kroha took part in the competition himself, as befitted a "national artist." Together with the sculptor Karel Pokorný he won second prize for a scheme that, admittedly, depicted Stalin as "friend and protector," but did not capture "the full scope of his personality" (Fig. 207). Instead the assignment went to the sculptor Otakar Švec, whose design showed Stalin at the head of the struggling Soviet and Czechoslovakian peoples.

1955. On May Day 1955 the unveiling ceremony was performed by the same Václav Kopecký who had been one of the prime movers. The work had not been easy. The laying of the foundations had been unexpectedly complicated and, to improve its integration with the site, the monument had been realigned. The main complication, though, was that Stalin had died on 5 March 1953, followed nine days later by his foremost representative in Czechoslovakia, President Klement Gottwald—presumably from a cold he had caught at Stalin's funeral. *Pravda* had already declared on 16 April 1953 that "collective leadership is the supreme form of leadership for the Party." Any such statement would have been inconceivable just a few weeks earlier. So it had gone on, and when the Prague monument was unveiled, Khrushchev's speech at the 20th Party Congress, marking the end of the cult of Stalin, was less than a year away. In Hungary and Poland, the emancipation was to spill over into rebellion. In Czechoslovakia and the DDR, on the other hand, events were

207 Design for a Stalin Monument in Prague by Jiří Kroha and Karel Pokorný, 1950.

to take a different course. Reluctantly and more cautiously than in the Soviet Union, the leaders set a new political course. As late as 1957, Zápotocký, while visiting Moscow, could place a wreath at the Lenin Mausoleum inscribed: "To J. V. Stalin, the great leader of socialism."

It was already clear, however, that Stalin was about to be revalued in Czechoslovakia too. In *Architektura ČSR* the results of the competition five years earlier had been presented in fifteen pages and with thirty-three illustrations. But now the end result received only one page and just a single picture, taken moreover by night, so that all the details were lost (1955:5; Fig. 208). Publicity remained sparse as time went on, and a few years later books were to be published about Prague in which the Stalin Monument was not even mentioned.

But what did this newly unveiled monument look like? In shape, it resembled a wedge pointing inward at the city. Stalin occupied the apex, the Soviet people one side, the Czech and Slovak peoples the other side. At the back, finally, was a relief of the hammer and sickle.

It was colossal. It was built of meter-high blocks of granite; the figure of Stalin was 13 meters high (Fig. 209). Bareheaded and with his right hand stuffed inside his long greatcoat, he gazed calmly and imperiously across the Moldau (Vltava) and away toward the Old

208 Stalin Monument in Prague. The scheme realized by Otakar Sveč, as presented in *Architektura ČSR*, 1955.

City. Behind Stalin there was a slight gap—to make him stand out as an individual, even if the monument was viewed from the side—and then, on both sides, came the nations rallying in his footsteps. They are each represented by four people only, but it was easy to see that they stood for the mass, the collective. At really close quarters one could see how this collective was composed—of representatives of the workers, the peasants, the intelligentsia, and the armed forces.

It is often said that monuments to dictators are invariably artistic failures, as if art, by virtue of some inherent strength, should refuse to lend itself to such dubious assignments. But is this really so? The history of art abounds in examples to the contrary.

Otakar Švec and his associates undeniably had accomplished the task they had been set, mastered the tremendous scale of it, and combined intelligibility at long range with legibility at close quarters. The ratio between leader and people was ingeniously formulated and the effect was truly monumental, not just a pompous stereotype as with the Stalin monuments of the Volga–Don Canal or the Moscow Agricultural Exposition.

But this was not a monument that provided balanced judgments and reasonably fair allowance for the artist's difficulties. It was a political monument and was rated as such: for or against. *For* in the few official mentions it rated, and *against* in practically every other connection.

1960. A brief digression. I visited Prague myself with a few contemporaries and with very little intellectual preparation: the ordinary reader's acquaintance with Kafka and the Good Soldier Schweik, a vaguely romantic notion of Prague as preeminently a *European* city, and at least a few facts about 1938, the war years, and 1948. Today, some decades afterward, only two experiences really come back to me from that visit: the remains of Jewish Prague, and the encounter with the Stalin Monument. The first of these experiences we were prepared for. The second was a surprise.

It was midday in one of the European capitals, at its biggest and newest memorial. There was not a soul in sight. And the monument was overwhelming. One of us climbed up on the base, so that the others could gauge the size of it all (Fig. 210). I just had time to take one photograph before a guard emerged from nowhere, angrily declaring that this was not a monument for climbing on.

An actor we got to know maintained that the money spent on the monument could have given Prague a whole new hospital. On returning home, we were told by Czechs in Sweden that Otakar Švec took his life the same year his great composition was completed.

209 Stalin Monument in Prague, photographed in 1960.

210 Stalin Monument in Prague. Another photograph from 1960, showing the difference between the human and monumental scales.

Later others told us that, in the rock beneath the monument, a fallout shelter had been constructed, a last refuge for the political leaders, reached by an underground corridor.

It is hard to make up one's mind about these three allegations. The cost of the monument was never openly accounted for. It is certainly true that Švec committed suicide, but he could have had several reasons for doing so. And stories about secret shelters are never easy to verify. But debatable or otherwise, the three statements were part of the criticism leveled against the monument and against the regime that built it.

1962. The year before this, Stalin's remains had been transferred from the Lenin Mausoleum to a grave at the Kremlin wall. Towns and cities, streets, squares, and factories that had been renamed got their old names back again or were given new ones of a more neutral kind. In Prague, though, the Stalin Monument remained standing.

In 1962, however, the leaders of Czechoslovakia's Communist

Party ordered a close scrutiny of the Slanský trial, the great sham trial in 1951 of Rudolf Slanský, former Secretary-General of the Party. This was one of several decisions marking dissociation from the past, and the 12th Congress of the Communist Party, in December 1962, marked the opening of a new period in the history of Czechoslovakia. Just before that, however, the Stalin Monument was demolished, and it has been said that it was this very action that heralded the events that concluded with the entry of Warsaw Pact forces on 21 August 1968.

Only the sculpture itself was removed, however. The base remained, together with the whole of the architecturally designed terrace, the sole purpose of which had been to support the colossal sculpture.

So the terrace and the empty base remained (Fig. 211). This rather puts one in mind of an aphorism by the Pole Stanisław Jerzy Lec: "Spare the bases when you pull down the memorials. They may come in handy again." That, however, was hardly the reason why the authorities made do with removing the sculpture. The reason was that they did not quite know what to do with the Letná Mountain.

It was a fatal perplexity, as a result of which the monument, even in its absence, invited comment. Here is an excerpt from Alexander Kliment's novel *Tedium in Bohemia*, published in 1979:

211 Empty terrace of the Stalin Monument, 1982. All that survives from 1960 is the brazier on the right.

On the left, in Letná Street, against the cloudy, misty sky, I could just make out the dark contours reminiscent of a gigantic catafalque. That was the terrace-shaped base left by the statue of Stalin, which today no longer watches over Prague. I would never have believed that the same people who had the statue put up could also have had it pulled down again so quickly. It is a pity, today it would have been a historic monument and a unique tourist attraction in Central Europe.

Pulling down monuments to politically odious predecessors is an ancient tradition, referred to in our previous section by its Latin name, *damnatio memoriae*, obliterating the memory. In many cases this obliteration was actually achieved, but remarkably often it has stopped short at half measures, both in ancient times and in postwar Eastern Europe. Rubbing out history is a risky undertaking, and the changes tend to show up, rather like emendations of a hand-written manuscript.

212 Stalin's name erased from the Polish worker's ideological textbook. Facade sculpture on the Palace of Culture, Warsaw.

The idealized Polish worker on the west front of the Palace of Culture in Warsaw holds a gigantic book with four lines of text on the cover (Fig. 212). Only three lines are legible, however: MARX/ENGELS/LENIN. The name that once stood on the fourth line has been chipped away, but it is all the more conspicuous by its absence. The name of Stalin is equally "visible" over the main entrance on the eastern side and in the big foyer.

Was it realization of this difficulty that prompted a shrewd answer by Deng Xiaoping when the journalist Oriana Fallaci asked him about the future of Mao's Mausoleum? "It was inappropriate to build it, but it would also be inappropriate to demolish it." Or did he really mean that suppressing and denying one's own former standpoints is bad politics?

In Budapest, the Stalin Monument was swept away by a rebellion. In Prague it was the regime itself that, late in the day, wanted to demonstrate a breach with the past. *Damnatio memoriae* can occur in many different forms and for many different reasons.

During the "normalization" the Husák regime embarked upon in 1968, embarrassing names were removed from history, national leaders like Thomáš Masaryk, awarded the title of "President-Liberator" on his retirement in 1935, and authors like Franz Kafka. The only Kafka mentioned in a guidebook to Prague published in 1983 is the sculptor Bohumil Kafka.

As regards the regime's handling of its own history, there is one example that Milan Kundera has made famous in the introduction to *The Book of Laughter and Forgetting*, published in Paris in 1978. The

Clementis referred to was Foreign Minister between 1948 and 1950 and was prosecuted and sentenced to death on trumped-up charges in the Slanský trial of 1952.

In February 1948, Communist leader Klement Gottwald stepped out on the balcony of a Baroque palace in Prague to address the hundreds of thousands of his fellow citizens packed into Old Town Square. It was a crucial moment in Czech history—a fateful moment of the kind that occurs once or twice in a millennium.

Gottwald was flanked by his comrades, with Clementis standing next to him. There were snow flurries, it was cold, and Gottwald was bareheaded. The solicitous Clementis took off his own fur cap and set it on Gottwald's head.

The Party propaganda section put out hundreds of thousands of copies of a photograph of that balcony with Gottwald, a fur cap on his head and comrades at his side, speaking to the nation. On that balcony the history of Communist Czechoslovakia was born. Every child knew the photograph from posters, schoolbooks, and museums.

Four years later Clementis was charged with treason and hanged. The propaganda section immediately airbrushed him out of history and, obviously, out of all the photographs as well. Ever since, Gottwald has stood on that balcony alone. Where Clementis once stood, there is only bare palace wall. All that remains of Clementis is the cap on Gottwald's head.

Clementis vanished, just as Trotsky had once done from the photographs in which he stood by Lenin's side.

But Kundera has also allowed himself to improve on reality. Or, rather, what he tells us is an anecdote, one of the political anecdotes so ubiquitous in the socialist countries. For the details of the text do not tally with those of the doctored photographs (Figs. 213, 214). Clementis was not obliterated. He was concealed behind the microphones, which were moved closer to Gottwald. What remained of Clementis was not the fur cap on Gottwald's head but his own hat.

In February 1968, the twentieth anniversary of Gottwald's speech, the newly appointed Party Secretary, Alexander Dubček, made a speech on the very same spot, in the square in the Old City. He spoke about the revolutionary traditions of Prague. That was the beginning of the short-lived Prague Spring. Clementis was reinstated. Before long, though, Dubček himself, in the Czechoslovakia of Gustav Husák, was to become a *nonperson*. One whose name could not be mentioned. One whose picture could not be shown. *Damnatio memoriae.*

213, 214 The retouched picture of history. Gottwald's speech in February 1948, with and without Clementis (and an irrelevant press photographer).

The Iconography of Pictorial Art

Just as there was a hierarchy of building assignments, so there was a hierarchy of pictorial art, a ranking order of subjects and themes, and this too was rooted in a long tradition. At the top of the ranking scale came the pictures of the leader, followed by historical painting, dealing either with prerevolutionary history or with the socialist contemporary scene. Then came genre pictures and landscapes—scenes from everyday life and working life—and, right at the bottom, still lifes. From top to bottom of this scale, however, the ideological content was ever-present. Two Romanian paintings will serve to illustrate this point.

Landscape from Bărăgan by Paul Atanasiu shows a plain being plowed up by two tractors (Fig. 215). The horizon is low, the color scale if anything pre-Impressionist. To the uninitiated beholder, this picture conveys little. But Bărăgan epitomized Romania's feudal backwardness; it was a place where formerly the rural population had led a wretched existence, completely at the mercy of the landowning boyars, whereas now the land was being plowed by the tractors of an agricultural collective. The landscape is a landscape in transition. Only the dry thistles in the foreground remind us of what used to be.

But there was a complication here. The title and the thistles put one in mind of a novel by the Romanian author Panait Istrati, published in 1928: *The Thistles of Bărăgan*. During the 1920s, Istrati's nov-

215 *Landscape from Bărăgan*, oil painting by Paul Atanasiu, early 1950s.

els, written in French, had made him one of the favorite authors of the European left, "the Gorky of the Balkans." Owing to his criticism of the Soviet Union, however, he had been ostracized.

Next, a genre painting, *The Little Chemists*, by Gheorghe Glauber (Fig. 216). This again apparently has little to say and looks indeed innocuous, but only to the uninitiated. Five children in a classroom, gathered round an experiment. As so often in genre paintings, however, the characters are acting in different ways, illustrating different attitudes to reality. If the painting were reproduced in color, we would see the point more readily: The most eager, most determined children wear red scarves. They are pioneers, the leaders of tomorrow. The scene in the classroom is an image of the leading role of the party.

Propagandist clarity was not confined to the Stalin monuments and oil paintings of construction workers. It permeated the entire scale of pictorial art and Socialist Realism.

Long after its abolition, Socialist Realism remains a key to the understanding of pictorial art in Eastern Europe. How are we to

216 *The Little Chemists,* oil painting by Gheorghe Glauber, early 1950s.

217 *Autobus,* oil painting by Bronisław Wojciech Linke, 1959–61.

account for a painting like Bronisław Wojciech Linke's *Autobus* (1959–61; Fig. 217), except as a protest by the artist against programmatic optimism and idealized realistic form? The scene is grotesque and crowded. The red bus is being steered by a robot. Nearly all the passengers have their eyes shut, including Stalin, who is sitting right at the back. This is the People's Republic of Poland on its way into the future.

This, however, is more than protest. If anything it is blasphemy, a Modernist, Surrealist taking in vain of all that Socialist Realism held sacred, a picture of human wretchedness, after the manner of Hieronymus Bosch. Beside a woman who is a celluloid dummy, below the man who is a dressed-up liquor bottle, we see a tremendous, huddled insect wearing a medal: the medal of Hero of Labor First Class.

Thaw and De-Stalinization

From the Death of Stalin till the End of the 1950s

XI

Stalin died on 5 March 1953, and three days later his embalmed body was carried into the Lenin Mausoleum in Red Square. His name was already displayed over the entrance, together with Lenin's. Khrushchev made the most important speech, as chairman of the burial committee, followed by Beria and Malenkov.

The twenty-four dignitaries on the tribune of the mausoleum also included the Eastern European leaders: Ulbricht and Grotewohl from the DDR, Bierut from Poland, Gottwald from Czechoslovakia, Rákosi from Hungary, Gheorghiu-Dej from Romania, Chervenkov from Bulgaria (Fig. 218). They were just as much committed to Stalin and his regime as their Soviet colleagues. This, as the saying goes, was a historic moment, and everybody was wondering, in their several ways, what the future held in store. Vast crowds had gathered in Red Square and its surroundings. So awful was the congestion that many people were trampled to death.

The twenty-three-year-old mausoleum by the Kremlin wall looked small and plain in the glow of rhetoric surrounding the death of the Leader and Teacher. The Central Committee and the Council of Ministers announced the construction of a Pantheon, "a monument in perpetual honor of the great personalities of the Soviet nation," that is, Lenin and Stalin primarily (*For a Lasting Peace,* 1953:11). It was to be built on the Lenin Hills, south of the new Moscow University. Ten specially invited designs, domed buildings in the grand Classical style, were presented in *Arkhitektura SSSR* (1954:9; Figs. 219, 220). In addition, an open competition was announced. Everything, however, was to remain on paper, and it has long since been forgotten that the leaders once looked so disdainfully on their holiest of shrines in the Soviet Union, the Lenin Mausoleum.

För varaktig fred, för folkdemokrati!

Nr 11 (227)
12—19 mars 1953

Bukarest. Organ för Kommunistiska och Arbetarpartiernas Informationsbyrå

VECKOTIDNING

Lösnummer 25 öre
I Norge och Danmark 35 öre
Finland 15 Mk

Proletärer i alla länder, förena er

Iosef Vissarionovitj Stalins begravning. På mausoleets tribun: kamraterna Gheorghiu-Dej, Boleslaw Bierut, Pak Den Aj, Walter Ulbricht, Dolores Ibarruri, Otto Grotewohl, Vylko Tjervenkov, Matyas Rakosi, Pietro Nenni, Palmiro Togliatti, Jacques Duclos, Klement Gottwald, N. A. Bulganin, V. M. Molotov, K. J. Vorosjilov, G. M. Malenkov, N. S. Chrusjtjev, L. P. Berija, M. S. Saburov, Chou En-lai, M. G. Pervuchin, L. M. Kaganovitj, N. M. Sjvernik.
Foto av F. Kislov och A. Ustinov

218 The Soviet leaders, together with Communist leaders from other countries, on the tribune of the Lenin Mausoleum at Stalin's funeral on 8 March 1953, as shown on the front page of the Cominform weekly, Swedish edition, for 18–19 March.

Stalin's death was a watershed, not only in political history but in all the fields that, directly or indirectly, were influenced by his regime. The change of political direction was already apparent by April, but it took different lengths of time in different fields and in different countries to become manifest.

The new leaders promised more scope for private consumption. The heavy political pressure was lifted, the cult of Stalin was toned down. Beria, the principal author of Stalinist terror, was deposed and executed in June. Before long the pressure was also lifted in the cultural sector. The journal *Novyi Mir* demanded candor in literature, which was a dig at the programmatic optimism of Socialist Realism.

The new signals were quickly perceived in the people's democ-

219, 220 Two of the designs for a Pantheon for the Soviet leaders on the Lenin Hills in Moscow: (left) by Michail Posokhin et al., and (right) by Dmitrii Chechulin et al.

racies too. Opposition and protest were no longer out of the question. Strikes and demonstrations took place during June in Plzeň, Ostrava, and other cities in Czechoslovakia, but without the regime losing hold of the situation. In the DDR that month, however, strikes and demonstrations threatened to turn into a general uprising, so that a state of emergency and Soviet tanks had to be resorted to. In the years to come the day of the uprising, 17 June, would be celebrated in West Germany as an annual festival.

In 1954 came Ilya Ehrenburg's novel *The Thaw,* which in the West has given a name to this period. The fall of Malenkov in 1955 was one of many signs of the power struggle taking place both in the Soviet Union and in the people's democracies during the years following Stalin's death. That same year came the Soviet Union's reconciliation with Tito's Yugoslavia and its admission of the existence of "several roads to socialism." Then came 1956, the big year of de-Stalinization and the most dramatic year in the international history of communism since 1917.

Although the cult of Stalin was already on the way out, Khrushchev's speech at the 20th Party Congress in February 1956 caused a political sensation. Even in the West, few had given such an unvarnished, negative character portrait of Stalin. Here are just a few phrases from the well-documented, four-hour speech: "...abuse of power...capricious and despotic character...cruel oppression...confessions extracted by torture...innocent victims...violence and terror...mass executions and deportations...executions without trial...intolerance...brutality...arbitrary rule...pathological suspicion..."

And as if this were not enough, Khrushchev severely criticized Stalin's performance during the war. "The strategic genius" had hesitated, had misunderstood, had refused to listen, and had made bad things worse. In his isolation from reality, Stalin had believed that life on the kolkhozes really looked the way it was shown in the propaganda films. He himself had created the cult of his person and everything was now blamed on this *cult of personality.* In the future this euphemistic expression would suffice. The name of Stalin did not even need to be mentioned.

Khrushchev's intention was to reinstate the Party, and this being a closed session, he appealed to the delegates to keep his speech a secret: "We must not give ammunition to the enemy, we must not wash our dirty linen before his eyes." These were probably the only words in the whole speech of which Stalin would have approved.

Even so, the impact of the speech was immense, though the text of it was publicized only in the West. In the people's democracies, not least, the 20th Party Congress aroused great expectations, both within the parties and outside them. But it also inspired fear among those who risked being pulled down with Stalin. Bolesław Bierut, President of Poland, died soon after the Congress, and before long it was an open secret that he had taken his own life.

In Poland and Hungary, above all, much was expected of a reform of the political system. Demands escalated and tensions rose, culminating in October 1956. But the political outcome was to be highly variable. In Poland, Gomułka was reinstated and hailed by enthusiastic crowds outside the Palace of Culture. The Party was reconciled with the Church, the peasants, and the intellectuals—at least, for the time being. Everything seemed possible and confidence in the Party was restored within wide circles. The philosopher Leszek Kołakowski, still a Marxist in 1956, wrote his remarkable *What Is Socialism?* Unprintable in Poland, it was circulated in transcript. Kołakowski wrote at great length describing what socialism *is not*, and the whole of his long list of examples consists of experiences from the Stalin era. No, this was not socialism. Finally he comes to what socialism *is:* "Well, socialism is a good thing." That is all we are told—confidence in socialism has been restored.

In Hungary, Rákosi had been thrust aside, for the second time and now for good. Great hopes were pinned on the previously dethroned Imre Nagy. Rajk, posthumously reinstated, was honored with a state funeral, as a gesture to critical opinion. But the Party lost control of things and, when a newly formed coalition government under Imre Nagy announced Hungary's withdrawal from the Warsaw Pact, only a couple of days were to pass before Soviet troops—following a short and bloody confrontation—were to put the Hungarians back in their place.

Events in Poland ended in a victory for the Party; those in Hungary ended in disaster, a disaster for all concerned. That verdict is unaffected by the completely different verdict eventually to be passed on János Kádár, the new leader.

Just before the Soviet troops invaded Hungary, Gyula Illyés had published his great poem "On Tyranny." Like Kołakowski's text, it gives a long, suggestive characterization of the Stalin era. But unlike Kołakowski it ends with no hope—"and even your ashes serve tyranny." But then that poem was written as early as 1951, when things in Hungary looked blackest. Events in 1956 seemed to inspire new hope, but they ended nonetheless in a relapse, the worst setback in the whole process of de-Stalinization.

And yet de-Stalinization continued, albeit less rapidly and with many interruptions. One step forward and one step back again. Not until 1961 did this chapter in the history of Eastern Europe come to an end. That was the year of the Berlin Wall (Fig. 221). No backsliding on the big issues! Europe was divided and the divison, so it seemed, was permanent. The year 1961 also witnessed the 22nd Congress of the Soviet Communist Party. The embalmed body of Stalin was moved out of the mausoleum in Red Square, a symbolic act that promised more than events were to justify: This far, but no farther!

The Deescalation and Abolition of Socialist Realism

The architectural journals noted Stalin's death with black-edged portraits and high-sounding declarations of the irreparable loss. And, of course, they made particular reference to his great importance for architecture.

These references to Stalin quickly disappeared. The political rhetoric was toned down. But Socialist Realism was not yet challenged, and a great deal of the published material on which this book is based actually dates from the years immediately following Stalin's death, 1953–55. It was then that the results of the proclamations from 1949 and the early 1950s began to materialize. Stalinallee began to take shape, as did Casa Scînteii in Bucharest and the new center of Sofia. Warsaw's Palace of Culture soared heavenward. Houses of culture, Party headquarters, and apartment blocks in the spirit of Socialist Realism were under construction everywhere in the people's democracies.

What is more, these projects showed that the architects were now fully in command of the new ideals. A project for Marszałkowska Street in Warsaw, designed in 1953 by Bohdan Lachert (one of the leading Modernists of the 1930s), shows an archi-

221 Berlin, 13 August 1961, the Wall under construction.

tecture closely resembling Soviet Academism in vocabulary and grandiloquence (Fig. 222). The same tendency was clearly apparent in a couple of competitions carrying high official status that were decided in Poland during 1954: the competition for the architectural surroundings of the Palace of Culture (Centralny Plac Warszawy) (Fig. 223), and the competition for a triumphal arch in Lublin to mark the tenth anniversary of the new Polish state, established with Soviet support in Lublin in 1944 (*Architektura*, 1954:7–8).

There was also another tendency, less observed by contemporaries and hardly at all noticed by posterity: a focus on the industri-

222 Warsaw, design for Marszałkowska Street, showing the Palace of Culture in the background. Architect: Bohdan Lachert, 1953.

223 Warsaw, competition entry for Plac Stalina, now Plac Defilad, opposite the Palace of Culture. Architects: Wacław Klyszewski, Jerzy Mokrzyński, and Eugeniusz Wierzbicki, 1954.

alization of building, on rationalization and prefabrication. People in the West have always spoken and thought as if Socialist Realism and industrialized building were mutually exclusive, but they were not.

Let us take an example from the DDR, an apartment block presented in the 1954 *Handbuch für Architekten* (Fig. 224). This is a four-story building, made up of prefabricated concrete elements. Both wall elements and ceiling/floor elements are big and heavy, 15 and 20 cm thick, respectively, and weighing up to 3 tonnes. They are assembled using a new building crane, the T 45, and they are intended for apartment blocks of between two and five stories. The technique, first tested in the Soviet Union, was introduced in the DDR in 1953 on an experimental construction site in Berlin. In the facade, the vertical joins are concealed by moldings made to look like pilasters, and in these pilasters we have a meeting point of modern technology and the tradition from Schinkel, which was the national vocabulary above all others in the DDR. Also part of this tradition are rustication, overdoor decorations, window proportions, and rooftop acroteria. This is rationalized building, but still on a small scale and without rationality acquiring sole command of architectural form.

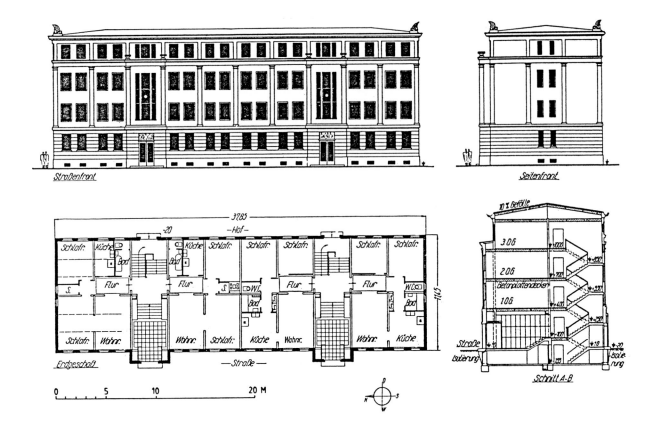

Straßenfront   Seitenfront

Erdgeschoß   —Straße—   Schnitt A-B

0   5   10   20 M

224 Elevations, ground plan, and section of an experimental building project in East Berlin, 1953. The apartment block used prefabricated concerete elements, with facade design in the spirit of Socialist Realism.

This tendency in favor of rationalized building was soon to give birth to a new architectural ideal. The process was a quick one. Once again, the new ideal came from the Soviet Union, where it was launched in two stages.

In the appeal of the All-Union Congress in Moscow in December 1954, fierce criticism was leveled against technical and economic shortcomings of the building program, against bad layouts, sloppy workmanship, uncompleted projects, poor efficiency, the lack of interest shown by architects in standard solutions and industrial building methods. The appeal also criticized the preoccupation of architects with outward effects and decorative facade designs, though as yet only in passing.

Eleven months later that criticism had expanded into a general attack on Socialist Realism: the Resolution of the Central Committee and Council of Ministers "On the removal of exaggerations in planning and building." That resolution was signed by Khrushchev and Bulganin and dated 4 November 1955, a date forming perhaps the sharpest boundary in the history of architecture. Newly unveiled major construction projects, such as the sumptuous Leningrad underground, were ruled right out of court.

What had recently been proclaimed as national form and Socialist Realism was now characterized as "shortcomings" and "exaggerations" and was blamed on the architects. Many were denounced personally, among them Mordvinov, the president of the Academy of Architecture. Some were sacked or deprived of their honorary titles. The new ideal, though nameless, was formulated clearly enough:

> Soviet architecture must be characterized by simplicity, austerity of form, and economy of layout. Buildings must be given an attractive appearance, not through the use of contrived, expensive decorative ornamentation, but by an organic connection between the architectural form of the building and its purpose, between good proportions and a proper use of materials, structures, and detailing, and through high-quality workmanship.

This declaration closed the gap between East and West. The resolution went on to say that the architects should learn from the foremost achievements of building in other countries, and no exception was made for the capitalist world. It was roughly at the same time that Soviet scientists and engineers began to be encouraged to "copy foreign experience." The Cold War was deescalated, leaving room for *peaceful coexistence.*

The de-Stalinization of architecture was already a fact three months before the 20th Party Congress, at all events on paper. But Khrushchev's speech, even though it made no mention of architecture, imparted further ideological content to criticism of Socialist Realism. The cult of personality in politics and the exaggerations in architecture had been one another's preconditions. They had developed together and must now be abolished together.

Some time was to pass, however, before Socialist Realism was abolished in practice. It disappeared fastest in housing production, where industrialized building on a new scale and in modern forms rapidly gathered speed. It went more slowly in the case of public buildings, where old projects were completed all through the 1950s and the instructions issued to the architects were often carried out to the letter. The exaggerations, the splendor, and the wealth of detailing were gone, the principles of composition remained. In the new building for the Finland Station in Leningrad, from 1960 (Fig. 225), we even find a modernized version of the national form: a distinct

225 The Finland Station building in Leningrad, rebuilt 1960. Architects: P. Ashastin, N. Baranov et al.

allusion to Zakharov's Admiralty building from the early years of the nineteenth century (see Fig. 132). There is a late harvest of Socialist Realism, a more discreet application of Classical and Traditional principles, which would be worth a whole chapter to itself.

But there was also a Soviet architecture of a completely new kind, already demonstrated at the World Exposition in Brussels in 1958 (Figs. 226, 227). The big glazed pavilion broke with everything that Soviet architecture had stood for during the past twenty-five years. But here again, in the prominent entrance section, there was a legacy from Academism and Socialist Realism. *Modernity*, however, was the new benchmark—modern form and modern materials; in that sense the Soviet and American pavilions at the Brussels fair were similar.

A breakthrough on the home front came with the Congress Palace in the Kremlin, built for the 22nd Party Congress in the autumn of 1961. Even the most representational building assignments could now be tackled using modern forms.

Not long before that, a protracted building question had finally been settled. The enormous Moscow Swimming Pool was opened officially in the summer of 1960 (Fig. 228). A use had at last been found for the base of Iofan's Palace of the Soviets, the building of which had been interrupted by the outbreak of war. A new competition in 1957–58 had come to nothing, and so the end product of the biggest prestige building project in the history of the Soviet Union and

226, 227 The 1958 World Exposition in Brussels. Above: Soviet pavilion, by Y. Abramov, A. Boretskii, V. Dubov, and P. Polianskii. Below: USA pavilion, by Edward Durell Stone.

228 Instead of the Palace of the Soviets—the Moscow Swimming Pool, 1960. Inscription in the foreground is an appeal from GTO, the "Ready for Labor and Defense" organization.

Socialist Realism turned out to be a swimming pool. But *bigger* than other swimming pools, and with warm water all year round.

Even contemporaries, of course, perceived a connection between the change of political climate and the changes in architecture. But what exactly was the connection? Was the new politics a cause for the new architecture? And if so, was the latter an expression of the new politics? We will have to put off answering these questions. Suffice it to say, for the moment, that during the years following the death of Stalin, de-Stalinization was to decide the ideological content of every change in architecture.

In the people's democracies, too, the 1954 appeal and the 1955 resolution were printed as quickly as possible. Architectural journals reproduced them in their first issues for 1955 and 1956, respectively. Even before that, however, the journals had begun to change their tune. They now contained less and less ideological material and more and more coverage of problems of structural engineering, as well as material about housing, hospitals, and industrial facilities. They also included material from the West and, before long, they adopted a new typography.

Changing direction and proclaiming the wisdom of the new course now being set was easy enough in that an overwhelming majority of the professionals were greatly relieved. But sarcasm and the forsaking of ideals that until recently had been above question was the political order of the day, as in the following cartoons published in 1955 in the Czech journal *Sovětská architektura*. The first of them shows six buildings of different kinds, each more fantastic than the other (Fig. 229). Most remarkable of all, however, are the statements of their different functions. What seems to be a church is a school, what seems to be a temple is a factory. The building said to be an exhibition pavilion looks like an apartment block (and on closer inspection appears to have been turned upside down). Most peculiar of all, however, is the apartment block, which looks like a mausoleum. Surmounting it is the statue of an architect, holding drawings and a ruler. Inscribed at his feet are the words: ONLY FOR

229 Satirical drawing, aimed at Socialist Realism soon after its denunciation and published in Czechoslovakia in 1955. From left: stables, school, factory, house of culture, exhibition pavilion, and apartment block.

stáje   škola   továrna   kulturní dům   výstavní pavilon   nájemný dům

HIMSELF (*Sám sobě*). This alludes to the famous motto above the proscenium of the National Theater in Prague, opened in 1881: "The Nation for itself." But there were no such lofty objectives involved here. The architects had only been out to glorify themselves. They had pursued their own cult of personality. One senses a new myth in the making: Socialist Realism was the architects' fault. The caption said as much: "How certain architects envisage the work of typologizing . . ." The appeal from Moscow had also put the blame on the architects.

In the second drawing we see a man who has just wrenched the temple porch away from the entrance of an apartment building. He is the architect of the building and is now going inside, taking the immense portico with him. The drawing is wittily captioned: "Away with all superfluity! Concern for mankind must be on the inside!" (Fig. 230).

The target of this irony is not only architecture but the political jargon of the Stalin era as well. Everything that was positive and a part of everyday life had been called "concern for mankind" (alternatively, "Stalin's concern for mankind"). The phrase had been worn threadbare as architects joked to one another about "putting in concern for mankind" when they really meant ornamentation, cornices, or temple porches.

Once again, the main butt of irony is the architect. The drawing hints that he is once again about to jump to conclusions and misinterpret the directives given. But there is a detail in the drawing that gives cause for reflection—the distinctive mark left by the decor that has been removed. Removing what was wrong is easier said than done. And it cannot be done inconspicuously.

No, least of all considering that so many buildings designed on the principles of Socialist Realism were not completed until now. They were published half-heartedly or not at all. Of the four volumes planned on the Palace of Culture in Warsaw, all that materialized was a plain publication with a print run of 720. Following a lengthy, profusely illustrated account of the competition for the Stalin Monument in Prague, the finished work rated only one page and a picture.

If Stalinallee, MDM, and Casa Scînteii had been films or plays, further performances could have been canceled. If they had been novels, the whole edition could have been withdrawn. But they were buildings, there for all to see, charged with many associations that should now be forgotten. But a large number of projects could be shelved permanently, such as the enormous governmental palace in Marx-Engels-Platz, East Berlin, or the magnificent city hall in Sofia.

The rejection of Socialist Realism was accompanied by a new

230 Another caricature: "Away with all superfluity! Concern for mankind must be on the inside!"

view of the architectural history of the twentieth century. The history of Modernism had to be brought into the limelight once more. But the Bauhaus, recently dubbed "the height of imperialist Cosmopolitanism," was an awkward case: too avant-garde and too experimental, even for the late fifties. It was not until the Moscow journal *Dekorativnoe iskusstvo SSSR* (1962:7–8) had published a favorable article by L. Pazhitnov that interest in the Bauhaus could also gather speed in the DDR. And a year later the article was published in brochure form in German, entitled *Das schöpferische Erbe des Bauhauses 1919–1933* (The fruitful legacy of the Bauhaus). Only then could there be any talk of restoring Gropius's famous building in Dessau, dilapidated and maltreated from the 1930s onward. At its official reopening in 1976, however, it ranked as one of the great historic buildings of the DDR.

When Socialist Realism was introduced, there could be cases—as, for example, with Ulica Krucza in Warsaw—of "realistic" forms being added at the last minute to the finished drawings of facades. Now there were many instances of the opposite happening. Projects already under construction were simplified and undressed. Detailing was dispensed with, sculptural decorations originally planned were never installed. Phases of construction that had not yet started were canceled, sometimes being replanned, but for the most part leaving just an empty space. There were very many projects for groups of buildings of which only fragments materialized. And the buildings that weren't completed were never integrated with their surroundings as intended. The magnificent main facade of the Ministry of Agriculture in Warsaw, built between 1951 and 1955, overlooks a back street and a demolition site.

Sometimes both the introduction and the abolition of Socialist Realism are illustrated by one and the same complex, as for example with the Institute of Technology in Budapest. Here one sees three phases in a single building: the early postwar period, Socialist Realism, and the de-Stalinization period.

Not all simplifications from the late 1950s are what they appear to be, however. Let us consider the example of the Bucharest radio station building, completed in 1960 (Figs. 231, 232). Compared with a project published in 1952, it looks exactly like the simplification of a detailed, sumptuous building in the spirit of Socialist Realism. So it seems at first, but is this really the case? The additive grouping of the volumes and the curved shapes—for example, those of the portico— do not tally with the aesthetic of Socialist Realism. The explanation must be that the first project is really the second, an attempt by the architects to adapt a Formalist project to a new aesthetic. That was

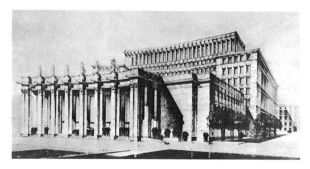

difficult, but it was all the easier afterward, during the late 1950s, to revert to the original project. That is how quickly the tide could turn in Eastern Europe during the 1950s.

The official breakthrough of a new Romanian architecture came with the Sala Palatului, the Palace Hall, adjoining the Palace of the Republic (the former Royal Palace; Fig. 233). Designed in 1958, it was completed in fifteen months, in time for the 8th Party Congress in June 1960. A squat metal dome surmounts an auditorium with seating for 3,100; modern vocabulary is employed without any historical or national associations. The main architect was the same Horia Maicu who had designed Casa Scînteii. It was typical of both the Soviet Union and the people's democracies that the architects were blamed collectively

231, 232 Bucharest radio station building. Left: Design by Joakim Beral, Leon Garcia, and Tiberiu and Mihai Ricci, published 1952; revision of an earlier, Modernist project. Right: The building as completed in 1960, after the "exaggerations" had been cleared away.

233 Sala Palatului, Bucharest, an addition to the former Royal Palace, intended for Party congresses. Architects: Horia Maicu, Tiberiu Ricci, and Ignatz Şerban; built 1960.

234, 235 Dresden,
Verkehrshochschule (College of
Communications) by Richard Paulick,
1954–62.

for what had happened but, as individuals, were allowed to go on working to new guidelines.

Lastly, here are four examples from Dresden, examples illustrating the road away from Socialist Realism and also illustrating the 1960s, which, before long, were to stand out as the absolute antithesis of that doctrine.

Our first example is the Verkehrshochschule (the College of Communications), designed by Richard Paulick. This building had a long gestation period, from planning in 1954 until completion in 1962. The first enfilades to be built betray distinct elements of local, Baroque tradition (Fig. 234). By contrast, everything is simplified in the nine-story main building, with its cladding of sandstone and pale ceramic tiles (Fig. 235). No balustrades or acroteria, as originally planned, no arched windows on the ground floor, no rhythmic repetitions, and hardly any decor. And yet the main building too is distinctly rooted in the Traditionalism of Socialist Realism, as witness

236 Dresden, Grunaer Strasse: two apartment buildings, one from the 1950s (right) and one from the 1960s (left).

the verticals of the facade, the proportions and profile surrounds of the windows, and the projecting entrance.

The second example comes from Grunaer Strasse, not far away from Pirnaischer Platz, and here we can see the contrast in housing construction between the fifties and sixties. On the right, a five-story brick building from the 1950s, instancing the everyday version of Socialist Realism; on the left, a fourteen-story complex of prefabricated concrete elements, built in 1966 (Fig. 236). In all six countries, gigantic apartment blocks like this came to typify the 1960s and 1970s. Housing production was rationalized and output rose, although, compared with the contemporary Million Homes program in Sweden, results were modest, both qualitatively speaking and in relation to national population.

The third example from Dresden is the new Palace of Culture (Figs. 237, 238). Instead of the imaginatively designed tower block intended as the end point of an Altmarkt rebuilt in Baroque style (see Fig. 76), what materialized toward the end of the 1960s was a low, rectangular box with glazed facades. From one extreme to another. A building that could just as well have been in the West, if it had not been for the 30-meter-long monumental device on one side of it, *The Path of the Red Flag*—from Marx and Engels to Walter Ulbricht and the DDR of the 1960s (Fig. 239). In the top right corner one reads: WIR SIND DIE SIEGER DER GESCHICHTE (We are the victors of history). It is a message that architecture was no longer called upon to transmit.

237, 238 Left: Palace of Culture, Dresden, opened in 1969. Architects: Leopold Wiel, Wolfgang Hänsch, and Herbert Löschau. Right: Design for the same plot by Herbert Schneider, 1953.

239 *The Path of the Red Flag,* monumental depiction on the west front of the Dresden Palace of Culture, 1969. Stained glass on concrete; collective work, headed by Gerhard Bondzin.

In the fourth and final example we see the new center of Dresden from the 1960s, Prager Strasse, near the Hauptbahnhof (Fig. 240). Construction work was still in progress when our picture was taken. For example, we do not see the Kosmos cinema, a big round building at the far end of the street. In the background we glimpse the Altmarkt and the new Palace of Culture. There are several hotels here and numerous shops, as in Western city centers, not so many offices but all the more flats. A pedestrianized street, dominated by the horizontals and plain facades of Modernism. The showpiece of the socialist consumer society, but useless for real parades. The architecture has been secularized, and once again it is pictorial art that

must carry the ideological message. To mark the twentieth anniversary, in 1969, of the foundation of the DDR, a 7-meter-high granite monument was unveiled in front of the Hauptbahnhof: Lenin together with a worker and a soldier of the Red Army.

240 Dresden, Prager Strasse from the Hauptbahnhof, looking toward the Altmarkt. Urban plan by Peter Sniegon, Kurt Leucht et al. Photograph taken c. 1969.

How the Other Side Built—Interbau in West Berlin

Well then, how did they build in the West? The answer to that would include the reconstruction of ruined cities like Cologne and Hanover, Le Havre and Rotterdam. It would include the way in which the architects related to tradition, the influence of Scandinavia during the early postwar years, the breakthrough of Modernism in the USA, and the important role played by the seminal figures of the interwar years: Walter Gropius, Ludwig Mies van der Rohe, Le Corbusier, and Frank Lloyd Wright. Further, it would include England's new towns and the large new buildings for the UN and Unesco, which in spite of the supranational character of those organizations turned out to be prominent examples of Western architecture. All this and much more besides. But an answer so exhaustive is outside the scope of this book. We will focus instead on West Berlin and its architectural response to the principles of Socialist Realism.

As was already remarked by way of introduction, the Cold War was not symmetrical. Its impact on architecture was much weaker in the West than in the East, and it was by no means ubiquitous. But, Socialist Realism reinforced the rejection of tradition, a rejection already existing after the collapse of the right-wing dictatorships. This was particularly apparent in West Berlin.

Berlin was the capital city of the Cold War. This was where the two systems confronted and denounced one another. To begin with, the confrontation was military and political. But after the Berlin blockade of 1948–49 it was above all ideological, visible in every field of cultural and political life, not least in architecture. The confrontation was visible, too, in urban planning, with both sides planning for a Berlin to be the capital of a reunited Germany, but on two quite different premises.

In his speech at the foundation-laying ceremony for Lange Strasse in Rostock, in January 1953, Ulbricht had spoken of the admi-

XII

ration that Stalinallee would arouse in visitors from West Germany. It would show them a *German* architecture, building that was no longer being "modeled on American crates and boxes." Expressions like this caused not a ripple of concern in the West, where Stalinallee was always presented as a cautionary example of what could happen to architecture. On the contrary, the new show street was thought of as a victory on points for the West—a false front, decked out in borrowed historical devices! The opportunity was too good to be missed, and while Stalinallee grew up in a spirit of socialist competition, plans began to take shape on the Western side for a big architectural countermanifestation.

In 1953 the West Berlin Senate decided to hold an international exhibition of architecture, modeled on the famous interwar exhibitions arranged by the Deutscher Werkbund, especially that in Stuttgart in 1927. Once again, the architects invited were to make individual contributions to what, after the exhibition, would become an ordinary housing estate. The exhibition was first scheduled for 1956, but this proved excessively optimistic.

Interbau opened in July 1957 (Fig. 241). All but two of the new buildings were in the Hansaviertel, at the western edge of the Tiergarten. They were deployed in accordance with a detailed development plan that had a great deal in common with Scharoun's "Stadtlandschaft," in particular the free grouping of volumes, the intermingling of different types of building, buildings in the park instead of buildings on a street, a complete rejection of the stone city of Berlin. The architects taking part included Alvar Aalto, van den Broek and Bakema, Egon Eiermann, Walter Gropius, Arne Jacobsen, and Oskar Niemeyer. The Hansaviertel also featured the exhibition *Die Stadt von Morgen* (The City of Tomorrow). At the other end of the Tiergarten was the Kongresshalle, the American contribution. Entirely on its own, near the Olympic Stadium, was Le Corbusier's housing complex, "Unité d'habitation type Berlin." Seventeen stories high and 135 meters long, it was too large for the real exhibition site.

In the exhibition catalogue, Theodor Heuss, President of West Germany, wrote that the Hansaviertel was a document of the mid-twentieth century and thoroughly adapted to the demands of the future. As an old Werkbund adherent, he was particularly gratified that the age of historicism was past: "Hankering for *tradition* elicits no response." The new Germany would be modern. The Federal Chancellor, Konrad Adenauer, expressed himself in few words: The ideas of the exhibition would "radiate both westward and eastward." On the other hand, Otto Suhr, West Berlin's Bürgermeister, was more explicit:

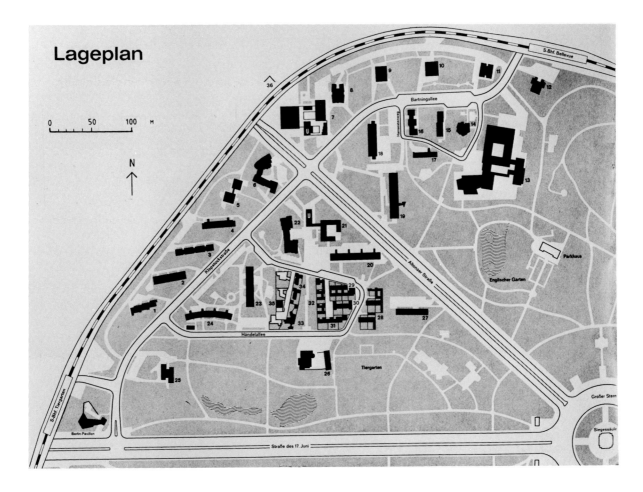

Lageplan

0   50   100 M

N ↑

241 West Berlin, Interbau 1957. Plan of Hansaviertel: no. 9, a sixteen-story tower block by van den Broek and Bakema; nos. 18, 19, 22, and 24 are apartment blocks of seven to nine stories by, respectively, Eiermann, Niemeyer, Aalto, and Gropius (TAC); no. 29, atrium building by Arne Jacobsen. Off the plan, nearly one km farther east, is the American Congress Hall.

Barely a kilometer away from INTERBAU there begins the other Berlin, another world, separated from us but still belonging to us. The new buildings, from now on, extend toward that boundary and will prove their powers of attraction.

The political rhetoric was more discreet than the opponent's, but it was clear enough. What did the buildings look like? Let's take a closer look at two of them: Gropius's apartment building and the American Congress Hall.

Interbau was primarily a housing exhibition, and this in itself was rather polemical: The focus of attention now was on housing construction, not on architecture as art or as symbol. But at the same time, in the spirit of 1950s Modernism, aesthetic variety was one of the themes of the exhibition.

The building by Walter Gropius—or rather by TAC, a collective

242, 243 West Berlin, Hansaviertel, apartment block by Walter Gropius (TAC), 1957. South elevation and ground plan.

practice founded by Gropius in the USA—was an eight-story building with an entrance floor and a rooftop story surmounting part of the building (Figs. 242, 243). On each floor there were eight apartments of three and a half rooms and a kitchen each. The stairwells projected from the slightly curved main volume of the building. The load-bearing structure was a reinforced concrete skeleton.

The consistently high standard of the apartments posed an aesthetic problem with which Western architects were familiar but which, as yet, was fairly unknown to their colleagues in the East: the monotony caused by the large number of balconies. Gropius and his associates tried to avoid the ordinary, vertical stacks by grouping the balconies in fours (two by two), except at the sides, where instead they were made to face outward.

As far as the architects of Socialist Realism were concerned, problems of this kind simply did not exist. As we have already seen from the examples of Dimitrovgrad and Sztálinváros, they could allow the facade composition to decide the number and positioning of balconies. In the West the opposite applied, but Interbau was intended to show that, even with a Modernist aesthetic and equality of housing standards, there was abundant scope for variety. This was above all apparent from the ground plans. These—as, for example, in Alvar Aalto's big apartment building—displayed an ingenuity to which the East had no counterpart (Figs. 244, 245).

The Congress Hall was the gift of the USA to West Berlin (Fig. 246, see Fig. 248). It was built in the eastern part of the Tiergarten, not far from the sectorial boundary, the Brandenburg Gate, and the gutted Reichstag building. It contained a theater, an exhibition hall, conference facilities, a restaurant, and, above all, an auditorium seating 1,200. The developer was the Benjamin Franklin Foundation, especially formed for the purpose. The moving spirit behind the project was Eleanor Dulles, responsible for Berlin affairs at the US State Department and sister of the Secretary of State, John Foster Dulles. The architect, Hugh Stubbins, had started as an assistant of Walter Gropius's at Harvard, but his architecture was more inspired by Marcel Breuer, who had also been at Harvard for some time.

The building was unusual, spectacularly modern. Technically it was an advanced structure of concrete, steel, and glass. The roof over the auditorium was at one and the same time a shell and suspension structure, convex on its longitudinal axis and concave in the lateral direction. And the aesthetic impression was directly dependent on the structure: not a building resting on foundations but something suspended that has just landed or is on the point of taking off. In the evening, although the two concrete arcs reached only 18 meters above ground level, the building was visible from a long way off.

And from this impression there emanated what were no small symbolic pretensions. In the rhetorical language accompanying the project from its first conception to the weeks around its official opening at the end of September 1957, the Congress Hall was a symbol of freedom of speech and of American determination on the question of Berlin, "a beacon toward the East" and "an expression of today."

Boldness and modernity were the symbolic assets of the American contribution. And so self-evident did this seem that hardly anybody noticed, as Barbara Miller Lane has pointed out, that it was actually the first *official* occasion on which the USA had made radical Modernism its own.

Insofar as the Congress Hall reached a body of opinion in East Berlin and the DDR, and insofar as it was looked on as architecture,

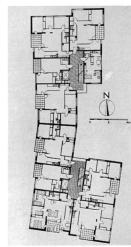

244, 245 West Berlin, Hansaviertel, apartment block by Alvar Aalto, 1957. West elevation and ground plan.

246 West Berlin, Tiergarten, American Congress Hall, designed by Hugh A. Stubbins and built for Interbau 1957.

247 West Berlin, *Luftbrückendenkmal* (Airlift Monument) at Tempelhof Airport, by Eduard Ludwig, unveiled 1951. Photograph taken in 1980.

there was an obvious candidate for comparison: the Deutsche Sporthalle from 1951 (see Fig. 121). That too was built for a big international event, had many functions, and, despite its name, could be applied to most purposes. It too had a symbolic and political significance. And it was also designed by a former associate of Gropius's. But there the similarity ended. The traditional vocabulary and iconography of the Deutsche Sporthalle lent additional emphasis to the modernity of the Congress Hall.

Stalinallee had its antithesis in the Hansaviertel, the Deutsche Sporthalle had its in the Congress Hall. And, just as the Treptow Monument in East Berlin commemorated "liberation from fascism" (see Figs. 19, 20), West Berlin had its memorial to "delivery from communism"—the *Luftbrückendenkmal* outside the Tempelhof Airport (Fig. 247).

This monument was designed by the architect Eduard Ludwig, who was awarded the brief following a competition, and it was erected in 1951 in memory of the allied airlift of 1948–49, which delivered West Berlin from the Soviet blockade and was the biggest Western success in the Cold War. The monument is a concrete arc, 20 meters high and slightly curved toward the west. Three ribs emerge from the arc, alluding to the three air corridors—Hamburg, Hanover, and Frankfurt am Main—which, during the blockade, were West Berlin's only links with the Western world. It is a kind of abstract victory monument, in the aesthetic tradition of the Bauhaus, based on the principle of "less is more."

Here, then, we have no aircraft or pilots, and no pent-up, famished Berliners. Still less do we see General Lucius Clay, the famous organizer of the airlift, and there is only a very subdued inscription to tell us what the monument is all about. From a Western European point of view in 1951, this was an elegant, sophisticated solution to the task. From an Eastern European point of view, it was symptomatic of the "lack of ideas and the Formalism" of Western art, of its lack of content, its denial of traditions.

This type of design was to be very much in vogue at the time of the Soviet space achievements in the 1960s, but that is quite another story (compare, for example, the big space monument outside VDNKh in Moscow of 1965).

The overt trial of strength in Berlin, however, was to end abruptly. It was too unfavorable for the DDR. On 13 August 1961, work began on building the Wall, "the antifascist rampart" as it was called by Walter Ulbricht and *Neues Deutschland*. From a practical political point of view, the Wall was to be a success for the DDR, but it was a costly one in terms of ideological prestige.

At the beginning of November that same year, Stalin's remains were moved out of the Lenin Mausoleum in Red Square. The statues of Stalin were taken down and Stalin names were done away with, in East Berlin as elsewhere. Stalinallee now came to be called Karl-Marx-Allee, and there was no longer a statue of Stalin to be seen outside the Deutsche Sporthalle. It looked like an escalation of the de-Stalinization process, but it was really the terminal point.

Stalin had been filed away and in future would not even be mentioned in the DDR, except by recalcitrants like Wolf Biermann, in his magnificent, cheerfully satirical couplet of 1973: "Acht Argumente für die Beibehaltung des Namens 'Stalinallee' für die Stalinallee" (Eight arguments in favor of Stalinallee continuing to be called Stalinallee).

Not only the Cold War but the thaw too was a thing of the past. West Berlin was no longer accessible to visitors from the East. And the ideological monument that attracted Western tourists was no longer Stalinallee and the Hansaviertel but the Wall. Stalinallee was superseded by Checkpoint Charlie.

The Deutsche Sporthalle was demolished in 1971, after only twenty years. It had been built in great haste and was no longer in keeping with the DDR's would-be image of a *modern* state. The dawning age of blue-jeans socialism did not know of any

248 American Congress Hall after its collapse, May 1980.

Vergangenheitsbewältigung—mastery of the past. On the site formerly occupied by the Sporthalle, a modern apartment block was built that did not fit in at all well with the socialist Classicism of its surroundings. And in a biography of Paulick, published in 1975, the Sporthalle is recalled only on account of its rapid completion, in 119 days.

The Congress Hall also came to be out-of-date, both architecturally and as a political symbol. In May 1980, one of the two concrete arches supporting the roof collapsed (Fig. 248, see Fig. 246). A young generation of West Berliners, as tired of Functionalism as they were of the Cold War, took a symbolic view of the event, which they celebrated with pamphlets and with picture postcards of the mishap. Not without an element of *Schadenfreude.* But the West Berlin Senate and the government in Bonn, no less aware of the symbolic implications, decided that the Congress Hall would be restored.

Architecture and Ideology: Discussion and Conclusion

In this final chapter, we will try to draw some conclusions on the subject of architecture and politics—on the relationship between architectural form and political ideology.

I. Three Comparisons

Comparisons are our best way of characterizing architecture, and where Socialist Realism in the people's democracies is concerned, there are two obvious comparisons to make: one with Modernism in the West, and the other with Socialist Realism in the Soviet Union. These were also the comparisons made by contemporaries. There is a third comparison—inevitable as soon as we touch on the theme of architecture and politics—a comparison with the architecture of Nazi Germany.

The Comparison with Modernism

For the reader who has got this far, it is probably needless to point out the differences between Socialist Realism and Modernism. They have been pointed out many times in the previous pages, and so perhaps it will suffice, once more, to recall the basic concepts presented in Chapter Three, "The Example of the Soviet Union." Progressing from small to large, they were as follows:

> ornament
> architectural detail
> facade
> street
> square
> block
> ensemble
> silhouette
> city as an artistic entity

These concepts also played an important role in the people's democracies, in practically all writings on Socialist Realism, but unlike many other ingredients of propaganda they did not remain on paper. They left their imprint on architecture. We can use them to describe what was built in Eastern Europe. And we can use their absence to describe what was built in the West, or at least, most of it. It is worth stressing that the study of Socialist Realism also sharpens our perception of Modernism.

Socialist Realism can be characterized correspondingly through the absence of positive qualities of Modernism: the derivation of form from material, from structure and technology, and from function. When Modernist qualities like these were mentioned in the East, they were called *fetishism* for material, for technology, and so on. Fetishism—in other words, a kind of superstition.

Descriptions and comparisons in these terms leave a good deal unsaid, however. The following six pairs of opposites—in the spirit of Wölfflin—focus attention on another side of the difference between Socialist Realism and Modernism.

diversity of form	simplification of form
plasticity	plainness of surfaces
verticality	horizontality
symmetry/axiality	asymmetry/repetition
hierarchy of forms	equalization of forms
hierarchy of functions	equalization of functions

As with nearly every attempt to generalize about big aesthetic questions, the well-informed student can find both borderline cases and exceptions, but we are talking here about the main characteristics of the opposing trends in architecture during the Cold War, and what counts is not the individual concepts but the comparison and antithesis between them.

The antithesis between *diversity of form* and *simplification of form* pinpoints perhaps the most striking difference and coincides partly with the next pair of opposites, *plasticity* versus *plainness of surfaces. Verticality* versus *horizontality* can be instanced right across the board, from window geometry to high-rise buildings (for in Modernism even the tower blocks had a horizontal emphasis). The antithesis between *symmetry/axiality* and *asymmetry/repetition* can also be applied from part to whole, from windows and portals to facades, ground plans, and detailed development plans. Another, more abstract way of expressing the same relationship was the antithesis

249 The aesthetic of Socialist Realism as instanced in *Deutsche Architektur*, 1952: facade from Mozhaiskoe Chaussé, Moscow, 1940.

between *hierarchy of forms* and *equalization of forms*. This can be used in order, among many other things, to describe vertical articulation: the clear hierarchical distinction made by Socialist Realism among different stories (often using a Classical tripartite division) and, by contrast, the frequently identical nature of stories in the case of Modernism. And so to our last pair of opposites: *hierarchy of functions* versus *equalization of functions*. The reference here is to differ-

250 The negative, Modernist antithesis according to *Deutsche Architektur:* Apartments in Weissenhofsiedlung, Stuttgart, 1927, by Ludwig Mies van der Rohe.

ence/equality of status among the rooms in a building or the buildings in a section of town, but also to the hierarchy/equalization of building types described in Chapter Five, "Socialist Content."

In the second issue of *Deutsche Architektur* for 1952, Kurt Liebknecht wrote about the importance of window proportions in architecture. In *Neues Deutschland* of 20 March that year, with reference to Stalinallee, he had brought up the question of the tall or broad window ("Hohes oder breites Fenster?"), and now he returned to the subject. The answer, of course, was a forgone conclusion, but not everybody had realized as much: For facades and interiors alike, vertical window shapes alone were admissible. The article had just two illustrations, in which Liebknecht contrasted the traditions of Socialist Realism and Modernism: in one picture, part of the facade of a seven-story building in Mozhaiskoe Chaussé, Moscow, built in 1940 and designed by architects A. M. Alkhasov and A. V. Mezer (Fig. 249); in the other picture, Mies van der Rohe's famous 1927 apartment building in Stuttgart (Fig. 250). These two examples do more than illustrate differences of window proportions, they instance *all* the pairs of opposites quoted above.

This was the way things ought to be—a hard and fast boundary against Modernism—but it was by no means always the case. In practice, aside from the big showcase projects, architecture in the people's democracies was often a matter of compromise.

The Comparison with Soviet Architecture

"The example of the Soviet Union" was paramount and unquestioned. It was indeed emulated, and from the end of the 1940s, it set the principal course of development for architecture in the people's democracies. Anything else would have been out of the question, but this is not to say that architecture in the people's democracies copied that of the Soviet Union. There were major differences between the two, almost as important as the similarities.

The clearest way of describing the differences is by reverting to the basic concepts and qualities we have just mentioned. All of them were *truer* of the Soviet Union than of the people's democracies. That which in the Soviet Union was a full-fledged academic architecture was matched in the people's democracies by a traditional architecture of a simpler kind. Viewed from the West—if any observers there had gone to the trouble of looking at the differences—it was more discreet, more moderate. Viewed from the East it was more modest, sometimes excessively modest, bordering on the Cosmopolitan and the humble.

There were various reasons for this, some of them intentional, others not. First, just as there was a hierarchy of forms and of building types, so there was a hierarchy of cities and states, and here again there were old notions that lived on in the body of Socialist Realism. Perhaps they were not refuted by the Modernists, but on the other hand they were not ascribed any formative significance, over and above that dictated by practical function.

Moscow towered high above all other cities, followed by Leningrad and then by Berlin—that is, the Berlin destined to become the capital of a united, socialist Germany, the Berlin for which Stalinallee was constructed. Next came Warsaw and the other capital cities of the people's democracies, followed by Kiev and the other capitals of the Soviet republics. *Within* the DDR, Berlin was followed by the four cities granted privileged positions in *das nationale Aufbauprogramm:* Dresden, Leipzig, Magdeburg, and Rostock. Much the same applied to Poland; after Warsaw and (undamaged) Cracow came Gdańsk, Poznań, and Wrocław. We are not concerned here with the obvious effects of the size of each city or with the reconstruction of what had been destroyed. Every city had its own rank, and that rank had to be made manifest by architects and urban planners. The same went for the states. First came the Soviet Union, in a class of its own, followed, at a respectful distance, by the people's democracies. Here, then, we have one cause of the differences.

A second cause has already been closely considered: Within the boundaries of Socialist Realism, the people's democracies were to develop an architecture of their own. They were to look to the Polish, the Hungarian, and so on, just as the non-Russian Soviet republics looked to the Georgian, the Armenian, and the other national traditions. And the traditions referred to in the people's democracies were, as it happened, very often more restrained than the corresponding traditions of the Soviet Union. Schinkel, for example, was a far cry from Carlo Rossi, his contemporary in St. Petersburg.

Then there was a third cause: The architects of the people's democracies were ten or fifteen years behind their Soviet colleagues in assimilating Socialist Realism. They were well on the way, but still had some distance to go. This argument often served as an excuse, because it was hard to spot the borderline between involuntary inertia and the deliberate resistance constituting a fourth cause. Even retrospectively, it is not easy to say where the line should be drawn. The resistance that, at the time, it was so perilous to mention lent itself all the more readily to self-commendation after the event.

The Comparison with the Architecture of Nazi Germany.

Mention of this comparison often produces two irreconcilable standpoints. On the one hand we have those who underline the similarities and seek to show that Socialist Realism and Nazi architecture were one and the same thing. On the other hand, we have those who reject or play down the comparison: It is absurd—the most one can find is ostensible similarities!

The genesis of this comparison is easily pinpointed. It must have come at the 1937 Paris Exposition, when the Soviet and German pavilions—designed, respectively, by Boris Iofan and Albert Speer—stood in a dramatic confrontation (Figs. 251, 252). Both were overwhelming, and with their national coats of arms and heroically allegorical figures, both were immensely symbolic. Erected only for the summer, they reiterated the aspiration of old architecture to defy the passage of time. They were far removed from the rationalist, technical character of German and Russian Modernism as it was just a few years earlier.

But there were also differences between them. Speer's pavilion, although more influenced by historical forms than its opposite num-

251, 252 The 1937 Paris Exposition. Left: Soviet pavilion, by Boris Iofan, surmounted by the sculpture *Worker and Kolkhoz Woman* (bearing hammer and sickle, respectively) by Vera Mukhina. Right: German pavilion by Albert Speer, surmounted by the German eagle and swastika.

ber, also came closer to Modernism. It had a simplicity of form and tastefulness that—let the ideologists on either side argue as they may—was akin to German Functionalism. Iofan's pavilion, by contrast, with its pronounced verticality, its silhouette effect, its dynamism (when viewed from the side), and its disproportion between building and surmounting sculpture, embodied a different, more immoderate aesthetic, in this particular case perhaps best described as residual Futurism about to be corralled by emergent Soviet Classicism.

During the years that followed, projects and buildings in Nazi Germany grew both larger and more grandiloquent, but still with the same austere, reticent Classicism as in Paris in 1937. This was the tradition of Prussian Classicism, from Schinkel and Gilly, and ultimately from ancient Greece. But the projects of the war years, at least in

Berlin, also presented a different tendency, a kind of New Baroque, a victory architecture in preparation for the triumph that never came.

Soviet architecture changed more. And instead of coming to an end in 1945 it went on developing. It became more and more academic, drawing more and more heavily on the traditional repertoire of architecture. And the tradition thus drawn on was of a different kind from the Prusso-Greek. In its diversity of form, its predilection for the exaggerated and sumptuous, the new Soviet architecture was rooted in Russian Classicism of the eighteenth and early nineteenth centuries, of the victorious year of 1812 and the ensuing period. And if, here again, one was reminded of the ancient world, allusions to Classical Greece were more the exception than the rule, the main emphasis being on the elaborate architecture of Hellenism and the Roman Empire. In the Soviet Union the architecture of victory came to be *realized*.

What really counts, then: the similarities or the dissimilarities between the architecture of Nazi Germany and that of Socialist Realism? Comparing the two as objectively as possible, the answer will depend on how detailed a comparison we make. If our comparison focuses on the deviation from Modernism, we will find great similarities. Most of the basic concepts of Socialist Realism—the detail, the facade, the street, etc.—were also valid for the architecture of Hitler's Germany. Things become more difficult, however, if the comparison is taken one step farther. The pairs of opposites expressing the differences between Socialist Realism and Modernism in the West are less helpful when we try to pin down Nazi architecture. That architecture, it is true, is every bit as subject as Socialist Realism is to the canons of symmetry and axiality. But at the same time, and in spite of the traditional nature of its architectural themes, it was characterized by an aesthetic of simplicity and repetition that came close to Modernism and that the advocates of Socialist Realism thought of as half-starved.

If we now also take into account the difference between Soviet architecture and the architecture of the people's democracies, the cases of Traditionalist architecture we are now referring to can be related *schematically* to Modernism in the following way: Farthest removed from Modernism is the Socialist Realism of the Soviet Union, then comes the Socialist Realism of the people's democracies, and one more step closer to Modernism we have the architecture of the Nazi era.

In many people's minds, observations like this are precluded by their ideological consequences, by the notion that they also imply something about the political ideology of the different patrons. But is the relationship between architecture and political ideology that simple? Can ideology be deduced from form? Let us now consider this question.

II. Alternative Interpretations

Three Views of Socialist Realism

The phenomenon in the history of twentieth-century architecture known as Socialist Realism has been interpreted as follows:

1. *Socialist Realism is the consistent, necessary, and sole expression of the socialist ideology.*

This was the official interpretation in the Soviet Union and the people's democracies during the years when Socialist Realism was the architectural style *de rigueur.* Above all, one finds it in a large number of magazine articles from the early 1950s, for example, in the first year's issues of *Deutsche Architektur,* published by the Deutsche Bauakademie in the DDR.

Also part of this interpretation is the converse, namely, that Modernism is the consistent expression of capitalist, bourgeois society, the architecture of imperialism. This interpretation lapsed after the mid-1950s, but it crops up in practically all the source materials.

2. *Socialist Realism is the expression of a totalitarian social structure and an anachronism—a counterpart of Lysenko's theory in biology.*

This interpretation has been and remains the usual one in Western Europe and the USA, where it has been so axiomatic that closer argument has for the most part been dispensed with. Mostly it has been manifested in derogatory passing mentions, known also to those who are otherwise uninterested in architecture: *Zuckerbäckerarchitektur* in German, and *wedding-cake architecture* in English. This phraseology ties in with the well-established criticism of nineteenth-century eclecticism, and there has been no risk of anyone missing the point: bad taste. Socialist Realism is vulgar and anachronistic. Its vocabulary belongs to the past, to authoritarian regimes of the past. It was just as badly out of step with the times as was Lysenko's biology.

Here again, it is important to note the converse message: Modernism is the consistent expression of modern, democratic society.

3. *Socialist Realism is the heir of the Classical tradition in architecture and implies a critique of Modernism.*

This third interpretation was at long last, toward the end of the 1970s, added to the first two, which confronted one another as the architectural standpoints of the Cold War.

This third interpretation is no compromise, however. It stands aside from the ideological conflict. It emanates from the growing criticism of Modernism during the sixties and seventies, above all by younger architects and architectural historians in Western Europe and the USA.

In both the previous interpretations, ideology has been the prime consideration. Here, suddenly, it is architecture. But it is easy to see that, in all three cases, we are dealing not so much with historical explanations as with various attempts at self-justification.

Three Diagrams

The long essay of Max Raphael, "Das Sowjetpalais. Eine marxistische Kritik an einer reaktionären Architektur," written in 1934 but not published until 1976, begins with a key sentence: "When the first works of the so-called functional architecture appeared, people soon agreed that they were communist."

The view that Raphael reproduces here of the relationship between architectural form and political ideology was one that he shared, though not uncritically. Schematically it can be depicted with the figure already presented in our introduction, with Aesthetics on the vertical axis and Politics on the horizontal, and with a dashed diagonal marking the covariation of the two (Diagram A).

In other words, the more modern, the farther left; and the more traditional, the farther right. And conversely: the farther left, the more modern; and the farther right, the more traditional. This still appeared to make sense at the beginning of the 1930s. Modernism and socialism pointed in the same direction. Everything was as it should be in the world picture of the radical intelligentsia. And before long, the architecture of National Socialism was to be chalked up as further confirmation.

But at the same time there took place the changes in the architecture of the Soviet Union that were the direct occasion of Raphael's essay. The competition for the Palace of the Soviets showed that the Modernists had now been thrust aside, while the Classicists and the Academic architects, who had never admitted defeat, were once more in the ascendant. The very title of Raphael's essay shows what he thinks of their architecture: It was *reactionary*.

What was one to make of this change? Had the Soviet Union also turned reactionary, or was the current idea of the relation between ideology and architecture misguided?

Neither was true, as Raphael saw it. The Soviet Union's desertion of Modernism was a deviation that could be put down to an

aesthetic
MODERNISM

political
LEFT

political
RIGHT

aesthetic
TRADITIONALISM

Diagram A

extreme political situation. Raphael was not disposed to give up the idea of the connection between the left and Modernism, and in this he was typical of the radical intelligentsia during the interwar years, if not during the whole of the present century. In the Soviet Union, on the other hand, a new theory was formulated on the relationship between ideology and architecture. That theory is illustrated, schematically, in the second diagram (Diagram C).

The dashed diagonal makes all the difference between this figure and the preceding one. Everything has changed. This time it is the left that covaries with Traditionalism, the right with Modernism. Socialism is the rightful heir of tradition!

In the Soviet Union itself, there was no lack of fertile soil for this kind of approach. But to Western friends and sympathizers of the Soviet Union it was quite unintelligible. They were prepared to go to great lengths in their understanding of political changes in the Soviet Union during the 1930s, but eclectic architecture was just too much.

Even in the West, though, the new Soviet architecture was to engender a new theory on the connection between architecture and ideology. The traditional political right-left scale no longer appeared capable of explaining variations in architecture. Instead it was the degree of democracy or dictatorship, quite irrespective of the left and right. Modernism was antitotalitarian.

This gives us a third schematic figure, with two new entities on the horizontal axis (Diagram D). In the West during the Cold War, this was the generally endorsed view of the connection between architecture and ideology. Tradition had been extolled in Hitler's Germany and to some extent in Mussolini's Italy as well. It was all the more important in Stalin's Soviet Union and in the people's democracies. The conclusion seemed obvious: Classicism is a *style belonging to dictatorship.* This argument, in its most simplistic application, could be made to imply that symmetry was undemocratic. This solves the difficulty presented by Socialist Realism to Raphael and his fellows—at the price of a complete reevaluation of the Soviet Union. But there were fresh difficulties lurking around the corner.

When, during the second half of the 1950s, the Soviet Union quickly and resolutely abolished Socialist Realism and developed a new architecture based on Modernism, what did this mean? The change coincided with the abolition of the cult of personality, but not really with any emergence of democracy. The system of government under Khrushchev was the same as it had been under Stalin.

To all this were added a growing number of right-wing dictatorships, blithely patronizing modern architecture and showing not the slightest interest in traditional architecture.

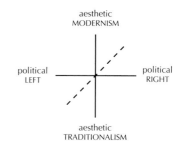

Diagram C

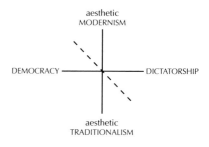

Diagram D

But for all the differences between our three figures, there is a fundamental similarity between them. They all presuppose that political ideology can be discerned in architecture.

Three German Condemnations

Now for some examples, chosen so as to be reasonably comparable with each other. They are three excerpts from three different German states, one from 1943 and two from 1954. All of them formulate the official view of the Traditionalism-Modernism antithesis in architecture, which they demonstrate by a critique of the architecture of the political opponent.

First, an excerpt from an anthology published in 1943 by Deutsche Institut für Aussenpolitische Forschung, with a preface by Foreign Minister Joachim von Ribbentrop: *Europa. Handbuch der politischen, wirtschaftlichen und kulturellen Entwicklung des neuen Europa* (Europe. Handbook for the political, economic, and cultural development of the new Europe). In the essay on architecture—"So baut Europa" (So builds Europe) by Wilhelm Lotz—we find the following argument concerning the origins of Functionalism:

> Compared with the great European architectural tradition, the movement of the years between World War I and our present fight for the freedom of Germany and Europe will at some future time be considered a mere episode, a movement that rejected any interest in style and tried to develop new architectural forms exclusively from the requirements of materials and external technical functions. This movement began in the Netherlands and spread to Germany, where it is closely connected with the name of the Bauhaus in Dessau. It is significant that these attempts derived purely from theory, a theory whose basis is easily traced to materialism and Marxism. . . . The stronghold of this peculiar stylistic phenomenon was communist Russia.[1]

---

[1] Gegenüber dieser grossen baukünsterischen Tradition Europas wird es später einmal wie eine Episode empfunden werden, dass in den Jahren zwischen dem Weltkrieg und dem derzeitigen Kampf Deutschlands für seine und der europäischen Völker Freiheit sich eine Bewegung geltend machte, die jeden künstlerischen Stilwillen verneinte und die baulichen Formen nur aus den Bedingungen des Materials und den äusserlichen technischen Funktionen neu entwickeln wollte. Diese Bewegung enstand wohl zuerst in den Niederlanden und griff auf Deutschland über. Hier ist die Bewegung eng mit dem Namen des Dessauer Bauhauses verknüpft. Bezeichnend ist, dass die Bestrebungen rein von der Theorie ausgingen, einer Theorie, deren Grundlagen unschwer in dem Materialismus und Marxismus zu erkennen sind. . . . Die Hochburg für diese seltsame Stilerscheinung ist das kommunistische Russland gewesen.

Modern architecture, then, is a passing phase, because it is out of touch with tradition and because it denies that architecture is art. It originated, we are told, in the Netherlands, spreading to Germany, but the Soviet Union has been its main bastion. We also read that it rests on the foundations of materialist and Marxist theories.

It is, of course, the first of our three figures (see Diagram A) that applies to this excerpt: Modernism belongs to the left, and, in a Nazi perspective, this is something negative. The left and Modernism discredit one another. Nazi hesitancy over Functionalism was long past in 1943, at all events for architecture with symbolic pretensions.

But the excerpt begs a question: Had it escaped the notice of Germany in 1943 that the Soviet Union had long since jettisoned Modernism in favor of Socialist Realism? This is in fact hinted at farther on in the text, but only to be played down: The "cloak of Classicism" was mere camouflage. "Barbaric Formalism" was the true stance of Soviet architecture. That was the way it should be and so that was the way things were.

Second, we have an excerpt from the DDR, from *Handbuch für Architekten*, published in 1954 by the Bauakademie in Berlin. The architecture of the Federal Republic is characterized in the following terms:

> As in other capitalist countries, building is predominantly formalist and subordinated to the cosmopolitan ideology of American imperialism. This is why buildings look alike whatever their location, whether they are in West Germany, Italy, France, or America. The housing, banks, administration buildings, hotels, and stores in the form of shapeless boxes are an expression of the profit hunger of monopoly capitalism under American dominance. The obliteration of all national character continues relentlessly. This is evident as well in the destruction of valuable historical complexes. Thus architecture is replaced by mere construction.[2]

The architecture of West Germany, then, is typical of the

---

[2] Man baut vorwiegend, wie auch in anderen kapitalistischen Ländern, formalistisch und unterwirft sich so der kosmopolitischen Ideologie des amerikanischen Imperialismus. Deshalb sehen die Bauten einander ähnlich, gleich wo sie stehen, ob in Westdeutschland, Italien, Frankreich oder Amerika. Die Wohnbauten, Bank- und Verwaltungsgebäude, die Hotels und Warenhäuser in Gestalt unförmiger Kästen sind ein Ausdruck der Profitgier des Monopolkapitalismus unter amerikanischer Herrschaft. Die Zerstörung aller nationalen Eigenarten schreitet immer weiter fort. Das Zeigt sich auch deutlich in der Vernichtung wertvoller historischer Ensembles. So wird die Baukunst durch das Bauen schlechthin ersetzt.

capitalist countries and of American imperialism: it is "formalist" and "cosmopolitan." These are two pejorative synonyms of the adjectives, more familiar to Western ears, *Functionalist* and *Modernist*. Formalist means having no content over and above the practical purpose, devoid of ideological content. Cosmopolitan means international, devoid of national character. But it means more than that. Cosmopolitan had been a positive word meaning a citizen of the world, but in the epoch of "socialism in one country" the citizen of the world was a dubious person, a traitor to his country.

The buildings of West Germany resemble each other, regardless of their location. Whatever their function they look like "shapeless boxes." Standardization obliterates national cultures. The demolition of places of historic interest has the same effect—and in this way is a tool of imperialism. Standardization is also an expression of "the profit hunger of monopoly capitalism," which no longer affords scope for building as an art. All that remains is "mere construction."

This is an interpretation based on analogy and association. International form is associated with imperialism, simplification of form with profit hunger, artlessness with capitalism.

Absence of tradition, artlessness, lack of ideas—this is partly the same characterization of Modernism as in the previous instance, but it is differently interpreted. This time it is applied, not to Marxism and the Soviet Union but to capitalism, imperialism and the USA.

Third, we consider this passage, from a handbook entitled *SBZ von A–Z*, published in Bonn in 1954 by the *Ministerium für Gesamtdeutsche Fragen* (Ministry for All German Questions). Its political standpoint is clear from its very title, which refers, not to the DDR, but to the SBZ, short for *Sowjetische Besatzungszone* (the Soviet zone of occupation). The entry for "Architecture" includes the following:

> Since architecture seems more capable than the other fine arts of simultaneously influencing and representing "social" development, the art policy of the SBZ, after a short period of uncertainty, embraced it with particular enthusiasm and soon stamped it with the dominant artistic trend, Socialist Realism. As an organ of the art policy of the regime, whose norm is the monstrous construction of Moscow's Lomonossow University, the German Bauakademie dictates an architectural style that,

in the aftermath of Hitler, displays a bombastic profusion of pseudoclassical elements, and in origin and attitude deserves rather to be called "antiquarian gigantism."[3]

Thus, the architecture of the DDR is dictated, its norm comes from Moscow, but all the same it fits in with "the aftermath of Hitler." In other words, it has been created by edict and modeled on both Nazi and Communist precedent. It is an architecture of dictatorship.

Thus, referring to the last of our three figures (see Diagram D), the aesthetic characteristic also holds good. The building setting the norm for architecture in the DDR is "monstrous." In the architecture of the DDR we find a "bombastic profusion of pseudoclassical elements" and the result is "antiquarian gigantism." We are faced, then, with eclectic architecture, imitative and retrospective, tasteless and immoderate.

All three of the passages we have quoted claimed universality. Even so, within a few years they had all been left behind by the march of events. Two of them were actually unprintable. Belief systems about the relationship between architecture and ideology appear to be variable, because, to a much higher degree than architecture itself, they mirror the ups and downs of politics.

III. The Negative Choice

The Principle of Rejection

What exactly happens when a society, a state, a political system chooses its style, say, in architecture?

Most historians of art and architecture apparently suppose that the choice is always of a positive kind: The people making the choice know what the new art and the new architecture are to be like. But how often is this true? Is there not a far greater likelihood of the

---

[3] Da die Architektur mehr als andere bildende Künste berufen erscheint, die 'gesellschaftliche' Entwicklung zugleich zu beeinflussen und zu repräsentieren nahm sich die Kunstpolitik der SBZ nach einer kurzen Periode der Unsicherheit ihrer mit besonderem Eifer an und drückte ihr bald den Stempel der herrschenden Kunstrichtung auf (Sozialistischer Realismus). Die Deutsche Bauakademie als Organ der Kunstpolitik des Régimes, für die das monstruöse Bauwerk der Moskauer Lomonossow-Universität als Norm gilt, diktiert einen Baustil, der in der Nachfolge Hitlers pseudoklassizistische Elemente in bombastischer Fülle aufweist und nach Herkunft und Haltung eher als 'antiqvarischer Gigantismus' bezeichnet zu werden verdiente.

choice being a negative one? In other words, is the "choice" based not on what is chosen but on what is rejected?

The greater the changes occurring in the history of art and architecture, the greater is the importance of this negative choice. Because, until something new has been established and infused with substance, rejection is the only ground available to stand on. The motivating force behind Neo-Classicism was not primarily desire for the revival of Classical antiquity, it was a rejection of the Rococo and of all that it stood for. The most convincing explanation of the genesis of Socialist Realism is very similar.

That explanation appears in an essay by Sheila Fitzpatrick, published in the *Slavic Review* in 1976 and entitled "Culture and politics under Stalin: a reappraisal." The essay begins by describing the closing years of the 1920s and the cultural revolution. All traditional values were challenged and a new, politicized cultural establishment was in the making. But Stalin and his administration would not hear of any such establishment. They demanded order and discipline, an order that was incompatible with the cultural revolution.

To summarize Fitzpatrick's argument briefly, the revolution could not survive without a counterrevolution. This is how the old professional establishment returned to power in art and sciences. Its members, unlike the cultural revolutionaries, had no political ambitions. The support of the class that had once been the making of them was long since lost, and they gratefully accepted the chance offered them by the counterrevolution. Professional competence had been rated low by the cultural revolutionaries, but now it was reinstated and tradition and the Classical art forms with it. From this point it is only a short step to architecture.

The Constructivists were left out in the cold. They were compromised. The age of Modernism was past. Academism returned, but this time under the name of Socialist Realism and with the motto "national in form, socialist in content." The name and the motto, though, were post facto rationalizations. It was the process of rejection that imparted meaning to the choice, not any connection between form and ideas. The ideas came afterward, like an interpretation of the form adopted. But they were very soon to be presented as the *cause* of the form.

Something similar applies to the implementation of Socialist Realism in the people's democracies: The important thing was the rejection of Western architecture. What was to be put in its place was far from clear to begin with. The new architecture had to be "national in form and socialist in content." Yes indeed, but this did not say exactly what it was to look like. Important, salient characteristics were determined by "experience from the Soviet Union," but national form had to be worked out separately in each country.

The new architecture which, after a time, began to emerge in the people's democracies, from the Baltic to the Black Sea, was often being taken to illustrate the Sovietization of Eastern Europe. This is not untrue, but the term *de-Westernization* is more accurate. It was the negative choice that mattered.

The same held true both in the Soviet Union and in the people's democracies, when Socialist Realism was done away with. Once again, rejection was the thing. In the West there was talk of the de-Stalinization of architecture. The official term was "overcoming the harmful consequences of the cult of personality" or, when the message was addressed to the architects directly, "removal of exaggerations in planning and building." And, again, some time was to pass before it became clear what the new architecture was to look like.

Rejection is the starting point, but after this an old idea, associated with the form chosen, can be revived and adapted to a new political situation. The new Soviet nationalism looked to the nationalism of old Imperial Russia for support. The victory architecture of 1812 and the victory architecture of 1945 gave each other meaning. The originally negative choice acquired a positive interpretation, supported above all by the wartime national atmosphere.

But this is not what happened in the people's democracies. Time was too short and the political and emotional resistance to Socialist Realism was too powerful, and thus it could be discarded all the more easily when the time came—much more easily than in the Soviet Union.

Modernism and Traditionalism

The antithesis between Modernism and Traditionalism in its various forms—from Classicism to national form—is one of the main characteristics of twentieth-century architectural history. Other antitheses of the twentieth century have been *projected* onto this one, specifically, anthitheses between the new century (the twentieth) and the old (the nineteenth); between European society as it was, respectively, *after* and *before* World War I; between left and right; between socialism and capitalism; between "cultural Bolshevism" and National Socialism; between "the permanent revolution" and "socialism in one country"; between democracy and dictatorship; between West and East in the Cold War; between the Soviet Union *after* and *under* Stalin; between "the development optimism of the 1960s" and "the disillusion of the 1980s."

All these interpretations stem from the idea of a close relation between social conditions on the one hand and art and architecture on the other, and from the idea that *style* is an expression of that connection. These notions are rooted in the development of humanistic disciplines during the second half of the nineteenth century and the early twentieth. Historians argued that the differences among artistic cultures were not only differences of taste but also differences of social system and ideology. There were feudal and bourgeois artistic cultures, Catholic and Protestant, monarchic and republican. But these relations between architecture and ideology were always historically conditioned, valid only in specified situations. The historians, while not laying down any laws, still helped to sustain anticipations of such laws being discovered in the future.

In the ideological climate following World War I, when demand for total explanations was equally great on both right and left, these expectations were revived. What was true of the past should also be true of the present and future, and in the absence of an answer book, it was easy to generalize, for example, about the connection between architecture and ideology.

It is a big step from the historian's idea of all being interconnected to the political leader's idea that society must be homogeneous, that lack of homogeneity is a defect in the social structure and must be redressed, but even so the two ideas are connected. The humanistic disciplines—willy-nilly—helped to supply arguments for a totalitarian cultural policy: Architecture must be an expression of the ideology of society, and style must be the vehicle of that expression.

From this perspective, Socialist Realism and Modernism in its radical form are not antithetical. They were both based on the idea of a congruence between social structure and aesthetic form, and the advocates on either side were equally intolerant. They were against diversity and pluralism. Each side had a total explanation and a conviction about the way the world ought to look. Their pretensions were total or even totalitarian, insofar as political circumstances permitted.

If we look more closely at this connection, which has always been taken for granted, at this uninvestigated relationship between form and political ideology, there is only one explanation that will fit in with all the interpretations we have just enumerated: There is no congruence between aesthetic form and ideological content. It is only with the aid of isolated, specially selected examples that the notion of such a congruence can be sustained. The more numerous the examples become and the more we compare different political systems with each other, the more difficult this operation will be.

It is impossible to deduce form from ideas or ideas from form, in the manner attempted by representatives of both Socialist Realism and Modernism. Ideological content is not a prerequisite of form, it is inserted into forms. The ideological content is interchangeable. This is the only possible way of understanding the three diagrams in our preceding section, as well as the interpretations we enumerated of the Modernism-Traditionalism antithesis.

Historical change keeps imparting new meanings to old forms. Instead of accumulating, however, meanings are *exchanged* as history goes on, and it is possible for several meanings of the same form to exist side by side, just as different forms can have almost the same meaning.

Does architecture, then, have no objective content, unaffected by historical change? It does, but we ought then to speak of *expression* rather than ideas. A hundred years have passed since Heinrich Wölfflin showed in his *Prolegomena zu einer Psychologie der Architektur* that there is a very definite connection between our experience of architecture and the character of its form. We experience down-thrusting weight and upward-soaring lightness, simplicity and abundance, unity and diversity; architecture can be inviting or forbidding, and these experiences can be rooted in our experience of form. But this is a question of ideas, not of feelings or psychological categories.

Architecture *does* have expression, but ideological meaning is *added* to it. This is a tenable distinction and one that would shed a great deal of light on things, if it were not for the fact that there is a wide margin within which expression can be received by the beholder, a margin determined by both individual and collective experience.

Form, alone and unaided, cannot be the vehicle of ideas. The ideas cannot spring from within the form. They are added from outside, through turns of phrase and through practical function, through *practice*. They are determined by the patron and his pretensions. Without the support of language and function, there can be no ideological content. A striking formal language may suggest that the patron has ideological pretensions, but it can never tell us exactly *what* ideas are involved. Even when, aided by analogy, we read an ideological message into the architecture, we are ultimately dependent on verbal formulae.

Conclusion

The perspective employed in this book has been that of power: What were the intentions of the political power and why did it choose to accomplish its ends in this particular way?

Architecture in the Western world has a long and rich tradition of manifestating power, fashioned over the centuries by the most accomplished architects. It is a tradition on which one has to take a stand, a tradition to be partly or wholly adopted. A tradition to be reformed or rejected and—no less important—to be *reinterpreted.* All depending on the purposes of those in power. And in our century especially, power shifts have led to drastic reversals of architectural development.

Architecture as the manifestation of power is interchangeable from the viewpoint of the subject people, but not in the same way. Architecture is judged in a wide perspective in which architecture itself is merely one of many factors. The crucial point is not architecture as formal language, nor ideological expositions of the meaning of architecture. The verdict on Socialist Realism in the people's democracies hinged on the *political* context. Architecture per se carried little weight compared with the fact of its being the architecture of the new rulers. It was the verdict pronounced on *them* that really mattered.

Architecture as the manifestation of power is interchangeable, but only in a certain sense. A choice, once made, becomes part of the determinants of the choices that follow. If Constructivism had become the architecture of the Stalin era, the repercussions on twentieth-century architectural history would have been very far-reaching indeed. And the subsequent history of Modernism would have been different, as indeed it would have been if Nazi Germany had made Modernism its own.

Insofar as Socialist Realism had any lasting effect at all on aesthetic values in Eastern Europe, that effect was paradoxical. From the aversion to Socialist Realism there emerged, quite contrary to the rulers' intentions, a new understanding for Modernism. Due to its rejection by Socialist Realism, Modernism in Eastern Europe became what it otherwise would never have become: *an aesthetic of resistance.* This it became to a much greater extent than in Western Europe, where from the 1950s onwards, Modernism was increasingly accepted, attaining almost official status. And Modernism has remained an aesthetic of resistance in Eastern Europe, almost across the board, from music and drama to pictorial art and literature.

And yet there is one field in which Modernism in Eastern Europe has lost this symbolical meaning, namely, architecture. But then architecture is the only field in which Modernism, in the East as well, became official, formalized, and mass-produced. It is only in architecture that, during the past thirty years, Party ideologists have made any attempt to put new life into Socialist Realism. It is the only field in which there have not been any lapses. Franz Kafka has been denounced at regular intervals, but not so Le Corbusier or Mies van der Rohe. The revived Bauhaus has not come in for any resurgence of criticism.

In contrast to Western Europe and the USA, however, the secularized view of architectural Modernism has not resulted in traditional, Classical architecture being revived and discussed as a possible source of inspiration for architects—not yet, at any rate. Recollections of the *national form* of the 1950s are too vivid for that, both in the minds of the architects and for the state that, until recently, was their only patron. The Stalin era remains a living memory, and Socialist Realism cannot yet be divorced from that memory in the Eastern European mind. It will take time for the Poles to look dispassionately at the Palace of Culture in Warsaw or the Romanians at Casa Scînteii in Bucharest.

Architecture is at one and the same time both dependent on the social system and independent of it. Socialist Realism was introduced for very definite political purposes in the Soviet Union at the beginning of the 1930s and in Eastern Europe at the end of the 1940s. But the forms that, on these two occasions, were made to express (among other things) strict de-Westernization were by no means the property of the system but were, paradoxically, part of the common European cultural heritage.

The question is not *whether* but *how* architecture depends on ideology. The answer is: not through firm, indissoluble links but through historically conditioned constellations of limited viability in both time and space.

Postscript

One last question, although at first it seems to have nothing to do with the subject of this book. When and where in Eastern Europe were publications of the classical treatises on architecture—those of Vitruvius, Alberti, Palladio, and Vignola—most numerous?

There might be different answers to this question but one of them is of special interest here, and perhaps surprising even to those who have read this book: Poland in the 1950s! Polish editions of the works of Vignola and Palladio, both in print runs of 15,000, were published in 1955. They were followed, the next year, by Vitruvius in a printing of 10,000. That adds up to 40,000 copies in two years in just one country. And these were not abridged economy editions. An

253 Warsaw, MDM, Plac Konstytucji, 1952.

edition of Alberti had also been in preparation, but it did not come out until 1960.

In a discussion in 1952 of MDM and the new Plac Konstytucji in Warsaw (Fig. 253), under the aegis of the Polish Architects' Association (SARP), the critics pointed out that the architects had not mastered the traditional vocabulary on which Socialist Realism was based. Edmund Goldzamt, the ideologist of the Polish architectural profession, had recommended a study of the classics, referring particularly to Palladio, Vignola, and Alberti.

That, then, was why the classical treatises on architecture were republished in Poland during the mid-1950s. It was in order to support the development of a new Polish architecture true to the principles of Socialist Realism. It was also closely allied to "the example of the Soviet Union," where the same classics had already been published in the 1930s.

The only trouble was that this time they were published too late. Socialist Realism was on the way out, and with it a demand for the classics. The overdue edition of Alberti was reduced to a run of 3,250 copies.

Vitruvius, Alberti, Palladio, and Vignola were enlisted to establish Socialist Realism, thereby assuming an unexpected ideological significance. But only in a certain context, and not for good.

Bibliography and Commentaries

Eastern Europe

There is a dearth of surveys of the architectural history of Eastern Europe, even as regards earlier periods. In his preface to *The Art of the Renaissance in Eastern Europe. Hungary, Bohemia, Poland*, Oxford 1976, Jan Białostocki names August Hahr, of Uppsala, as his only true precursor.

In those surveys that do exist, Socialist Realism is mentioned only in passing. This applies, for example, to vol. 12:2 of the great Soviet reference work *Vseobshchaia istoriia arkhitektury* (General history of architecture), published in 1977, which in this connection is alluringly subtitled *Arkhitektura zarubezhnykh sotsialisticheskikh stran* (The architecture of the foreign socialist countries). This volume includes long, exhaustive chapters on architectural development in the Eastern European countries after 1945, but it does not make clear that Socialist Realism was the all-pervading doctrine for an important part of the postwar era.

The same can be said concerning a work by the Polish architect Edmund Goldzamt, *Urbanistyka krajów socjalistycznych*, Warsaw 1971 (German edition: *Städtebau socialistischer Länder*, Berlin/O 1974). The importance of Socialist Realism in urban development is not made clear, and the bibliography does not even mention Goldzamt's own major contribution to the theoretical literature on the subject: *Architektura zespołów śródmiejskich i problemy dziedzictwa* (Architecture in city centers and problems of tradition), Warsaw, 1956. The 1950s are also given very cursory treatment in the only survey to have been published in the West, *Zeitgenössische Architektur in Osteuropa*, Cologne 1985, by Udo Kultermann.

A substantial essay on the early 1950s in Poland, Czechoslovakia, Hungary, and Romania was published in the March issue of *The Architectural Review* in 1953. Entitled "Retreat to Moscow. Architecture in the Soviet Satellites" and written by Harold A. Meek, it was based on official material. Its critical tone led to an exchange of opinions in the July issue that year. Andrew Boyd maintained that the rejection of Modernism had been brought about by professional opinion among the architects, not by political interference. But Meek was not convinced.

Material from all six countries can be found in the Cominform political weekly, published 1947–56, first in Belgrade, then from 1948 onward in Bucharest, and in a growing number of languages. An English edition, *For a Lasting Peace, for a People's Democracy,* existed from the very beginning.

As regards general surveys of Eastern European history, mention should be made of *Eastern Europe 1740–1980. Feudalism to Communism,* by Robin Okey, London 1982. So should two collections of specialized studies, *Communist Power in Europe 1944-49,* ed. Martin McCauley, London and New York 1977, and *Stalinism. Essays in Historical Interpretation,* ed. Robert C. Tucker, London 1977. The latter collection also includes a section entitled "Stalinism and the 'People's Democracies'" by Włodzimierz Brus. Brus, who worked as an economist in Poland during the 1950s, is also the author of *Economic History of Communist Eastern Europe,* 1981.

DDR

Three publications provide a solid foundation for studying architecture and building in the DDR. In the journal *Deutsche Architektur,* which began publication in 1952, one finds not only projects and completed buildings but also a large number of articles energetically and lucidly proclaiming the principles of Socialist Realism. *Handbuch für Architekten,* Berlin/O 1954, is a summary of the theory and practice of architecture early in the DDR (two editions the same year, total print run 13,000). Among other things, this reproduces "Grundsätze des Städtebaues," the government enactment on "principles of urbanism." *Chronik Bauwesen. Deutsche Demokratische Republic 1945–1971,* Berlin/O 1974, records the outward course of events and is compiled from announcements and articles in newspapers and professional journals. An historical account and collection of documents illustrating political developments and published in the West is *Von der SBZ zur DDR,* I–II, by Hermann Weber, Hannover 1966–67.

The first decade in the history of architecture in the DDR was summarized in *Architektur und Städtebau in der Deutschen Demokratischen Republik,* Berlin/O 1959. Later and briefer surveys are to be found, for example, in Gerhard Krenz, *Architektur zwischen gestern und morgen,* 2d. ed., Berlin/O 1975, and in *Kunst der DDR 1945–1959,* Leipzig 1982, ed. Ullrich Kuhirt.

Mention should also be made of the political speeches of Walter Ulbricht, published in *Zur Geschichte der deutschen Arbeiterbewegung. Aus Reden und Aufsätzen,* Bd IV, Berlin/O 1958, and covering the period from 1950–54. The statements on the political function of architecture that historians have so often looked for in vain from the lips of Frederick the Great or Napoleon are to be found here in superabundance. The same is also fairly true of the corresponding publication of speeches by Otto Grotewohl, *Im Kampf um die einige deutsche demokratische Republik,* especially Bd III (1952–53), Berlin/O 1954.

Kurt Liebknecht was the greatest authority among professionals. Especially worth mentioning, besides his many articles in *Deutsche Architektur,* is *Das grosse Vorbild und der sozialistische Realismus in der Architektur und in der Malerei,* Berlin/O 1952, published together with Kurt Magritz. Second to him was Hermann Henselmann, whose essays, speeches, and projects were assembled with a commentary by Wolfgang Heise and Bruno Flierl in *Hermann Henselmann. Gedanken Ideen Bauten Projekte,* Berlin/O 1978. We also have the first part of Henselmann's memoirs, *Drei Reisen nach Berlin,* Berlin/O 1981, dealing with the period down to 1949. Richard Paulick is the subject of a popular biography by Manfred Müller, *Das Leben eines Architekten,* Halle/Saale 1975.

Very interesting are a number of essays by Christian Borngräber: "Das nationale Aufbauprogramm der DDR" in *Arch+,* 56, 1981; "Un futuro per quale passato? La Stalinallee e L'Hansaviertel" in *Casabella,* 474/475, 1981; and "Residential Buildings in Stalinallee" in *Architectural Design* 11/12, 1982. His contribution to *Exil in der UdSSR,* Leipzig 1979, deals with the foreign architects in the Soviet Union, among them Liebknecht and Weiner.

The genesis of Stalinallee can be traced in detail in the first few volumes of *Deutsche Architektur.* Western views of Stalinallee are reflected, for example, by articles in *Der Spiegel,* 14 May 1952, and *The Manchester Guardian,* 19 September 1953. To illustrate the official view in the East, there are articles in *Aufbau* (DDR), 1952:8, and *For a Lasting Peace, for a People's Democracy,* 1953:1. The development of Stalinstadt can also be followed with the aid of *Deutsche Architektur,* especially the 1952 and 1953 issues. Kurt W. Leucht, principal architect of Stalinstadt, published *Die erste neue Stadt in der Deutschen Demokratischen Republik. Planungsgrundlagen und -ergebnisse von Stalinstadt,* Berlin/O 1957. That, however, is a doctored account of both architecture and ideology, as the publication year might lead one to expect.

An excellent survey of postwar Germany between 1945 and the early 1950s is Hartmut Frank's essay "Traditionelle und moderne Architekturen im Nachkriegsdeutschland," in *Grauzonen Farbwelten*, ed. Bernhard Schulz, Berlin/W 1983. Frank deals above all with Berlin and the future Federal Republic, but he also takes in the future DDR.

Further material for comparison with the architecture of West Germany is available, for example, in *Neues Bauen in Deutschland*, by Bruno E. Werner, Munich 1952, and in the survey *Bauen in Deutschland 1945–1962*, Hamburg 1963. Hansaviertel is presented in the catalogue *Interbau Berlin 1957*, Berlin/W 1957. Among more recent publications, special mention is merited by an essay by Barbara Miller Lane, "The Berlin Congress Hall 1955–1957," in *Perspectives in American History* (Cambridge, Mass.), new series, vol. 1, 1984.

Poland

The journal *Architektura*, revived at the end of 1947, furnishes a wide-ranging account of postwar building and clearly reflects all the ideological complications. For questions of urban development, see the journal *Miasto* (City), published from 1950 onward, and for questions of building conservation—of great moment in Poland—see *Ochrona zabytków* (Protection of historic buildings), published from 1948 onward. As regards building in Warsaw, there is a fair amount of material in the popular weekly *Stolica* (Capital city), published from 1946 onward.

The most important single publication is *Architektura polska 1950–1951*, ed. Bohdan Garliński, Warsaw 1953. This is a presentation of thirty-two big projects, complete with photographs and drawings, and also of the architectural and ideological discussions attending them. The Congress of 20–21 June 1949, which opened the way to Socialist Realism, forms the subject of a special publication, *O polską architekturę socjalistyczną* (On Polish socialist architecture), Warsaw 1950. The resolution is also reprinted in *Architektura* (Warsaw), 1949:6–8.

One publication that, through its profusion of illustrated material, vividly presents the role of building in the new Poland is *Sześcioletni plan odbudowy Warszawy* (The six-year plan for the rebuilding of Warsaw), Warsaw 1950, published in the name of Bolesław Bierut. A German edition, *Der Sechsjahrplan des Wiederaufbaus von Warschau*, was brought out the following year by the Bauakademie in the DDR. Both versions have twenty pull-out plates showing what Warsaw was going to look like in 1955. Similar in kind is *MDM. Marszałkowska 1730–1954*, ed. Stanisław Jankowski, Warsaw 1955. The rebuilding of the Old City also formed the subject of a publication, though with more emphasis on documentation, namely, *Stare miasto w Warszawie. Odbudowa*, Warsaw 1956 (with parallel editions in several languages). The Palace of Culture, as we have already seen, was given very subdued publicity, *Budowa PKiN*, Warsaw 1957. A more recent commentary is "Morfologia Pałacu Kultury" by Piotr Witt in *Sztuka* (Warsaw), no. 4, 1975. That is where the comparison with Jules Verne comes from.

Polish architecture was also presented in Sweden, at an exhibition in Stockholm in 1953 organized by the Swedish-Polish Association and the Swedish Association of Architects. The catalogue, "Arkitektur i Polen," appeared as no. 9, 1953 of *Det nya Polen*. It was very skeptically reviewed by Lennart Holm in *Att bo*, 1953:3.

Budownictwo i architektura w Polsce 1945–1966, ed. Jan Zachwatowicz, Warsaw 1968, was published the same year in English as *Building and Architecture in Poland 1945–1966*. Far more detailed on the 1950s and Socialist Realism is a not very widely distributed work by Adam Kotarbiński, *Rozwój urbanistyki i architektury polskiej w latach 1944–1964* (The development of Polish urban planning and architecture, 1944–1964), Warsaw 1967.

Bohdan Pniewski was the subject of an exhibition in 1967 at Muzeum Narodowe in Warsaw, from which there is a catalogue, *Bohdan Pniewski 1897–1965*. Pniewski and Szymon and Helena Syrkus are presented in the comprehensive catalogue *Avant-garde polonaise. Urbanisme. Architecture 1918–1939* (with text also in Polish and English), Paris and Warsaw 1981.

Relations between Polish authors and the new regime are the subject of *The Captive Mind* by Czesław Miłosz, 1953. This is a great book and the remote precursor of my own chapter herein, "The Logic of the Situation: Eight Biographical Sketches."

Socialist Realism has attracted revived interest in Poland since the end of the 1970s and is being studied with a frankness unmatched by any other country, with the possible exception of Hungary. There is much to be learned from a long essay by Krzysztof Stefański in *Kwartalnik architektury i urbanistyki* (Warsaw), XXVII:1-2, 1982: "Architektura polska 1949–1956" (originally a degree thesis at the University of Wrocław). *Socrealizm. Sztuka Polska w latach 1950–54*, by Wojciech Włodarczyk, was published in Paris in 1986 but before then had been presented as a doctoral thesis in Cracow. This is an analytical work, concerned primarily with pictorial art, but it also deals with architecture (MDM). One section was published previously in English in *Polish Art Studies* (Warsaw), IV, 1983: "How to paint a good socio-realist painting?" One should also mention an essay by Waldemar Baraniewski: "Rola, 'tradycji' w architekturze polskiej lat 1949–1956" (The role of 'tradition' in Polish architecture, 1949–1956) in *Tradycja i innowacja. Materiały sesji stowarzyszenia historyków sztuki 1979*, Warsaw 1981.

My characterization of the 1937 World Exposition as something midway between Functionalism and Socialist Realism is derived from an essay by Andrzej K. Olszewski, "Styl 1937 w świetle krytyki i historii," in *Myśl o sztuce*, Warsaw 1976. Adam Zagajewski is quoted from *Polen. Staat im Schatten der Sowjetunion*, Hamburg 1981, a long historical and political essay written in West Berlin before and during the Solidarity period.

Czechoslovakia

The journal *Architektura ČSR* came back into publication as early as 1946, one of the first architectural journals in postwar Eastern Europe. It reflects more clearly than any other journal the vicissitudes of politics.

Between 1951 and 1955 there was the specialist journal *Sovětská architektura*, which also provided a certain amount of space for native material. Ideological articles on architecture were published in the political weekly *Tvorba* (e.g., in 1950, no. 22–24, "K situaci v naší architektuře," and no. 50–52, "Národní tradice v české architektuře").

Postwar housing construction is dealt with in a generous overview, *Bydlení v Československu. Přehled bytové výstavby od roku 1945*, Prague 1958, with text also in Russian, English, and French. Urban development is treated in *Urbanismus socialistického Československa*, by Oleg Švidkovskii, Prague 1966, a work published in Russian three years earlier.

Publications in recent years have paid scant attention to Socialist Realism. This is true both of *Československá architektura 1945–1977*, by Josef Pechar, Prague 1979, and of *Česká architektura v proměnách dvou století 1780–1980*, by Marie Benešová, Prague 1984. All the more worthwhile is the feature issue of *Architektura ČSSR* (1968:9–10), published in the eventful year of 1968 to mark the fiftieth anniversary of the foundation of the state of Czechoslovakia. In it the postwar period is treated with a frankness unthinkable in the 1970s and 1980s.

Karel Teige's book on Czechoslovakia between the wars, *Modern Architecture in Czechoslovakia*, was published in Prague in 1947 (also in Czech and French). An excerpt from Teige's contemporary, unpublished polemic against Socialist Realism is included in *Archithese* (Niederteufen), 19, 1976, in connection with an article by O. Mácel, "Zur Theorie des sozialistischen Realismus in der Architektur." Jaroslav Seifert's depiction of Teige's last year comes in his memoirs, published in Swedish in 1986 as *All världens skönhet.*

A presentation of Kroha's earliest works, *Jiří Kroha s úvodem od/mit einer Einleitung von Jaroslav B Svrček,* was published in Geneva in 1930. In addition to his own articles in *Architektura ČSR*, the section on Kroha is based on particulars furnished by a couple of his students.

The exile journal *Svědectví,* no. 60, 1980, published in Paris, reproduces the minutes of the State Commission that organized the Czech celebrations of Stalin's seventieth birthday and took the initiative leading to the Stalin Monument in Prague.

In addition, there are three works on political history to be mentioned: *Der Kurze Marsch. Kommunistische Machtübernahme in der Tschechoslowakei 1945–1948,* Munich 1981, and *Dans les archives du comité central,* Paris 1978, both by Karel Kaplan, and *Communism in Czechoslovakia 1948-1960,* by Edward Taborský, Princeton, N.J. 1960. It was Taborský who supplied the term de-Westernization.

Hungary

Journal succeeded journal. *Tér és forma* (Space and form), which had existed since the 1920s, went out of publication at the beginning of 1948. *Új építészet* (New architecture) came out in 1946–49 and *Épités-Építészet* (Building-architecture) between 1949 and 1951. *Magyar Építőművészet* (Hungarian architecture), which is still extant, began publication in 1952. "The progressive tradition in Hungarian architecture" was presented in *Magyar építészet haladó hagyományai,* Budapest 1951.

Important contributions to the postwar debate on architecture are reprinted and commented on in an anthology edited by Máté Major and Judit Osskó, *Új építészet, új társadalom 1945–1978* (New architecture, new society), Budapest 1981. This gives generous scope to the debate on Socialist Realism, with contributions by György Lukács, Máté Major, and the Minister of Culture József Révai, among others. Révai's 1951 speech (see Chapter Nine, on Máté Major) achieved widespread currency and was printed, not only in *Épités-Építészet,* 1951:9–10, but also in *Architektura ČSR,* 1951:10–12, *Aufbau* (DDR), 1952:2, and *Architektura* (Warsaw) 1952:2.

The building of the first postwar decade was documented exhaustively in *Magyar építészet 1945–1955,* Budapest 1955, but the complete omission of the projects results in an unduly strong impression of moderation on the part of Hungarian architects in their practice of Socialist Realism. Subsequent overviews have toned down the 1950s and Socialist Realism still further, e.g., *Neue Architektur in Ungarn,* Munich 1978, by Jenő Szendrői et al. Not until *Magyar Építőművészet,* no. 3, 1984, is it subjected to fresh appraisal. This is a highly informative issue whose contributors include both veterans from the 1950s and latter-day observers. The latter include Ákos Moravánszky, who has also published a couple of essays in the West: "Die dorischen Säulen des Überbaus" in *Um Bau* (Vienna), no. 5, 1981, and "Asplund's impact on Hungarian Architecture" in *Lectures and Briefings from the International Symposium on the Architecture of Erik Gunnar Asplund,* Stockholm 1986. This latter question is also treated in an article by Fredric Bedoire and Eva Lampel, "Samband mellan skandinavisk och ungersk arkitektur" in *Arkitektur* (Stockholm), 1976:1. The plans for Sztálinváros were published in 1953 in *Sztálinváros Városközpont Városterv.* This was a difficult volume to come by, but there is a copy in Intercisa Múzeum, Dunaújváros.

The journal *Budapest a főváros folyóirata,* no. 9, 1981, contains an article by József Fischer, "Amikor újjáépítési kormánybiztos voltam..." (When I was Commissar for Reconstruction...). The Hungarian CIAM, of which Fischer and Major were both members, is described in *A CIAM magyar csoportja (1928–1938),* by Eszter Gábor, Budapest 1972. Máté Major's activities can be traced in his bibliography, "Dr Máté Majors Fachaufsätze, Fachbücher," in *Periodica Polytechnika, Architecture-Arkhitektura* (Budapest), vol. 18, 1974:1–2. At the time of his death he was praised in *Magyar Építőművészet,* no. 3, 1986, among other things for his resistance of "false" Socialist Realism. Mention should also be made of my own meetings with Fischer and Major in Budapest during October 1982.

The course of events in Hungary during October and November 1956 is documented in detail in a cyclostyled UN report in two volumes, *Report of the Special Committee on the Problem of Hungary,* I–II, 1957. That report is the sole result of the rebellious Hungarians' appeal to the UN during the 1956 crisis. Further particulars concerning the demolition of the Stalin monuments have been taken from *Uprising!* by David Irving, London 1981, and from *In the Name of the Working Class* (1979), by Sándor Kopácsi, Chief of Police in Budapest in 1956, New York 1987.

Romania

The journal *Arkhitectura R.P.R.* began publication in 1953. Data from earlier years have been taken from the weekly *La Roumanie Nouvelle* published since 1948 and the daily newspaper *Neuer Weg*, published since 1949, both appearing in Bucharest, the latter being addressed to the country's German-speaking minority. An art journal for Western readers began to appear in 1949, its earliest issues being in French, *L'art dans la République Populaire Roumaine* (1949 and 1950), while subsequent issues were in English, *Arts in the Roumanian People's Republic*, from 1951 onward. No. 3 (1951) included a detailed presentation of Casa Scînteii by Horia Maicu.

Both tradition and new building are described in *Arkhitektura rumynskoi narodnoi respubliki*, Bucharest 1952, first published in Russian and then, the following year, with slightly fewer illustrations and in a somewhat plainer format in French *(L'architecture roumaine)* and German *(Rumänische Architektur)*.

A good survey of Romania in the 1950s can be found in a feature issue of *Deutsche Architektur*, 1956:5–6, in which, for example, Horia Maicu writes about Casa Scînteii and Gustav Gusti about Romanian urban planning. For an ideological commentary there is *Rumanian Summer. A View of the Rumanian People's Republic*, London 1953, written by two British Marxists, Jack Lindsay and Maurice Cornforth, on the occasion of the World Youth Festival in Bucharest. There are several works by the architectural historian Grigore Ionescu, among them *Arhitectura în România perioada anilor 1944–1969*, Bucharest 1969, and *Arhitectura pe teritoriul României de-a lungul veacurilor*, Bucharest 1972, published in French the same year as *Histoire de l'architecture en Roumanie. De la préhistoire à nos jours*.

Göran Börge's *In i Rumänien*, Stockholm 1973, makes a comprehensive introduction to the culture and history of Romania, including the 1940s and 1950s.

In Romania during the 1980s, there was a revival of the big projects, the monumental proportions, and the national tradition. Here we can refer to an article in *Der Spiegel*, 1984:48, and to a feature program by the Eastern European Department of Austrian Television, *Später Cäsar* (alluding to Ceausescu's "imperial" building plans), 1986.

Bulgaria

The journal *Arkhitektura i stroitelstvo* (Architecture and urban development) was published in Sofia from 1951 to 1953 and is not to be confused with the Moscow journal of the same name. It was then divided up into *Arkhitektura* and *Stroitelstvo*, published from 1954 onward. Schemes for the center of Sofia and for Dimitrovgrad pre-1951 are to be found in a work by Liuben Tonev on the theory of urban development, *Ploshtadut*, Sofia 1949. Tonev, who before the war practiced with Auguste Perret in Paris, occupied a powerful position among Bulgarian architects all through the postwar period.

Political rhetoric played a large part in the architectural journals, but it can also be studied in a journal for Western readers, *La Bulgarie d'aujourd'hui,* published from 1952 onward.

A survey of postwar building will be found in the detailed volume *Arkhitekturata v Bulgariia sled 9 septemvri 1944,* Sofia 1954, in Bulgarian, Russian, and French. Also very rewarding is an unnumbered fascicle in the 1955 volume of the East German journal *Deutsche Architektur,* entitled "Bulgarische Architektur," with contributions from both Bulgarian and German specialists such as Tonev, Tashev, and Liebknecht. To supplement these, there is *Arkhitekturata v Bulgarija 1944–1960,* by Liuben Tonev, Sofia 1962. More recent publications have ignored the 1950s, with the partial exception of the center of Sofia, as for example in the case of *Arkhitekturata na Sofiia,* by Georgi V. Labov, Sofia 1979.

The national tradition was explored by Todor Zlatev in *Bulgarska natsionalna arkhitektura,* 1–3, Sofia 1955–58. Mention should also be made of *Arkhitektura Bolgarii,* Moscow 1953, by the Soviet architectural theorist M. P. Tsapenko.

The Soviet Union

The architectural history of the Soviet Union is the necessary background to a study of postwar Eastern Europe. A number of publications in the DDR, Poland, and Czechoslovakia have already been mentioned in Chapter Four under the heading "How the example was transmitted." Of these we can once more mention *Dreissig Jahre sowjetische Architektur in der RSFSR,* Moscow 1950 (also in Russian and Czech). This should be supplemented by overviews of the non-Russian republics, such as *Arkhitektura respublik zakavkazia* (The architecture of the Caucasian republics), Moscow 1951.

A very useful bibliography, compiled by Anatole Senkevitch, Jr., is *Soviet Architecture 1917–1962. A Bibliographical Guide to Source Material,* Charlottesville 1974, listing and commenting on nearly 1,200 titles, both Soviet and foreign, magazine articles included. Just a few publications from the 1970s and 1980s will be mentioned here.

A major work on Soviet Modernism is *Pioniere der sowjetischen Architektur,* by Selim O. Chan-Magomedow, Dresden 1983, written in the Soviet Union but published in the DDR. The same goes for *Ideen-Projekte-Bauten. Sowjetische Architektur 1917/32,* by Kyrill N. Afanasev, Dresden 1973.

Part 12:1, Moscow 1975, of the great reference work *Vseobshchaia istoriia arkhitektury* is devoted to "Arkhitektura SSSR." This is a very detailed work, even as regards the Stalinist era, but bland in its approach. All the more original is a work by the Soviet architectural historian Vladimir Papernii, now practicing in the USA, *Kultura "dva,"* published in Ann Arbor in 1985, but so far only in Russian. This is a virtually structuralist study of the architecture and culture of the Stalin era—"culture two." It is full of ideas, critical of previous writers, opposed to the concept of a "left-wing architecture," but not very firmly rooted in concrete examples.

Adolf Max Vogt, in his *Russische und französische Revolutions-architektur 1917 1789,* Cologne 1974, has perceived a pattern: from revolution and radical, geometrical form to political stabilization and Classicism under Stalin and Napoleon. Its true subject, however, is the revolutionary phase, not Soviet Classicism and Socialist Realism.

Also worthy of note is a work by Anatole Kopp, *L'Architecture de la période stalinienne,* Grenoble 1978. Its background is Kopp's great admiration of Soviet avant-gardism, to which he devoted two previous works. To a corresponding extent he regards Socialist Realism as an apostasy, so much so that he hardly takes it seriously.

It is taken very seriously indeed, though, by another author who has also written about the Soviet avant-garde. In addition to his works on Konstantin Melnikov (1978) and the history of Soviet jazz (1983), S. Frederick Starr has also written about "The social character of Stalinist architecture" in the *Architectural Association Quarterly* (Oxford and New York), 1979:2.

Kopp's real antithesis, however, as regards both values and knowledge of source material, is Christian Borngräber (already mentioned in the section on the DDR). Pending his magnum opus on Academic architecture in the Soviet Union, mention will be made here of only a couple of his essays: "The Moscow Metro" in *Architectural Design,* 1979:8–9 (with a retort by Anatole Kopp in the same journal 1980:7–8 and a reply by Borngräber in 1981:3–4); "Akademiker und Konstruktivisten. Die ersten fünfzehn Jahre der sowjetischen Architektur," in *Journal für Geschichte* (Braunschweig), 1981:3; and "Nationale und regionale Bauformen in der sowjetischen Architektur. Die Landwirtschafts-Ausstellung in Moskau 1939" in *Archithese* (Niederteufen), 1981:3.

There are also a couple of Swedish works: *Byggande i Sovjetunionen,* by Claes Caldenby and Aleksander Wolodarski, Stockholm 1973, and *Kollektivhus. Sovjet och Sverige omkring 1930,* by Claes Caldenby and Åsa Walldén, Stockholm 1979. The former includes a brief but well-written chapter on "The Architecture of the Stalin Era" and translations of the Soviet resolutions of 1954 and 1955, which, in the people's democracies too, spelled the demise of Socialist Realism. The latter includes a critical scrutiny of the history of Soviet architecture as viewed by Kopp and Vogt.

Parts of this book have been published previously, in slightly different form, in other connections: the section on the Palace of Culture in Warsaw in *Arkitektur*, 1983:3; the section on Stalinallee in East Berlin in *Arkitektur*, 1984:7; "The Stalin Monument in Prague" in *Tiden*, 1982:1; "Pass me a Brick!" in *Tvärsnitt*, 1983:1; and "The Logic of the Situation" in *Tvärsnitt*, 1987:2. "Iconography, Rhetoric, and the Cult of Stalin" was published as "Symbols and Rituals in the People's Democracies during the Cold War" in *Symbols of Power. The Esthetics of Political Legitimation in the Soviet Union and Eastern Europe*, Stockholm 1987; and parts of the section "Architecture and Ideology" as "Sozialistischer Realismus—Zum Problem Architektur und Ideologie" in *Klassizismus. Epoche und Probleme. Festschrift für Erik Forssman*, Hildesheim, Zürich, and New York 1987. There are also the articles "Det kalla kriget i arkitekturen" in *Tvärsnitt*, 1980:3, and "Den socialistiska realismen—Östeuropas arkitektur efter 1945" in *Magasin Tessin*, 1982:1.

Illustration Credits

CHAPTER ONE: 1. Gerhard Krenz: *Architektur zwischen gestern und morgen*, 2d ed., Berlin/O 1975. 2. *Polska 1944–1965*, I, Warsaw 1966. 3. Stanisław Jankowski: *MDM. Marszałkowska 1730–1954*, Warsaw 1955. 4. Deutsche Fotothek, Dresden. 5, 7. Adolf Ciborowski: *Warsaw. A City Destroyed and Rebuilt*, Warsaw 1964. 6. *Architektura* (Warsaw), 1949:11–12. 8. AÅ 1981. 9. *Bydlení v Československu. Přehled bytové výstavbý od roku 1945*, Prague 1958. 10. *Magyar épitészet 1945–1955*, Budapest 1955. 11, 12. Jan Zachwatowicz: *L'architecture polonaise*, Warsaw 1967. 13. *Arkhitektura rumynskoi narodnoi respubliki*, Bucharest 1952. 14. Okruzhen tsentur za fotopropaganda, Burgas 1987. 15. *The decline and rise of Budapest*, Budapest 1946. 16. Josef Pechar: *Československá architektura 1945–1977*, Prague 1979. 17. *Architektura* (Warsaw), 1948:6–7. 18. *Hans Scharoun. Ausstellung in der Akademie der Künste*, Berlin/W 1967. 19. Volker Frank: *Antifaschistische Mahnmale in der DDR*, Leipzig 1970. 20. Joachim Schulz and Werner Gräbner: *Berlin Hauptstadt der Deutschen Demokratischen Republik (Architekturführer DDR)*, Berlin/O 1974.

CHAPTER TWO: 21. *Neuer Weg* (Bucharest), 14 August 1949. 22. *Pravda* (Moscow), 22 December 1949. 23. *Neuer Weg* (Bucharest), 7 January 1953, after *Pravda* (Moscow), 28 December 1952. 24. Sven Öste: *Gränsen: Järnridån från Ishavet till Kaukasus*, Stockholm 1963. 25. *Mitten in Deutschland. Mitten im 20. Jahrhundert. Die Zonengrenze*, 8th ed., Bonn and Berlin/W 1964. 26. *La Bulgarie d'aujourd'hui* (Sofia), 1953:6. Cf. Nikola Mavrodinov: *Ivan Funev*, Sofia 1955 (Biblioteka izobrazitelno izkustvo, 5). 27. *Arta plastică în Republika Populară Romînă 1944–1954*, Bucharest 1954. 28. Preben Kannik: *Flaggor från hela världen*, Stockholm 1957. 29. From originals. Cf. *Zumstein Briefmarken Katalog. Europa-Ost*, 65th ed., Berne 1982. 30. From an original. 31–33. *Gedenkstätten. Arbeiterbewegung. Antifaschistischer Widerstand. Aufbau des Sozialismus*, Leipzig, Jena, and Berlin/O, 2d ed., 1974 (cf. the Polish equivalent, *Stätten des Kampfes und des Märtyrertums 1939–1945. Jahre des Krieges in Polen*, Warsaw 1965). 34, 35. *Przegląd artystyczny* (Warsaw), 1953:3. Cf. *Katalog polskich plakatów politycznych z lat 1949-56*, Warsaw 1978. 36. Bolesław Bierut: *Sześcioletni plan odbudowy Warszawy*, Warsaw 1950. 37. *La Roumanie Nouvelle* (Bucharest), no. 51, 1950. 38. Richard M. Ketchum, ed.:*What is Communism?* New York 1955. 39. *Dimitrovgrad*, Sofia, 1959. 40. *Den nya tiden* (Moscow), 1954:1, parallel Swedish edition of *Novoie Vremia*.

CHAPTER THREE: 41. *Vladimir Tatlin* (Moderna Museet), Stockholm 1968. 42–45. Selim Chan-Magomedow: *Pioniere der sowjetischen Architektur*, Dresden 1983. 46. Hans Schmidt: *Beiträge zur Architektur 1924–1964*, Berlin/O 1965. 47, 48. *Arkhitektura moskovskogo metro*, Moscow 1936. 49. *Deutsche Architektur*, 1954:6 50. Edmund Goldzamt: *Wieżowce radzieckie* (Instytut polsko-radziecki), Warsaw 1953. Also in B.M. Michajlow: *Die Architektur der Völker der Sowjetunion*, Berlin/O 1953; *Handbuch für Architekten*, Berlin/O 1954; and *Arhitectura R. P. R.* (Bucharest), 1955:3. 51, 52. AÅ 1985.

CHAPTER FOUR: 53. Centralna Agencja Fotograficzna, Warsaw. Cf. Bohdan Garliński, *Architektura polska 1950–1951*, Warsaw 1953. 54. Herbert Ricken: *Der Architekt. Geschichte eines Berufs*, Berlin/O 1977. 55. Stanisław Jankowski: *MDM. Marszałkowska 1730–1954*, Warsaw 1955. 56, 57. AÅ 1979 and 1982, respectively.

CHAPTER FIVE: 58. *Deutsche Architektur* 1955:9. 59. *Ostravsko ve fotografii*, Ostrava 1958. 60. *Deutsche Architektur* 1953:5. 61. Same as no. 13. 62. Same as no. 10. 63. Same as no. 27. 64. Bolesław Bierut: *Der Sechsjahrplan des Wiederaufbaus von Warschau*, Leipzig 1951 (not included in the Polish edition). 65, 66. *Architektura ČSR*, 1953:7–9. 67, 68. *Arkhitekturata v Bulgariia sled 9 septemvri 1944*, Sofia 1954 (plan redrawn). 69. *Handbuch für Architekten*, Berlin/O 1954 (redrawn). 70. Bohdan Garliński: *Architektura polska 1950-1951*, Warsaw 1953. 71. *Kultura Polski Ludowej. Wybór fotografii z lat 1945–1955*, Warsaw 1956. 72. AÅ 1980. 73. Same as no. 71. 74. *Deutsche Architektur* 1959:1. 75. AÅ 1982. 76. *Deutsche Architektur* 1953:4. 77. AÅ 1985. 78. Hermann Henselmann: *Gedanken Ideen Bauten Projekte*, Berlin/O 1978.

CHAPTER SIX: 79. *Exposition universelle. Le panorama*, nouv. série 11, Paris 1900. 80–82. *Dreissig Jahre sowjetische Architektur in der RSFSR*, Leipzig 1951. 83. *Deutsche Architektur* 1954:3. 84. Kurt Liebknecht and Kurt Magritz: *Das grosse Vorbild und der sozialistische Realismus in der Architektur und in der Malerei*, Berlin/O 1952. 85. *Deutsche Architektur* 1953:1 (after Schinkel: *Sammlung architektonischer Entwürfe*). 86. AÅ 1976. 87. *Deutsche Architektur* 1954:4. 88. Deutsche Fotothek, Dresden. 89. *Deutsche Architektur* 1952:3. 90–92. Bohdan Garliński: *Architektura polska 1950–1951*, Warsaw 1953. 93, 94. Centralna Agencja Fotograficzna, Warsaw. 95. Juliusz A. Chróscicki and Andrzej Rottermund: *Architekturatlas von Warschau*, Warsaw 1978. 96, 97. *Architektura ČSR*, 1951:10–12. 98, 99. Same as no. 9. 100. AÅ 1985. 101. Imre Fejős and József Korek: *A magyar nemzeti múzeum története*, Budapest 1984. 102. Same as no. 10. 103. *The Architectural Review* (London), March 1953 (illustrated in an article by Harold A. Meek). 104, 105. Same as no. 10. 106. Same as no. 13. 107. Vasile Cucu and Marian Stefan: *Sehenswürdigkeiten in Rumänien*, Bucharest 1978. 108, 109. AÅ 1979. 110. Grigore Ionescu: *Arhitectura pe teritoriul României de-a lungul veacurilor*, Bucharest 1982. 111. AÅ1979. 112. Postcard from the World Youth Festival in Bucharest, 1953. 113, 114. *Deutsche Architektur*, 1956:5/6. 115. AÅ 1982. 116. Mihály Zádor: *Bulgária építészete*, Budapest 1979. 117, 118. AÅ 1982 119. Georgi V. Labov: *Arkhitekturata na Sofiia*, Sofia 1979.

CHAPTER SEVEN: 120. AÅ 1983. 121. Postcard, East Berlin 1960. 122. Deutsche Fotothek, Dresden. 123. *Architektur und Städtebau in der deutschen demokratis-*

chen Republik, Berlin/O 1959. 124–126. Deutsche Fotothek, Dresden. 127. Same as nos. 5, 7. 128. Same as no. 36. 129. *Plakat polski 1944–1953*, Warsaw 1953. 130. Centralna Agencja Fotograficzna, Warsaw. 131, 132. Same as no. 69. 133, 134. *Budowa PKiN,* Warsaw 1957. 135. Same as no. 130. 136–138. Same as no. 133. 139. *Deutsche Architektur* 1956:5/6. 140. AÅ 1979. 141, 142. *Arts in the Roumanian People's Republic,* no. 4, 1952. 143. *Deutsche Architektur* 1956:5/6. 144. Same as nos. 141, 142. 145–149. AÅ 1979. 150. *La Roumanie Nouvelle,* no. 52, 1950. 151. Postcard, Bulgaria, 1982. 152. Liuben Tonev: *Arkhitekturata v Bulgariia 1944–1960,* Sofia 1962. 153.Georgi V. Labov: *Arkhitekturata na Sofiia,* Sofia 1979. 154. Same as nos. 67, 68. 155, 156. AÅ 1982. 157. *Bulgarien av idag* (Stockholm), March 1955. Cf. *Arkhitektura i stroitelstvo* (Sofia), 1953:7–8.

CHAPTER EIGHT: 158, 159. *Deutsche Architektur* 1952:3 160. Kurt W. Leucht: *Die erste neue Stadt in der DDR,* Berlin/O 1957. 161. Same as no. 54. 162. Same as no. 3. 163, 164. Same as nos. 90, 91. 165, 166. AÅ 1980. 167. *Det nya Polen* (Stockholm), no. 8, 1953. 168. Same as nos. 90, 91. 169. *Internationale Kunstausstellung Berlin 1951,* Berlin/O 1951. 170–172. Same as no. 10. 173. *Sztálinváros Városközpont Városterv,* Budapest 1953. 174, 175. Same as no. 10. 176. *Dimitrovgrad,* Sofia 1959. 177, 178. AÅ 1982. 179. *Vseobshchaia istoriia architektury,* 12:2, Moscow 1977. 180. *Deutsche Architektur,* 1955 (Sonderheft Bulgarische Architektur). 181. Same as nos. 67, 68. 182. Josef Pechar: *Československá architektura 1945–1977,* Prague 1979 (erroneously attributed there to Havířov). 183. Oleg Švidkovskij: *Urbanismus socialistického Československa,* Prague 1966. 184, 185. Same as nos. 90–92.

CHAPTER NINE: 186. *Slovník českých spisovatelů,* Prague 1964. 187. *Jiří Kroha s úvodem od/mit einer Einleitung von Jaroslav B. Svrček,* Geneva 1930. 188. Supplied by József Fischer. 189. *Magyar építőművészet* 1986:3 190. Edmund Goldzamt: *William Morris und die sozialen Ursprünge der modernen Architektur,* Dresden 1976. 191. Same as no. 130. 192, 193. Same as no. 54.

CHAPTER TEN: 194. Muzeum Narodowe, Wrocław. 195. *Architektura* (Warsaw), 1952:9. 196. Swedish Film Institute. 197. Michał Krajewski: *Fachkunde des Kollektivmauerns* (translated from the Polish), Leipzig 1953. 198. Olle Björklund, 1981. 199. *Ausstellung Otto Nagel zu seinem 65. Geburtstag,* Berlin/O 1959. 200. Associated Press, London, 1956. 201–204. Arkivbild, Stockholm. 205, 206. DN, Stockholm, Folke Hellberg. 207. *Architektura ČSR* 1950:3–4. 208. *Architektura ČSR* 1955:5. 209, 210. AÅ 1960. 211. AÅ 1982. 212. AÅ 1980. 213. Alain Jaubert: *Le commissariat aux archives. Les photos qui falsifient l'histoire,* Paris 1986. 214. Olle Häger and Hans Villius: *Brännpunkt Prag,* Stockholm 1971. 215, 216. Same as no. 27. 217. Agnieszka Morawińska: *Malarstwo polskie od gotyku do współczesności,* Warsaw 1984.

CHAPTER ELEVEN: 218. *For a Lasting Peace, for a People's Democracy* 1953:11. 219, 220. *Architektura SSSR* (Moscow), 1954:9. 221. *Berlin 13 August* (Bundesministerium für gesamtdeutsche Fragen), 2d ed., Bonn and Berlin 1963. 222. Same as no. 130. 223. *Architektura* (Warsaw), 1954:7–8. 224. Same as no. 69. 225. Göran Lindahl, 1986. 226. *The Architectural Review,* August 1958. 227. Gerd Hatje, ed.: *Knaurs Lexikon der modernen Architektur,* Munich and Zurich 1963. 228. AÅ 1972. 229, 230. *Sovětská architektura* (Prague),

1955:4. 231. Same as no. 13. 232, 233. Grigore Ionescu: *Arhitectura în România perioada anilor 1944–1969*, Bucharest 1969. 234–236. AÅ 1979. 237. *Deutsche Architektur* 1953:4. 238. AÅ 1979. 239. "Manfred Schröter and Wolfgang Grösel: *Kulturpalast Dresden*, Leipzig 1974. 240. Same as no. 1.

CHAPTER TWELVE: 241, 242. *Hansaviertel Berlin*, Stuttgart and Berlin 1964. 243. *Interbau Berlin 1957*, Berlin/W 1957. 244. *Bauen in Berlin 1900–1964* (Akademie der Künste), Berlin/W 1964. 245. *Interbau Berlin 1957*, Berlin/W 1957. 246. Barbara Miller Lane: "The Berlin Congress Hall 1955–1957," in *Perspectives in American History* (Cambridge, Mass.), new series, vol. 1, 1984. 247. Akademie der Künste, Berlin/W. 248. Postcard, 1980.

CHAPTER THIRTEEN: 249, 250. *Deutsche Architektur* 1952:2. 251, 252. Postcards from the exhibition. 253. Same as no. 130.

Index of Names

Index of Places

In the text, the official forms of names applying in each instance has been used whenever possible.

This index includes only references to buildings, urban developments, and monuments, some of which are unrealized projects.

Caption references appear in italics following page references.